From the Valley of Making

David Wojahn

From the Valley of Making

ESSAYS ON THE CRAFT OF POETRY

UNIVERSITY OF MICHIGAN PRESS

Ann Arbor

Published in the United States of America by the
University of Michigan Press
Printed and bound by CPI Group (UK) Ltd, Croydon, CR0 4YY

2018   2017   2016   2015   4   3   2   1

A CIP catalog record for this book is available from the British Library.
ISBN 978-0-472-07250-7 (hardcover : alk. paper)
ISBN 978-0-472-05250-9 (pbk. : alk. paper)

For Noelle, Luke, and Jake,
and for Louise Crowley

Acknowledgments

Grateful acknowledgment is made to reprint the following copyrighted works.

Andrew Allport, "Poem Ending with an Icepick Lobotomy," from *The Body of Shape in the Space of the Human*. Copyright © 2012 by New Issues Press. Reprinted by permission of New Issues Press.

Jon Anderson, "Tucson: A Poem About Wood," from *The Milky Way: Poems 1968–1982* (New York: Ecco Press, 1983). Reprinted by permission of the estate of Jon Anderson.

John Berryman, from *The Dream Songs* (#91, #51, #46, sections of #29) (New York: Farrar, Straus, and Giroux, 1968).

Linda Bierds, "The Whim Gin," from *The Ghost Trio*. Copyright © by Linda Bierds. Published 1994 by Henry Holt. Reprinted by permission of Linda Bierds.

Robert Bly, "Driving into Town Late to Mail a Letter," from *Silence in the Snowy Fields* (Middletown, Connecticut: Wesleyan University Press, 1962).

Hayden Carruth, "Emergency Haying," from *From Snow and Rock, From Chaos*. Copyright © 1973 by New Directions Publishing Corp. Reprinted by permission of New Directions Publishing Corp.

C. P. Cavafy, "Hidden Things," and "Days of 1909," from *C. P. Cavafy Selected Poems*. Copyright © 1992 by Edmund Keeley and Philip Sherrard. Reprinted by permission of Princeton University Press.

Tom Sleigh, "Airport Economy Inn," from *Spacewalk* (Boston: Houghton Mifflin, 2007). Reprinted by permission of Tom Sleigh.

Mark Strand, "Viewing the Coast," from *Pushcart Prize XII: Best of the Small Presses*, ed. Bill Henderson. Copyright © 1988 by Pushcart Press. Reprinted by permission of Mark Strand.

Tomas Transtromer, "The Open Window," section of "After the Attack," from "The Gallery," *Selected Poems 1957–86*, ed. Robert Hass (New York: Ecco Press, 1987).

Joe Wenderoth, "The Home of the Brave," from *No Real Light*. Copyright © 2007 by Wave Books. Reprinted by permission of Wave Books.

James L. White, "An Ordinary Compose," from *The Salt Ecstacies*. Copyright © 2010 by The Estate of James L. White. Reprinted with the permission of The Permissions Company, Inc., on behalf of Graywolf Press, Minneapolis, Minnesota, www.graywolf-press.org.

I am grateful to the editors of the following journals and anthologies for publishing these essays, often in earlier versions:

American Poetry Review:
"'Of Course I Would Have Saved Them if I Could': On Capaciousness"
"'Tell Me if It Is Too Far for You': On Sympathy"

Blackbird:
"'In All Them Time Henry Could Not Make Good': Reintroducing John Berryman"

Notre Dame Review:
"The Coast Is Never Clear: On the Poetry of Happiness"

The Planet on the Table: Poets and the Reading Life (Sarabande Books):
"From the Valley of Making"

Writers' Chronicle:
"Maggie's Farm No More: The Fate of Political Poetry"
"'To the Betrayed World': Darth Howard, Ashurbanipal, and a Defense of Poetry"
"'If You Have to Be Sure Don't Write': Poetry and Self-Doubt"
"'And Not Releasing the Genie': The Poetry of Knowledge vs. the Poetry of Stuff"

"'If You Have to Be Sure Don't Write'" was reprinted in *The Ivor Guerney Journal* and in *Words Overflown By Stars: Creative Writing Instruction and Insight from the Vermont College MFA Program* (Writer's Digest Books).

Thanks are also due to David Jauss, William Olsen, and Tony Whedon for their ongoing advice, and especially Noelle Watson, who read each of these essays multiples times and with exquisite care. Thanks also to Lynda Fleet, and to Marilyn Hacker and Kazim Ali for their belief in this book. Special thanks are due to my students and colleagues at Vermont College of Fine Arts, where early versions of many of these essays were presented as lectures.

Contents

Preface

Much has been made in recent decades about the supposed marginalization of poetry. Books of verse rarely sell more than a few thousand copies, and the readership of those books is limited largely to other poets—or to the authors' students, for we all know that almost the only way a contemporary poet can make a living is by teaching others to write poetry. We're frequently told that the present situation has fostered a creative writing "industry," but if that is so, poetry writing remains very much a small product line within companies that are far more interested in peddling fiction, memoir, and screenwriting. Furthermore, the arrival of the digital age hasn't done much to change poetry's less-than-exalted status, save that it is now more likely that readers will encounter new poetry in online journals rather than in print publications. Given the state of things, what would possess someone to devote a goodly portion of his or her life to a discipline that is seen by the world at large as impenetrable at best, and more typically as effete and trivial? A coterie discipline whose language and practice might with some justification be characterized as oddball and cultic? A discipline that is, furthermore, immensely hard to master? And finally, what would possess someone to engage in the exponentially marginal activity of composing poetry *criticism?*

After writing both poetry and poetry criticism since the time of the Carter administration or thereabouts, I can offer some provisional answers to these questions. (And of course, if you want to offer truthful answers about anything having to do with literature, those answers *must* be provisional.) I write poetry because the discipline insists, no matter how unsuccessful the product happens to be on a given day, that the inner life of the individual has some worthiness, has a meaning that evolves in its urgencies and its intricacies whether one likes it or not. And, increasingly over the years, I write poems simply because the act of writing is its own reward. When I write a poem I am making a small reckoning with myself and with my world that challenges and delights me in a way that seems comparable to almost no other activity. And in an inscrutable but essential way the writing of a poem is a moral and political act. When I write a poem I am, for a brief time, no longer a demographic, no longer someone at the receiving end of a robo-call, and no longer involved in a servitude to social media. Freed from such constraints, I can be alone with my interests and obsessions, my expressions of gratitude or of condemnation, with the bewilderingly rich tradition of the English language in general, and the writing of verse in particular. Berryman infamously defined poetry as a man or woman alone in a room with the English language. At one time I thought this definition bleak. But now I see it as a prescription for delight, for possibility, and even for subversion.

Interest, obsession, gratitude, condemnation: the essays in this collection emerge from the same wellsprings as I would like my poetry to derive from. Although a few of the pieces in this volume were commissioned for books or journals, most developed simply because I was interested in exploring a topic, or because the subject seemed to me in some way timely. They are the product of a dozen years of work, and most were written during the first decade of a new millennium, a strange and perilous time for American culture. They were written in the wake of 9/11 during the Iraq and Afghanistan wars, and amid the poisonous skullduggery of the Bush administration. American poetry, in ways we are now only beginning to understand, was forced to re-appraise and re-align itself during these years. And it is my hope that these essays help to document that reappraisal. At the end of each essay I have noted its year of composition, for they are very much the products of their *particular* time.

As a reader and as a critic, I would like to think my tastes are relatively catholic, although the poets who have been most sustaining for me are of course of special interest. The so-called middle-generation poets—Lowell, Berryman, Bishop, among others—appear often in these pages, for I find in their work a vitality, an ambition, and a desire to express the intricacies of the relationship between selves and the world that was sometimes lacking in their Modernist forebears, and I fear these qualities are often lacking in the work of poets of my own and later generations. And, like many American poets who began publishing in the 1970s and 1980s, I have often looked to modern international poetry for inspiration and instruction; hence the presence in these essays of figures such as Transtromer, Milosz, Herbert, and Cavafy. There is still much to discover and to praise among the poets on this list, and much to appreciate in the work of my fellow Boomer poets, several of whom are also discussed here at length.

My first hope is that *From the Valley of Making* offers a fairly comprehensive snapshot of the situation of American poetry at the start of a new century. My second hope is that its essays are above all readable, personal, and fair-minded in the Jarrellian sense (for Jarrell sets the critical standard that all decent poet-critics who have followed him must aspire to); I want these essays to be passionate in expressing my enthusiasms, and equally impassioned in condemning the cant and frivolity that too often seems to afflict contemporary poetry.

An exasperated Wallace Stevens once complained that the problem with readers and writers of verse is simply that too few of them remember that "one writes poetry because one *must*." Practically no critics of poetry would claim that their endeavors arise from a similar sense of inevitability. And readers of poetry criticism? Readers turn to it, if they turn to it at all, largely because they want poems and poetry *explained*. I very much hope to disappoint such readers. But I do hope to reach those readers who understand that the mysteries and delights of contemporary poetry must always remain mysteries—and, at least some of the time, delights.

—**Richmond, Virginia, September 2013**

From the Valley of Making

Poetry "survives in the valley of its making, where executives would never want to tamper": most of us know these lines from Auden's elegy for Yeats, and all of us likely know the line which immediately precedes them, that famously blunt assertion: "poetry makes nothing happen." I imagine that when poets look at Auden's stanza, they are less interested in the oratorical flatulence of the contention that poetry won't make anything happen than they are in determining how poetry survives in the valley of its making. Where is that valley, and why do the executives want to steer clear of it? The trope is quintessential Auden, a rather loopy metaphor that, on the other hand, is instantly recognizable; in some alternate universe it is surely a well-worn cliché. And in fact, Auden implies that it is only *in* a kind of alternate universe where poetry survives, for the valley of its making calls forth images of an obscure and inaccessible backwater, some Appalachian hollow where the inbred inhabitants still speak a kind of Elizabethan English, and not even a new satellite dish will distract the populace from their dulcimers and back-porch banjo-picking. No wonder the executives won't go there. It is also perhaps a lost valley, where creatures thought extinct still roam, something out of the boys' adventure books that the youthful Auden cherished—it is Conan Doyle's *Lost World*, Edgar Rice Burroughs's *Land that Time Forgot.*

And yet, whether from neglect or because it always will remain, for most of the world, a region unmapped and unexplored, the Valley of Making is not often disturbed, and its odd little culture continues to survive, if not to prosper. Here a small number of inconsequential lives go on, lives devoted largely to useless activity. For poetic endeavor is very much akin to the great polar explorer Fridjof Nansen's definition of "polar endeavor." It is "about nothing, in nothing, for nothing." And nothing, we know, will come of nothing, neither the nothing that is not there, nor the nothing that is. In the Valley of Making, the same old wearisome nothings prevail: there is no audience for poetry, no money in poetry, no respect for its virtues, and nothing new for it to say. No wonder there's a brain drain in the valley: the real talent leaves as soon as it can: outside the valley there are novels to write, scripts to crank out, agents to contact; the dollar signs and memoirs of dysfunctional families beckon. The real talent boards the Greyhound Bus, and it never looks back.

How strange, therefore, that in the Valley of Making those who choose to stay do not feel left behind. For uselessness exerts a powerful appeal. The poets in their uselessness know something that the Real Talent never suspects. It is the very uselessness of poetry, its economic insignificance, and its political and cultural irrelevance that are in fact the sources of its greatest subversive power. Let us therefore talk uselessly a while, let us, in the words of that supremely subversive figure Walt Whitman, sit down a while and loaf.

Let us begin with a small, flawed, and quirkily exquisite poem by Kenneth Rexroth, likely written within a year or two of Auden's Yeats elegy, and published in his 1944 volume, *The Phoenix and the Tortoise*:

The Advantages of Learning

I am a man with no ambitions
And few friends, wholly incapable
Of a living, growing no
Younger, fugitive from some just doom.
Lonely, ill-clothed, what does it matter?
At midnight I make myself a jug
of hot white wine and cardamom seeds.
In a torn gray robe and old beret,
I sit in the cold writing poems,
Drawing nudes on the crooked margins,
Copulating with sixteen-year-old
Nymphomaniacs of my imagination.[1]

One could hardly imagine two poets more different than Rexroth and Auden. Yet in the early years of World War II the pair faced similar aesthetic crises, and addressed them in roughly parallel ways. The activist 1930s were dead and gone; Marxism had lost its promise in the wake of the Moscow show trials, the defeat of the Spanish Republic, and the Hitler-Stalin nonaggression pact. And now the world was plunged into its second huge conflagration in less than thirty years. Auden flees to Manhattan, abandons the Marxist-inflected sloganeering of his early poems, and instead embraces his newfound Christianity. The rhetoric of his poetry cools, the fiercely stentorian refrain of "Spain"—"today the struggle"—is replaced by the end of the low dishonest decade with something which, in hindsight, we must read as a form of plea rather than as ultimatum: we must love each other or die, or so we are told in "September 1, 1939." In time, even this assertion was called into question by the poet. Now his poems, for all their didacticism, would venture inward, a transformation toward what Jarrell called "a vaguish humanitarian mysticism."[2]

Unlike Auden, Rexroth had actually been a member of the Communist Party, but by 1938 his romance with the Left had also soured, and by the start of World War II he had sought conscientious objector status. He was reading a wide range of mystical literature, from Jacob Boehme to the Tao Te Ching, and trekking for weeks on end in the Sierras. Now his subjects would be love and death and the changing of the seasons—or "bearshit on the trail poetry," as one of Rexroth's later detractors put it. But perhaps confusion and ambivalence are the only proper response during this particular historical moment: the world is on the brink of war, the dream of world revolution has been betrayed. How could a cohesive artistic position be possible now, when the first order of business was to acknowledge the breadth of world violence, and the meaninglessness of activism? Auden and Rexroth were back to where Pound had been in 1917, witnessing the carnage from afar, yet with the same infuriated bile that animated his Mauberly sequence. Where does a poet turn when faced with conditions such as these? Pound of course turned to crank economic theories, a choice disastrous for both his poems and his life. Auden turned to the church, a choice that seems equally dubious, at least as far as Auden's later poems are concerned. Rexroth made a third choice, the way of homesickness and exile, of aestheticism and armchair anarchism. And to the Valley of Making he went to live out his remaining years.

So let's return to "The Advantages of Learning." In the manner of T'ang Dynasty poems he would later translate, the poet begins with a deadpan account of his shabby condition: "I am a man with no ambitions / And few friends, wholly incapable / Of a living, growing no / Younger. . . ." But in the context of the poem's title, the flatness of the statements and the terse enjambments give its opening a bitter irony, an irony made even more pronounced when we remind ourselves that Rexroth, for all his much-vaunted erudition, was an autodidact: in the world's eyes, his learning meant nothing, quantifiable by no advanced degree, no marketable skills. The poem quickly becomes a tongue-in-cheek imitation of Li Po or Tu Fu, who themselves were adept practitioners of self-mockery. As the poem moves from statement to narrative, Rexroth trots out the familiar stereotypes.

> At midnight, I make myself a jug
> of hot white wine and cardamom seeds.
> In a torn gray robe and old beret,
> I sit in the cold writing poems,
> Drawing nudes on the crooked margins,
> copulating with sixteen-year-old
> Nymphomaniacs of my imagination.

I see far more whimsy here than I see self-pity. Rexroth characterizes himself as a bohemian out of central casting, up late to drink and write poems, sporting his beret while alone in the house. And of course, when it actually comes to writing poems, the speaker's been distracted; he's instead drawing nudes, and indulging in some male fantasies which are themselves as stereotypical as the robe and the beret. But the buffoonery isn't all there is. Something in the poem—perhaps it's the flatness and precision of the language and its detail—asks us to also see the speaker's plight as genuine. He traffics in clichés in part to reinvigorate their legitimacy. He is poor, solitary, and he can't even finish the poems for which he has given up his hopes of worldly success. And no one is better able to see his ridiculous plight than the poet himself, who documents his condition with a kind of anti–ars poetica. It is a poem that conveys both conviction and detachment at once, and a detachment decidedly different from the lofty remove that permeates a good many of Rexroth's other poems. The tone instead recalls the dry, fastidious irony of contemporary Eastern European poets such as Zbigniew Herbert and Czeslaw Milosz: it is not the effete irony practiced so benumbingly by poets in the heyday of the New Criticism, but instead what A. Alvarez calls, in characterizing Herbert's poetry, "the irony of a vulnerable man."[3] "The Advantages of Learning" refutes all the romantic precepts of lyric poetry: neither the poet nor poetry itself can make any special claims to significance. But the "advantage" of poetry is its capacity to allow the poet to dwell outside the parameters of significance, be they aesthetic or economic. The advantage of poetry, that dialect spoken in the Valley of Making, is its uselessness. It is the argot, sometimes ironic, sometimes enacting the entrancement of detachment—what Elizabeth Bishop called "a perfectly useless concentration"—of the vulnerable men and women who dwell in the Valley. The subversive power and authority of poetry thus derive from two main sources, one linguistic—the idiosyncratic speech and regional accent of the valley dwellers—and one geographical or spatial, for the Valley of Making is a backwater, far removed from the bustle of the capital.

Special lingo, special perspective: from grade school onward we are told that this is what poetry is about. But these characterizations tend to come with valorizing strings attached. Poetry's "specialness" is somehow connected to notions of the sublime, of obscurity, of deadly earnestness. The popularizing of verse-writing through poets-in-the-schools programs and collegiate creative writing classes hasn't done much to dissuade the world at large from holding these notions. Nor has the legacy of literary Modernism, and it's the High Church Modernists whom young readers are apt to first encounter. Eliot, Pound, and Yeats are still the gatekeepers, despite the efforts of anthologists to enlarge the canon. And it's Rainer Maria Rilke, that Sultan of Sublime, who occupies the most shelf space in the poetry sections of B&N and whatever independent booksellers still remain. The result of all of this, aside from making bad translations of *The Duino Elegies* a kind of cottage industry, is to reinforce a decidedly Victorian notion of poetry's mission: it is quaint, good for you in an oat bran sort of way, and above all domesticated. It is this declawed, spayed, or neutered version of poetry that causes the Language poets to rant against Official Verse Culture. Poetry that falls outside the parameters of these sanctioned norms tends to be neglected, or at worst, its practitioners are punished and silenced: witness the fates of Gumilev and Mandelstam.

The product of the Imagination's Party Line, whether it is a Yevtushenko ode to a new hydroelectric dam or a laureate doodle on something-safely-quotidian by Billy Collins, is not the kind of writing which first attracts us to poetry. Tyro poets tend to be drawn either to poetry's subversive playfulness with language—to a hit parade which includes Hopkins, Roethke, and more recently James Tate and John Ashbery—or to its postures of rebelliousness: this is why the Beats are still read, and why a talent as indifferent as Thomas Chatterton could so inspire the Romantics. The Minions of Official Verse Culture (among which I reluctantly count myself), whether consciously or not, try to wean the kids away from these interests and these models. And in a short time they learn just enough to know they should regard these first poetic mentors with suspicion. Not too many years ago my then-colleague Dean Young taught a graduate seminar on Dada and surrealism, and apparently subversiveness and nihilism don't play well anymore. Stein, Breton, Cage, O'Hara: despite the students' knowledge of these writers' impact on postmodern thinking, they resisted them all, for lots of dutiful but inchoate reasons, all of them vaguely PC. In one particularly puzzling conversation, O'Hara got branded as a sexist and a racist (an accusation that certainly would have startled O'Hara himself). The class in essence reenacted the miserable tale of the surrealists' flirtation with international communism, with poor Dean playing the role of Breton and company, and the students the role of the Stalinist hacks, baffled and threatened by the convulsive transgressiveness of surrealist poetics, its call for "a revolution of the mind."

And of course a revolution of the mind has little institutional value, whether it is debated around a seminar table or presented naively to the Comintern as a weapon for destroying the Beast of Capitalism. Revolutions of the mind are always useless, always subjective—and almost always poetry's first order of business. The revolution of the mind is for the young poet not some major upheaval, but a kind of initiation to the transformative properties of language, and of poetry's role in self-transformation. And yet, in the way of all revolutions, it is followed by a counter-revolution, a Thermadorian Reaction where a kind of aesthetic zealotry prevails. My friend Dean's students seem caught in the throes of such a reaction, for better or for worse, but they're not untypical. Some poets are trapped in that reaction—and the embitterment that accompanies failed promise and failed allegiances—for long and sorrowful stretches of their writing careers. It causes some to turn to silence, some to turn to new fidelities (Auden to the church, Wordsworth to the Tories). And some—at the risk of muddying my analogies—will pack their books and papers up and move off to the Valley of Making, and come full circle, back to poetry's initiating thrall and vigor, back to its useless but astonishing delights.

An archetypal pattern, then? Maybe, but this sounds too grandiose. Yet I see my own career as following it, and I see it enacted in many of the poets I most admire, provided they live long enough, and escape the choice of punishment or silence. I am now forty-seven years old, Mandelstam's age when he last was sighted, scavenging a Gulag garbage heap in search of food, and the age when Paul Celan chose to leap from a bridge into the Seine. According to Dante, old age begins at forty-seven: you're a graybeard now, entering geezerhood: you can lay down your lyre and quill. But I'm lucky enough to feel persecuted only by myself, to have no suicidal inclinations, and to have no intention of putting down my pen. In the Valley of Making, in the subdivision called Minor Poet in Mid-Career, there's still a great deal that I want to say.

Oddly enough, the journey takes me again to Kenneth Rexroth, and again to "The Advantages of Learning." For in 1970 there were precisely three books of contemporary poetry to be found on the shelves of the Washington County Pub-

7

lic Library's Lake Elmo branch. I was seventeen, and I'd been reading poetry with a sort of desultory avidness for a couple of years. Pound, Eliot, Stevens—I'd read them, but not closely, read them because my high-school English teacher suggested them to me, but frankly they left me cold. I sensed in them the same sort of mock-profundity and declamatory self-importance that I got from my Emerson, Lake and Palmer LPs. (Stevens was, admittedly, a little more interestingly weird, more like Pink Floyd. . . .) But the High Modernists, in their loftiness, were high in the wrong way. I was ready for something else, and into my life there came—serendipitously, and thanks to the exquisite taste of an anonymous rural Minnesota librarian who no doubt spent a hefty portion of the little library's purchasing funds on three new poetry books—*The Collected Shorter Poems* of Kenneth Rexroth, *Silence in the Snowy Fields* by Robert Bly, and, most importantly, the 1971 *Collected Poems* of James Wright. I read them in precisely that order, and I read them and read them. Rexroth I liked, Bly I liked better, and Wright I adored. When the library books came due I bought my own copies, and battered they sit on my desk as I write this, paper yellowed, spines unglued, their dust jackets long ago turned to shreds, worn like the woodworking tools my father kept in his basement shop. After all the years of reading and rereading this trio, it's hard to pinpoint what first attracted me to their work, but I know my love of them sprang in part from their attention to place, and in the case of Bly and Wright to a landscape that was my own: the snowy windswept fields were right before me, but suddenly they no longer suggested the dreary tedium of Sinclair Lewis and his purgatorial Gopher Prairie—after all, we'd read *Main Street* and *Babbitt* in English class, and I and my friends all suspected that real life occurred somewhere else. But now, in a single stroke, real life was happening right before me, and it was a mysterious, occult, and hugely sensual reality—"a cloister, a silence, / closing around a blossom of fire," as Wright put it in "The Jewel."[4] "Frail shadows" everywhere, everywhere "cathedrals in the wind"—an exquisitely mystical vista of Swedenborgian correspondences, of shadowy hermetic revelation: "we are all asleep in the outward man," said Bly in his epigraph to *Silence in the Snowy Fields*, quoting Jacob Boehme. But the means to wake the inner man were all around you, if only you had the wherewithal to look—here "the moon drops one or two feathers in a field," and there "the dark wheat listens." I did not know in those days what pain and self-torture the poems of James Wright emerged from: that understanding of Wright would wait for later. In those days his were purely poems of ecstasy, poems that subverted the natural order through the revelatory astonishments of their imagery, and by rhapsodizing places and situations that I knew, but now saw x-rayed, revealing a hitherto hidden luminosity. A hammock in Pine Island, Minnesota, Indian ponies in a field off Highway 55 to Rochester, and on the South Dakota border, "where the moon is out hunting," at last we understand that we "are lost in the beautiful white ruins / of America."

Here you could voyage to the inner life, but you could also drive to it, as my friend Pete Mladinic and I did one afternoon, trying to locate that roadside field where Wright set "A Blessing." (Admittedly, we'd smoked a lot of hash that day. . . .) Wright and Bly weren't trendy in the way the Beats were, but they still possessed some countercultural cachet. I knew they wrote in protest of the war, and Bly in his readings liked to wear a serape. They lauded the simple pleasures of doing nothing, pleasures that to me seemed a lot like getting high. I didn't know the hammock poem could be seen as a self-indictment, didn't understand its desperate homage to "The Torso of an Archaic Apollo." I read the poems as if they were ways to jump-start the inner life, and even at their most trivial they seemed profound. And it didn't hurt that no one else but my friend Peter seemed to get the point. My mother, who not many years earlier had banned all comic books from our house save those from the Classics Illustrated series, thought well of my interest in reading poetry, until one day she picked up my copy of *Silence in the Snowy Fields.* I'd dog-eared a poem she found easy to judge:

Driving into Town Late to Mail a Letter

It is a cold and snowy night. The main street is deserted.
The only things moving are swirls of snow.
As I lift the mailbox door, I feel its cold iron.

There is a privacy I love in the snowy night.
Driving around, I will waste more time.[5]

"Billy Shields could write better than that," she said, referring
to the mentally disabled kid who lived up the street. My mother
valued learning, but she also had a cruel streak. The learning
that this poem exemplified, a learning without quantifiable values, a learning whose purpose is sometimes to educate us in the
value of useless pleasure, wasn't something her accountant's
mind could grasp. It made me love the poem all the more.

But I also suppose that even then I knew in some vague way
that Bly's poem was ultimately a trivial thing, a kind of Wordsworth Lite. The World That Is Too Much With Us is, in so many
of the Deep Image poems that Bly and Wright spawned, very
easy to reject in favor of atavistic symbolism and a fuzzy romantic pantheism, and there is no cost to pay. When you could so
readily drive to the inner life, cruising at sixty in what Bly inane-
ly termed "the iron solitude of the car," using barely a quarter
tank of gas, revelation came to seem like a cheap thrill. Bly himself was shaken out of this sort of quietism by the Vietnam War,
and the most enduring poetry of the Deep Image group—most
notably W. S. Merwin's *The Lice*—sets the retreat into the self
against a backdrop of imperialist war-mongering and the threat
of atomic Armageddon. Yes, you can still drive to the inner life,
but there are many roadblocks along the way, and when you get
there you must face your own extinction; you see that in fact
you have crawled off like a wounded animal to die: "It is March
and black dust falls from the books / Soon I will be gone / The
tall spirit who lodged here / Has left already," says Merwin in
a poem from *The Lice*.[6] No consolation here, and certainly no
delight. But after book upon book of this sort of thing, Merwin's
testimony seemed inauthentic.

But the models came, and there are two of them I now want
to speak of in more detail, for their lessons apply here in ways
that perhaps no others can. Both poets are provincials, writing in
languages that, even in an era of diversity and multiculturalism,
are apt to be branded as marginal. Tomas Transtromer writes
in Swedish, Constantine Cavafy in modern Greek. Their work
comes to me infused with the distortions, inaccuracy, and feed-

back which attends any work of literary translation, for I have no knowledge of what their poems might sound like in their original form. Transtromer will probably never be awarded the Nobel; for the Swedes to give the prize to one of their own would be an act of . . . provincialism.[7] Cavafy, one of the last century's greatest poets, never issued a book of poetry during his lifetime, unless you count the stapled and mimeographed productions he'd put together from time to time for his friends. As an Alexandrian Greek, speaking Arabic in the cafés he frequented and English in his workplace—the Dantescan-sounding "Third Circle of Irrigation"—Cavafy spoke the tongue he wrote his poems in only occasionally. And *fin de siécle* Alexandria, once the greatest Greek city of all, was in his time neither Greek nor much of a city. One of the things which links these two very different poets is a stance which does not and cannot assume centrality: they must position themselves in the cheap seats, the outermost districts, far from the foci of cultural or political power. They cannot assume the roles of smiling public men, or pen aristocratic odes to Union or Confederate fallen. Yet they remind us that even in the sticks life goes on, and that distant vantage points are often the ones which permit us the most acute and truthful view: both of history and of ourselves, and sometimes of the ways in which selves and history must inextricably commingle. Like Chekhov's three sisters, they'll never visit Moscow, but in time the most fortunate of them learn to turn their very obscurity, marginality, and insignificance into their strongest assets. The process of this transformation is a complex one, and it entails more than writing diddly-squat epiphanies in Midwestern cornfields in the manner of Robert Bly, and yet—ironically—it was Robert Bly who helped to teach me this.

The lesson took place on a Monday in early November 1972. Specifically, it was the eve of Richard Nixon's re-election, not the grimmest day in American history, but certainly a shameful one, and surely a time of profound and benumbing despair. Four more years of Nixon's criminality and our genocidal war in Asia seemed to loom before us, and nothing appeared to stop him or to slow him down. Marches and moratoriums had failed, and the well-meaning earnestness of George McGovern would inevitably fail as well. I could say that times such as these are the ones in which we turn to poetry for solace, but I have to report that I wasn't thinking very clearly in those days. Yet somehow I found myself in an auditorium on the University of Minnesota campus, and before me and a few dozen others stood Tomas Transtromer, accompanied by his translator Robert Bly. Had I not been there that night, I doubt if I'd have continued to write poetry.

That only a handful of listeners had come to the reading was no surprise. Transtromer was at that time represented in English by only two collections, a small *Selected* which Pittsburgh had issued, and an even smaller volume which Bly's Seventies Press had printed. I'd never read the Swedish poet's work; like most of the audience, I was there to hear Bly, whose manic delivery and marathon readings lasting hours had in those years taken on a kind of cult cachet. Bly didn't disappoint: he hulked and strutted about the classroom, punctuating his translations of Transtromer's poems with speedy and pontificating between-poem banter. Transtromer's presence was entirely different. Tall, thin to the point of gauntness, with angular Nordic features which made him look for all the world like Max Von Sydow, blond hair going to gray, Transtromer looked quietly commanding, relaxed above the podium, but standing very still. He recited his poems in Swedish, but also read several of them in translation, slowly and in an almost accent-free English. Transtromer and Bly were a study in contrasts, but also oddly symbiotic. Bly paced, circled, and generally filibustered around Transtromer at his podium, orbiting him like a wayward asteroid. Transtromer presented a kind of Zen-like awareness, quietly attentive toward both his poems and the audience; he seemed strangely ego-less, more like a shrink than a poet—listening and observing in an intense but nondirective fashion, and putting his poems under the same sort of benign scrutiny a therapist would give a client's self-appraisals. ("Were your needs being met by this metaphor?" "Do you still feel angry toward this stanza?" "Tell me more about the image of the horse's flank.") That night as he introduced a poem entitled "After the Attack," I discovered that Transtromer was, in fact, a psychotherapist, working in a boys' reform school. As the decades passed, I came to understand that a stance of detachment that is at the same time utterly attentive was a principal source of Transtromer's authority as a poet. In his famous poem about Vermeer, it is neither the painter himself nor his human figures which have the last word, but a ray of light, corporeal and incorporeal at once, which utters the poem's conclusion:

The clear sky has set itself against the wall.
It's like a prayer to emptiness.
And the emptiness turns its face to us
and whispers
I am not empty; I am open.[8]

In this poem, as in so much of Transtromer's work, the hidden world of inanimate and abstract things is invariably personified, sometimes consolingly, sometimes frighteningly. "Memories Look at Me" is in fact the title of an autobiographical sketch in Transtromer's book *For the Living and the Dead,* and a passage in "The Gallery," a long and nightmarish lyric that functions as a kind of ars poetica, has this to say about the poet's creative process:

Often I have to stand completely motionless.
I'm the partner of the knife-thrower in the circus!
Questions I threw from me in a fit of rage
come whining back
don't hit but nail down my shape
in coarse outline
stay there when I've left the place.[9]

Critics in Sweden, especially those with a Marxist bent, have condemned this stance throughout Transtromer's career, seeing in it a kind of apolitical Olympian indifference—one of them went so far as to label him "a buzzard poet."[10] And indeed, many of his poems do seem to arrive at an aerial perspective, or at the vantage point of someone who suddenly finds himself to be experiencing astral projection. One poem concludes with a vision of "islands [which] crawl like huge moths over the globe." In another the shadow thrown by an airplane covers a man at work in a field, and "for a fraction of a second he is right at the center of the cross." These are not moments of potential rapture, in the way that even the most ambivalent images at the conclusion of many of James Wright's poems can be; they instead seem prophesies of conflagration, whether an annihilation of the self or destruction on a cosmic level; sometimes they point to both at once. Certainly this is the case with the poem that Transtromer chose to read at the close of his reading:

The Open Window

I shaved one morning standing
by the open window
on the second story.
Switched on the razor.
It started to hum.
A heavier and heavier whirr.
Grew to a roar.
Grew to a helicopter.
And a voice—the pilot's—pierced
the noise, shouting:
"Keep your eyes open!
You're seeing this for the last time!"
Rose.
Floated low over the summer.
The small things I love, have they any weight?
So many dialects of green.
And especially the red of housewalls.
Beetles glittered in the dung, in the sun.
Cellars pulled up by the roots
sailed through the air.
Industry.
Printing presses crawled along.
People at that instant
were the only things motionless.
They observe their moment of silence.
And the dead in the churchyard especially
held still
like those who posed in the infancy of the camera.
Fly low!
I didn't know which way
to turn my head—
my sight was divided
like a horse's.[11]

An unsettling poem, surely; despite its imagistic pyrotechnics, it is telegraphic and brusque. By line eight Transtromer is out his window, once again becoming a buzzard poet. Yet the experience of being airborne is hardly that of a delightful flying dream, where our wings spread and we coast upon thermals. This final glimpse of the world beneath us permits no consolidating clarity—the poem ends abruptly, with a startling image of bifurcation: our sight is "divided / like a horse's." Although the image is striking, the poem seems to stop in mid-thought.

The audience greeted this with a stunned silence, and it took awhile for someone to remember to applaud. A halting Q & A began—not because Transtromer seemed uncomfortable with English, but because the audience seemed puzzled by the oddness of perception and the quiet gravity of the poems. Yes, they were surreal, but the images seemed to derive from something far different from the slick romanticism of Deep Image verse. Bly tried to play ringmaster to this all, joking that he'd initially made a huge blunder in his translation, mistaking *rockerapparater*, the Swedish word for electric razor, for "rocket apparatus"—thus his initial version of the poem had its speaker strap on some sort of Buck Rogers device and literally rocket out his open window. The audience lobbed some of the usual questions reserved for such events—asking Transtromer about his influences and writing habits. But one question was openly hostile: the questioner was wearing a Mao cap, a red star in its center: "How, at a time like this, can you write such introspective poems? How can you be so apolitical? You're like an ostrich with his head in the sand."

Clearly Transtromer had heard this sort of accusation before, and often. "I write poetry because I believe in the value of individual lives. By writing about my private life I hope to remind my readers of theirs. In a world such as ours, where the individual is little valued, this position seems to me a highly political one." The dignity and wisdom of this reply stunned me: it is of course the kind of statement that has been uttered in countless ways in the past two centuries; you hear it in Blake and Wordsworth as well as in the Language poets. But I'd never heard this sort of formulation before, and never again would I hear it without recalling that evening in 1972. Years later, during a winter in which

Transtomer stayed in Provincetown, I mentioned that Minnesota evening to him. He sheepishly confessed that he couldn't recall it, though he still agreed with the content of his statement. Some friends and I were chauffeuring him to a reading he was to give in Boston. On the way there, he asked to be driven on a side trip through Roxbury. He'd never seen an American slum before. The talk turned to politics, and he told me that he'd written "The Open Window" during the week of the Cuban Missile Crisis: the notion of having a final view of life on earth was at that moment not by any means a mere metaphor.

In some ways the most radical—or surreal—aspect of Transtromer's poetry is its manipulation of spatial relationships, its willingness to suddenly alter our physical perspective—at one moment we are shaving, in the next we are flying high above the planet: tracking shots suddenly become close-ups, and vice versa. We never are allowed to stay in a position long enough to grow comfortable with our point of view. These devices are wrenching and unsettling rather than simply virtuosic; it is not the frenetic jump cutting of an MTV video or the latest Lexus commercial that Transtromer gives us, but a warning that we will never see *anything* from the best or the right perspective, and never do we remain at a single vantage point for long. Transtromer asks us to stand in the way that E. M. Forster cannily noted that Cavafy stood—"at a slight angle to the universe."

Like Transtromer, Cavafy sees displacement as the single thing that most characterizes the human condition, and yet he too finds in these states of exile and rupture the content of his most enduring poetry. This is of course a paradox, but Cavafy's oeuvre abounds in paradox. No other great poet—with the possible exception of Thomas Hardy—employs such a restrictive palette. Metaphor is nearly absent from his work, his language is spare and minimalist, and his themes are limited to three: memory, desire, and the failure of ambition. Yet the scope of Cavafy's poetry is immense; somehow the tilt of Cavafy's perspective— that vantage point comprised of views from café tables, a single apartment balcony, windows in homosexual brothels, and an untidy desk in the Third Circle of Irrigation—begat a body of work of tremendous vitality. It is peopled with a nearly Shakespearean variety of characters, but it is also autobiographical, infused with a self-reflective intelligence considerably different from the reportorial drabness of American confessional verse. Yet no other poet will ever sound much like him. No other poet of the Modernist era speaks to us with such straightforwardly lucid intimacy; yet Cavafy remains unapproachable, even unknowable, a figure of baffling complexity and reserve. "Hidden Things," an early but crucial poem, offers up an aesthetic which is based upon a striking paradox, at once baldly direct and poignantly self-protective:

For all I did and said
let no one try to find out who I was.
An obstacle was there that changed the pattern
of my actions and the manner of my life.
An obstacle was often there
to stop me when I began to speak.
From my most unnoticed actions,
my most veiled writing—
from these alone I will be understood.
But maybe it isn't worth so much concern,
so much effort to discover who I really am.
Later, in a more perfect society,
someone else made just like me
is certain to appear and act freely.[12]

It is easy to read this poem as a denunciation of the closet, but this is to oversimplify the intricacies of the dance between self-disclosure, impersonation, and self-concealment that lies at the heart of Cavafy's writing. It is not a question for him of being closeted or out, but of selfhood being permeable, malleable, vibrantly in play within the matrix of his trio of thematic concerns. And to some degree you need a highly educated theologian of Cavafyism to separate the attributes of this trio, for in the poetry of Cavafy memory, desire, and history often seem one and the same: historical monologues and recollective love poems occupy identical regions of the past.

The means by which art and politics commingle in Cavafy's world parallel those in which eros and memory are conjoined. Cavafy's historicizing impulses encompass the erotic life with a similar ruefulness. Memory's imaginative power derives not from comprehensive evocation, but from selectiveness, flattening to a kind of shorthand the ephemeral nature of erotic beauty as well as the tawdriness within which it is set. Memory is thus both the ash of experience and its base metal alchemized to gold, causing rapture and bitterness to alternate from line to line. "Days of 1909, '10, and '11" is one of the best examples of this strategy:

> He was the son of a harassed, poverty-stricken sailor
> (from an island in the Aegean Sea).
> He worked for a blacksmith, his clothes shabby,
> his workshoes miserably torn,
> his hands filthy with rust and oil.
>
> In the evenings, after the shop closed,
> if there was something he longed for especially,
> a fairly expensive tie, a tie for Sunday,
> or if he saw and coveted
> a beautiful blue shirt in some store window,
> he'd sell his body for a dollar or two.
>
> I ask myself if the glorious Alexandria
> of ancient times could boast of a boy
> more exquisite, more perfect—lost though he was:
> that is, we don't have a statue or painting of him:
> thrust into that awful blacksmith's shop,
> overworked, tormented, given to cheap debauchery,
> he was soon used up.[13]

The acuteness and gruff realism of the portraiture give way in stanza three to idealization, but only for a moment, and with the dual goal of insisting upon the young man's beauty while linking it to the long-departed glories of the Classical world. Yet memory has but one horizon: both the beauty and the glory are equally extinct. All that remains are chiseled letters weathered smooth, composed in a language which itself is dead. It is a poor and fragmentary metonymy, but in its flat insistence, in its ardor to preserve some essence in spite of these relentlessly eroding forces, Cavafy's cameo of the blacksmith boy is richly poignant. But he does not let us savor this poignance: the brutal closing lines have seen to that. Like Dickinson, that other great miniaturist, Cavafy refuses to dwell in a single emotive state for long.

When Cavafy was asked by friends why he had lived for twenty-five years in the same apartment, in a shabby neighborhood deemed unbefitting an educated man with a private income, in an apartment above a bordello, looking out upon a decrepit church and a charity hospital, he famously replied that in fact his street had everything: "Where could I live better?" he said. "Below, the brothel caters to the flesh. And there is the church which forgives sin. And there is the hospital where we die."[14]

What of this myth, beyond the poems, now remains? Our driver and our guide have been lost for half an hour, circling street after narrow street, from the waterfront to the coliseum ruins and back again. The Greek-speaking Alexandria of Cavafy's day has now been thoroughly Arab-ized, and the address we're seeking is no longer 10 Rue Lepsius, but its current incarnation, 4 Sharia Sharm Al-Sheikh. Heesham, our guide, knows Alexandria well, but no one's ever asked to visit the dwelling of a long-dead Greek poet. The guidebooks are of little help: the big *Blue Guide to Egypt* says nothing of Cavafy or his house; the *Knopf Guide* notes the existence of a Cavafy museum, but it's unstarred and without an address. Cavafy's poem "The City"—typeset as prose—appears beside a drawing of the poet. "Upon his death in 1933," says the guide, "his apartment was converted into a museum."[15] Here again the guide's mistaken. When the translator and Cavafy scholar Edmund Keeley visited here in the early 1970s, the poet's apartment was a transient hotel, the Pension Amir, "each room a dormitory crammed with sway-backed beds and peeling wardrobes."[16] The purchase of the apartment by the Greek consulate and its conversion to a museum happened much later. "Are you sure the house is in Alexandria?" asks our guide. "Perhaps it's actually in Cairo."

I'm starting to think the house is not just off the tourist map, but that it may never have existed, is as mythic as the city of Cavafy's poems. It's been a long drive from Cairo. My wife and Heesham are growing impatient; they're ready for lunch. "I know it's near a Greek church," I say, "and maybe near a hospital." So we circle again, finding at last the Church of St. Shara, and then a winding street called Sharia Sharm Al-Sheikh, and on it number four, among a row of nineteenth-century apartment buildings, brightly colored in stucco, three and four stories high, bristling with TV antennae. The doors are flush with the sidewalk; it's like the French Quarter in New Orleans, but much worse for the wear. Beneath the paint's garish maquillage, the pinks and iridescent greens, the buildings are about to crumble. But several plaques have been affixed to number four, Arabic above, Greek in the middle, and English below: CONSTANTINE CAVAFY HOUSE. Below the plaques is a handwritten wooden sign: "open ten o'clock to three." And below it, a message has been stuck with masking tape: "asend the stare on top floor please ring bell." The door we push open is huge and weathered, carved with arabesques. Before us, a courtyard, cat-cradled with hanging laundry, line upon line of sheets and t-shirts, thick old-fashioned torpedo-pointed bras, men's white briefs with tears badly mended, semaphores of handkerchiefs and blue and red bandanas. Behind them, almost invisible, the stairway: *part these curtains and "asend."*

But we can never approach great writing by rising up. When reading poetry, Hélène Cixous insists, we always must descend, ever downward in a slow deliberate katabasis, down to the realm of the eloquent shades. So it's downward to the top floor, downwardly ascending to the bell, the gatekeeper telling us, in halting English, that "the most substantial poet of the modern Greeks" wrote only some one hundred poems; downward to the shuttered little rooms, slats of light on a rickety display case where the old man's death mask floats atop a purple cushion (weirdly garish, like the head of John the Baptist on its jeweled plate) beside a chapbook of his poems, a tattered mimeographed affair, bound with a stickpin—one of the "collections" he'd present to friends. Downward to a hulking writing desk, inlaid floridly with mother-of-pearl, to a rickety teak armoire and a huge Victorian four-poster; and beyond them, downward further, downward to the bottom-most place, the lowest rung, the deepest cavern, we step out on the balcony to the scalding Mediterranean sun, blinded and groping for our sunglasses. Car-horns and a distant siren, the dome of the church which forgives your sins, the hospital where you go to die. "You'll always end up in this city," says the poem. "Don't hope for anything elsewhere. / There is no ship for you, there is no road." There is only this crucible, inside which lies the city, this necropolis, this citadel. The Valley of Making and its ancient capital.

2002

Notes

1. Kenneth Rexroth, *Selected Poems*, ed. Bradford Morrow (New York: New Directions, 1984), p. 31.

2. Randall Jarrell, *Kipling, Auden and Company: Essays and Reviews 1935–64* (New York: Farrar, Straus, and Giroux, 1980), p. 38.

3. A. Alvarez, introduction to *Zbigniew Herbert: Selected Poems*, trans. Czeslw Milosz and Peter Dale Scott (Harmondsworth, UK: Penguin, 1968), p. 14.

4. James Wright, *Collected Poems* (Middletown, CT: Wesleyan University Press, 1971), p. 114.

5. Robert Bly, *Silence in the Snowy Fields* (Middletown, CT: Wesleyan University Press, 1962), p. 38.

6. W. S. Merwin, *Selected Poems* (New York: Atheneum, 1988), p. 120.

7. Happily, my powers of prediction are limited: Transtromer at long last received the Nobel in 2011.

8. Tomas Transtromer, *Selected Poems 1954–86*, ed. Robert Hass (New York: Ecco Press, 1987), p. 187.

9. Transtromer, *Selected Poems*, p. 147.

10. Robin Fulton, introduction to Tomas Transtromer, *New Collected Poems* (Newcastle upon Tyne: Bloodaxe Books, 1997), p. 5.

11. Transtromer, *Selected Poems*, p. 101.

12. C. P. Cavafy, *Collected Poems*, trans. Edmund Keeley and Philip Sherrard, ed. George Savidis, rev. ed. (Princeton, NJ: Princeton University Press, 1992), p. 195.

13. Cavafy, *Collected Poems*, p. 161.

14. Edmund Keeley, *Cavafy's Alexandra: Studies of a Myth in Progress* (Cambridge, MA: Harvard University Press, 1976), p. 53.

15. *Knopf Guide to Egypt* (New York: Knopf, 1995), p. 185.

16. Keeley, *Cavafy's Alexandra*, p. 5.

Maggie's Farm No More

The Fate of Political Poetry

The most controversial performance of Bob Dylan's career took place during the Newport Folk Festival on July 25, 1965, and to Dylan aficionados the event is the stuff of legend. Dylan, the young acoustic troubadour of the folk music revival, singer of earnest protest songs, and during the previous two years the darling of Newport Fest, strode onto the stage with an electric guitar, wearing a leather jacket. To the consternation of many of his devotees and to the outright horror of the folk performers who had gathered backstage, Dylan had "gone electric," eschewing the postures of folkie authenticity and the leftist pieties of what Dylan later disdainfully referred to as his "finger-pointing songs." He looked to many of his fans to be making a shameless appeal for commercial success among the teenybopper crowd. Backing him was an electric group, members of the Paul Butterfield Blues Band, featuring the brilliant young guitarist Mike Bloomfield, who had earlier that summer played on what is arguably Dylan's greatest recording, "Like a Rolling Stone." Emerging from the barrooms and juke joints of Chicago's Southside, and among the first genuinely integrated bands in pop music, the Butterfield ensemble followed in the tradition of Muddy Waters, Howlin' Wolf, and the other Chess Records greats, and—like them—they knew how to play loud. And play loud they did, so loud that folkie paterfamilias and Gandhi disciple Peter Seeger reportedly wanted to find an ax with which to sever the electrical cord to the sound system. A few bars into the first song, and the booing and catcalls began. Some chroniclers of the event claim the crowd was booing the murky sound system, better suited for acoustic guitars and autoharps than the feral Stratocaster vampings of Bloomfield and his cohorts. But the more likely scenario is that the crowd hated what they heard, hated it just as acutely as did the folk music elite who had gathered backstage. As Greil Marcus puts it, "the music was the cigarette butt, and people made up their minds about its significance on the spot."[1] Dylan played three songs with the band and left the stage.

The conventional wisdom has it that Newport marked Dylan's definitive break with his past; from this point on, he would be a folk balladeer and finger pointer no longer, no longer a spokesman for civil rights, no longer a shy and lanky prophet warning of apocalyptic doom, no longer a custodian of the traditional songs he had learned from the Childe Ballad books, the Harry Smith anthology, and the interchangeable singers of the Greenwich Village scene. Not only had Dylan gone electric, he had traveled inward. Now his music would resemble the turbulent associative complexity of Rimbaud and the surrealists and the jittery improvisations of Kerouac and the Beats. The music would be cramped, subjective, hermetic, and the songs which Dylan performed in the next two years would be celebrated as among the most revolutionary in twentieth-century music. Dylan would make rock and roll a respectable art form, but his new songs, gathered on the groundbreaking albums *Highway 61 Revisited* and *Blonde on Blonde,* would chart the inner life; he would leave the ethos of social protest behind. Of course, the conventional wisdom is always only partly true, and we are reminded of this now that a clear-sounding official recording of Dylan's often-bootlegged Newport concert has been released. Dylan opens his Newport set with a searing version of perhaps his most striking "protest" song, "Maggie's Farm," first recorded in early 1965 for his *Bringing It All Back Home* album, and also over the years released in four live versions. Yet the Newport version, done as a haunting and relentless blues shuffle, seems to me the best, Dylan's definitive finger-pointing song.

"Maggie's Farm" is a truculent absurdist parable, an outcry against servitude in any form. The song's refrain is a bracing cry of negation—the speaker has had it, and he's not going to take it any longer: "I ain't gonna work on Maggie's Farm no more. / No, I ain't gonna work on Maggie's farm no more," he sings in the song's refrain.[2] And Maggie's Farm is a Boschian place, run by a family of sadists. Maggie's father "puts his cigar / out in your face just for kicks," and Maggie's brother "hands you a nickel / he hands you a dime / he asks you with a grin / if you're having a good time / then he fines you every time you slam the door." In the familiar fashion of totalitarianism, Maggie's family claims moral superiority while at the same time spewing out falsehood. Maggie's mother "talks to all the servants/about man and God and Law. . . . / She's sixty-eight but she says she's twenty-four." The song's memorable concluding verse contains one of those Dylanisms that seemed to those of us growing up in the 1960s and 1970s to be almost scriptural: "I try my best / to be just like I am / but everybody wants you / to be just like them / They say sing while you slave / and I just get bored." The important thing is that the speaker refuses to play the game. He's done with Maggie's farm; he's not looking back. A comparison to "Penny's Farm," a 1927 recording by the Bentley Boys included in Harry Smith's *Anthology of American Folk Music* that was Dylan's obvious model for the song, is instructive here. The lament of sharecroppers oppressed by a greedy landlord, "Penny's Farm" was a favorite among Dylan's fellow folk revivalists. (Dylan had already plundered its lyrics and melody for one of his earlier songs, a piece of juvenilia entitled "Hard Times in New York.") The narrator of the Bentley Boys' recording possesses none of Dylan's certainty or rage; his protest is almost apologetic, as the song's first verse attests:

> Come you ladies and you gentlemen
> And listen to my song,
> I'll sing it to you right but you might think it's wrong,
> May make you mad but I mean no harm,
> It's all about the renters on Penny's Farm.
> It's hard times in the country,
> Down on Penny's Farm.[3]

"Maggie's Farm" is an early and important example of the kind of jeremiad that would soon be very common in the era, a surrealist-tinged condemnation of injustice in its manifold forms. The song's finger-pointing is not directed at specific social ills; the song instead insists that the causes of the corruption and absurdity of contemporary society are too great to be identified or analyzed. And yet we cannot tolerate their results. The position set forth in "Maggie's Farm" is echoed in works as diverse as the poems of W. S. Merwin's *The Lice* and Robert Duncan's *Bending the Bow,* the manic Brechtian filmscapes of early Bertolucci and middle-period Goddard, and the music of African American musicians not normally associated with Dylan, among them the Marvin Gaye of *What's Goin' On* and the Sly Stone of *There's a Riot Going On.* These are all familiar works, representative in key ways of a new kind of art of social engagement that emerged in the 1960s. As Morris Dickstein puts it in his now-classic study of that decade, *Gates of Eden*—tellingly, the volume takes its title from another Dylan song, recorded shortly before his Newport appearance—"the sixties gave impetus to both revolution and reform, and tried to combine the quest for social justice with the search for personal authenticity."[4]

Unfortunately, for a number of reasons, this new variety of socially engaged art failed to evolve, failed to fulfill its early promise. The new art of social engagement was predicated upon the belief that a symbiosis between a desire for social reform and "personal authenticity" was not just possible, but inevitable, and it was fueled by the work of now half-forgotten social theorists and psychologists such as Herbert Marcuse, Norman O. Brown, and Wilhelm Reich, whose work sought a utopian fusion of Marx and Freud. It was an era afflicted by the same sort of tautology that troubled Western art and literature in the years immediately after the Russian Revolution: the quest for social justice would beget a new and revolutionary art, and a new and revolutionary art would further the cause of social justice. Yet very few artists in any discipline were capable of convincingly blending personal authenticity and social concerns. Leftist political poetry of the 1930s as often as not devolved into mere agit-prop, and its naive expressions of Popular Front antifascism and solidarity with the oppressed working classes soon turned to bitterness and confusion thanks to the fall of the Spanish Republic and news of Stalin's show trials. The work of a good many of the American poets of the 1960s who spoke out against the Vietnam War now looks equally simplistic and dated. While figures such as Robert Duncan, W. S. Merwin, and George Oppen found the means to blend a desire for personal myth with social consciousness, poets as considerable as Denise Levertov, Robert Bly, and Muriel Rukeyser could not, and when we read these latter writers we tend to skip over their Vietnam War–era protest poetry, much of which is decidedly bad. (Levertov's publisher has recently seen fit to reprint a new selection of her antiwar poetry, yet I doubt if this repackaging will win many new admirers for this work.)

Furthermore, by the middle of the 1970s, in the aftermath of the Nixon resignation and the fall of Saigon, the zeitgeist had changed. Although a few poets, most notably Adrienne Rich, appeared to have discovered in their antiwar poems the sort of mixture of the personal and the social which would allow them to powerfully address issues such as feminism and gay rights, most American poets—regardless of whether they were writers of color or white, gay or straight, male or female—simply turned inward. The 1970s and 1980s were the era of the implosive atavism of the Deep Image, the nattering chattiness of confessional writing, the wise-cracking solipsism of the way Ashbery's followers had diluted his approach, and the similarly hermetic navel-gazing of the nascent Language poetry movement—which, for all its efforts to dismantle the received pieties of autobiographical poetry and talk up Marx, managed to be even more self-centered than Sharon Olds at her worst and more elitist than James Merrill. Granted, ever since the advent of Romanticism it has been common to insist that the act of developing a rich and emotionally sustaining sense of personal history is itself a political gesture, and in many respects I believe this claim is true. It is furthermore a belief which is all the more crucial in the era of late capitalism; when you write poetry, you insist that you are a self and not a consumer, and the commodities which you do consume—the felt-tipped pens and black notebooks, the issues of *APR*, the skinny poetry collections with their print runs of a couple thousand—don't count for much in the eyes of the marketing departments and ad agencies.

The point of all this, however, is that the direction American poetry has taken during the past three decades has been overwhelmingly subjective and hermetic. At some point in the early 1970s poets, like artists of the various other disciplines, surveyed the ruins of 1960s culture and concluded that the quest for social justice and the desire for personal authenticity were an oil-and-water mixture. As surely as Wordsworth did two centuries before them, poets gave up the urge to combine radical politics with poetry; they bunkered down, left the politics behind, and went on and on about their inner lives. (Insightful studies of the ramifications of this process can be found in poet-critic Kevin Stein's *Private Poets, Worldly Acts: Public and Private History in Contemporary American Poetry,* and in Charles Altieri's *Sense and Sensibility in Contemporary Poetry.*) Fortunately, most American poets did not become Tories in the way that the elderly Wordsworth did, but the results can seem almost as depressing. One might think that the arrival in the late 1960s of poetic schools deriving from identity politics—beginning with the Black Arts movement and the feminist reawakening—should have triggered a different sort of trend, but identity politics begat its own forms of insularity. As progressive critics ranging from former SDS member Todd Gitlin to the Marxist Terry Eagleton have insisted, the rise of identity politics—and by implication the poetic movements which we might associate with it—has in many respects served only to blunt the Left's ability to mount a sustained and collective program for social change. As Gitlin witheringly observes in his *The Twilight of Common Dreams,* what remains of the Left is a melee of coteries and special interests: "There is no *it* there. What we have instead is an ill-fitting sum of groups overly concerned with protecting and purifying what they imagine to be their identities. Yet the conscience they still tug on is the conscience of the Left. The energies they drain are the energies of the Left. What we are witnessing in the culture wars is not the triumph of the Left, but its decline."[5]

Thanks in part to this exasperating situation, American poets seem to have lost the means to compellingly address political concerns in their work. We may read Czeslaw Milosz, Zbigniew Herbert, Nazim Hikmet, Ko Un, Cesar Vallejo, and other figures in twentieth-century world poetry who have written about the intricate relationship between self and politics, but thanks to some general sense of inferiority before these greats we have rarely permitted ourselves to be influenced by them in any but the most superficial of ways. Certain poets with political or topical concerns may enjoy a brief vogue—Carolyn Forché in the 1980s, for example, or more recently Iraq War veteran Brian Turner—but their writing as often as not soon passes into oblivion. Attempts are made to revive the reputations of unjustly forgotten poets of the Left such as Thomas McGrath, Edgell Rickword, and Kenneth Fearing, but these writers are still not represented in the major anthologies. There are of course a few figures at work today who bring to their writing a compelling sense of political and historical import: Adrienne Rich again comes to mind, as well as Yusef Komunyakaa, but this pair is the exception rather than the rule. American poets may choose to look up from their laptop screens and out their windows long enough to add a couple of snide observations about their neighbors' SUVs or to bemoan the latest example of Bush administration hubris, but their efforts at combining the personal and the political remain for the most part failures, plagued by reductive thinking, a clumsy shuffling between anemic anecdote and simplistic rhetoric, and a pervasive sense of futility—we know how marginal we are, but don't know how to change our status.

Furthermore, we tend to look askance at poems of political protest which do not fit the restrictive aesthetic and political confines (i.e., mildly left-leaning but never far left) of the period style. As Piotr Gwiazda notes in a highly perceptive essay entitled "The Aesthetics of Politics/The Politics of Aesthetics," the controversy over Amiri Baraka's "Somebody Blew Up America" was notable less for the media frenzy caused by the poem's alleged anti-Semitism and its crackpot conspiracy theories about 9/11 than it was for the decidedly half-hearted defenses of Baraka which came out of the mouths of mainstream poets such as Gerald Stern, Robert Pinsky, and David Lehman, all of whom made some consternated and conflicted statements to the press about the Baraka affair. Admittedly, sound bites and replies to reporters' questions are not the best way to gain access to a poet's aesthetic, but the press interviews Gwiazda quotes leave you to understand that the poets just wanted Baraka to go away. He offers a very credible reason for this: "the assumption that poems of well-pronounced political and social views are merely forms of versified polemic rather than potentially valuable works of art is still taken very much for dogma."[6] In the pages that follow, I want to see if something can be done about the present situation, and try to posit some solutions that do not seem anemic, simplistic, or futile. I want to see if the bracing spirit of "Maggie's Farm," with its manic allegory and sly finger-pointing, can be revived to create a different sort of poetry of social engagement. And it is obvious to me that "Maggie's Farm" is far more interesting than what passes for political poetry today. Witness the dubious achievement of Sam Hamill's Poets Against the War movement. Shortly before the beginning of the second Iraq War, a number of American poets were invited by Laura Bush to a White House shindig intended to honor the poetry of Whitman, Dickinson, and Hughes. The first lady subsequently canceled this event when word got out that many of the poets intended to read work in protest of Bush policy regarding Iraq. Sam Hamill, founder of the esteemed Copper Canyon Press and one of the disinvited poets, then started a web site featuring anti–Iraq War poetry. Hamill invited poets to submit poems to be posted on a site, and he soon received a staggering number of submissions. Fifteen hundred arrived within the first four days of the site's inception, and as of January 2007, over twenty thousand poems had been posted on the site.[7] In 2003 Hamill also published a small print anthology of poems and statements by poets against the war. Some of the contributors were big shots like Merwin and C. K. Williams; others were unknowns. Hamill did the right thing at the right time; he galvanized the poetry community, and in some respects made it *seem* like a community again, bringing writers of various aesthetics and schools, writers who often speak of one another with disdain, together to express an important common cause. And Hamill, a hugely energetic figure, whose list when he ran Copper Canyon Press shows him to be both catholic and discerning in his literary tastes, was a very suitable person for this task. Hamill furthermore has a reputation in the literary world for being something a huckster—a quality that can't hurt if you're going to appoint yourself as a kind of spokesman for the poetry community. Hamill's activities and anthology garnered a fair amount of attention.

Unfortunately, a disproportionately large percentage of that attention came from the right-wing press in the form of some very nasty appraisals. Bruce Bawer, writing in the *Hudson Review,* speculated that Hamill's actions were simply a means of getting attention for his own poetry.[8] The *Weekly Standard* ran a lengthy piece on the controversy, starting with a headline that read, "THE APPALLING MANNERS AND ADOLESCENT PARTISANSHIP OF OUR ANTIWAR POETS." The article, by one J. Bottum, pilloried Hamill and found a way to malign a long list of highly regarded contemporary poets. Bottum let everybody have it—Mary Oliver, Adrienne Rich, Galway Kinnell, Robert Bly, W. S. Merwin; he even got a couple digs in at the centegenarian Stanley Kunitz, and bemoaned the fact that the single American poet whom Bottum seemed to admire—Richard Wilbur, whom one would never think unmannerly—appeared to have bowed to peer pressure and (horrors!) signed an antiwar statement.[9] Although the *Weekly Standard* is one of the few right-wing journals that pay any attention to the arts, the piece was tainted with the same pugilistic anti-intellectualism you find on the Fox network, and the tone was typical of the way the right greeted Poets Against the War. Of course, anyone expressing reservations about administration policy is regarded by the right in general as unpatriotic. But the poets, with their quaint sense of moral outrage and Quixotic 1960s nostalgia, must have been seen as especially tasty prey.

But Bottum and his cohorts in the neo-con press were right about one thing: the quality of the antiwar poetry they surveyed was generally pretty dismal, and as the war drags on and more and more poems pile up on the Hamill web site—he's received over twenty thousand poems, remember—they don't seem to be getting any better. Each week there are new postings on the site, and though I may visit it to sign the antiwar and human rights petitions that appear in its pages, or to read the quarterly newsletter, I rarely spend any time with the poems. Some of the offerings are by well-known poets, but writers of all ages and from all walks of life have contributed work, and each featured poem is accompanied by a short explanatory note or bio statement. The bio notes are frequently touching, just as the poems themselves are frequently bad. And I mean *merely* bad. Baraka's "Somebody Blew Up America" may be offensive to some readers thanks to its anti-Israel stance and fringe politics; and it may represent a discredited Beat aesthetic: but the poem is defensible as art. This can't be said about many of the postings on the Poets Against the War site. Some representative passages:

> We speak mountains of blank pages
> To deafened ears.
> Eyes blind to the rights of the wronged
> Offer no vision to those seeing it all.
>
> Freedom doesn't fit the oppressed.
> Liberty now holds a snuffed torch.
> Apathy silences the shouting voices.
>
> To whom can unread letters be written?
> Dysfunctional functionaries on the hill?
> Greed is a tight diet . . .[10]

Or this:

> Let us honor the lost, the snatched, the relinquished,
>   Those vanquished by glory, muted by shame.
> Stand up in the silence they've left and listen:
>   Those absent ones unknown and unnamed—
> *Remember!*
>
> Their whispers fill the arena.[11]

The first passage is by a sixty-seven-year-old retired architect from Fayetteville, Arkansas. The second is by Rita Dove, whose offering seems not at the level of her best work.

It is of course entirely legitimate to answer my complaint about the poetic insufficiency of efforts such as these by saying that they represent something important that is fundamentally extra-literary: a grassroots effort at political protest and consciousness raising that will combine with other such efforts and eventually help to bring the war to an end, change Bush administration policy, or, better still, send George W. in ignominy back to Crawford before his second term is up. Maybe it is better to regard Poets Against the War as a version of moveon.org, with some dead metaphor and clumsy scansion thrown in. But what troubles me about the majority of the poems on the Poets Against the War web site is that their bad writing connotes a lot of silly, sentimental, and sanctimonious thinking—the very sort of thinking which, allied with greed, helped to bring America into Iraq in the first place. The poems may be attempts at consciousness raising, but they often reflect a sadly low level of consciousness. W. S. DiPiero, reviewing the Hamill anthology in *Poetry*, comes up with a persuasive—and distressing—list of reasons why the book fails, both in its antiwar message and as poetry. His observations are worth quoting at length:

> If poets suppress ambiguity, generative vagueness and destabilizing inquiry, they collude with the media circus we all criticize for its depredations on language. The media thrives and dominates because it insists on sentimental simplifications. If poets so indulge, they become their own enemy. . . . Then there's this. The nice idioms cultivated and encouraged in the hothouses of writing programs are inadequate to the worst (and best) of experience. Some poets write almost as proxies for past poets who had a fuller, formal, rhetorical range. One piece in *Poets Against the War*, after stating the occasion ("Early in the day reports said our planes / have bombed a wedding in a distant country"), comes round to this: "It was exactly the sort of thing which in a Greek play / would initiate a sequence of events / that turns inexorably back to bite / the hand that set it in motion." This is shadow-boxing—there's no resistance. . . . In a sense, the poems can't win for losing. Many are preacher man poems hollered at the choir. A good holler clears the air. But I suspect the writers know in their hearts how ineffectual poetry is in greater American society. I don't think American poets should speak as if they're goddamn right.[12]

Would Milosz have been able to turn into the sort of poet he became if he'd been born into a culture where he watched a lot of TV as a child, grew up in a ranch house in the 'burbs, ate a lot of junk food, and then went to Botox State for an MFA before winning the Vachel Lindsay Memorial Prize from Pumpernickel Press for his very promising first collection? After you read what Di Piero says, you suspect that the answer to this question has to be no. The curious bipolar shuffle between self-satisfaction and feelings of inadequacy which afflicts most American poets, coupled with their training in MFA programs which tacitly favor competence over risk-taking, isn't conducive to a poetry of Milosz-ian grandeur and moral seriousness. Of course, Milosz faced much greater challenges than we face, and we needn't aspire to be Milosz. But we shouldn't on the other hand aspire to be the sort of poets who are represented in the Hamill anthology and the Poets Against the War website.

What needs to be done to change all this? I suspect that one answer lies in reviving the reputations of long-neglected poets of the Left in the way that the critic Cary Nelson has so tirelessly done in books such as his *Repression and Recovery* and *Revolutionary Memory*. But I have to say that many of the poets Nelson makes a case for don't generally interest me. The American Left can boast four figures who to me seem unquestionably major poets—Langston Hughes, Thomas McGrath, George Oppen, and Muriel Rukeyser. But we also look at the work of this group for reasons other than simply to admire their poetry of social protest. They are rich and abiding figures, various in their concerns and ambitious in the way that we expect major poets to be. But you can't say the same for the likes of Lola Rudge, John Beecher, Edwin Rolfe, and a host of even lesser writers whom Nelson would add to this pantheon. Is their poetry defensible as art? Sure. Just not particularly so—and it is certainly not great. Still, Nelson and others have done important work in realigning the canon to give poetry of social engagement its proper due, and doubtless more such work will be done.

Another answer may be to go the way which Brecht, Neruda after his conversion to communism, and Auden in efforts such as "Spain" did, and try to formulate a well-crafted and merciless poetry of invective against oppression and political injustice, a poetry which overtly calls for action and which is by no means meant to be nuanced or subtle. Thomas McGrath called such poetry "tactical" verse, and opposed it to "strategic" verse, which is meant to raise awareness and consciousness.[13] The problem with the former sort of poetry is that it is hard to write well, and its success rate even among masters of the form like Neruda and Brecht is fairly low. Furthermore, in the hands of American writers poems of political invective always start to sound like fourth-rate versions of "Howl." Yet I share with Gwiazda the wish that this sort of poetry weren't so far out of favor; besides, the challenge of composing a well-written screed might be just the thing that certain so-called mainstream poets need in order to shake themselves out of their various forms of complacency: the tutelage of Amiri Baraka might in this respect do many of our mainstream poets a world of good. We need at the very least to study with some seriousness the art of the polemical poem, be it in the form of the epigraphs of Martial and Catullus, the topical "libels" of Jonathan Swift, or the late satires of Bertolt Brecht. American poets, who go to such extraordinary lengths to prove how sensitive they are, may find the writing of these decidedly insensitive poets to be refreshing, and perhaps even instructive.

Yet the solution to our problem which most interests me does in fact have to do with sensitivity, if we define authentic sensitivity as, among other things, resistance to the "sentimental simplifications" which Di Piero sees as afflicting both our poetry and our culture. The poem will be sensitive thanks to its emotional complexity and dividedness rather than through its adherence to period-style mannerisms and PC posturings. It will proceed by contraries, those qualities of ambiguity and "destabilizing inquiry" which Di Piero praises, and its forms will reflect that dividedness, a dividedness that cannot be resolved by resorting to easy dichotomies. It will combine social engagement with personal authenticity, yet it will not proceed from predetermined definitions of the social or the personal. Nevertheless, it will be intensely aware of how, as Kevin Stein puts it, "history inscripts our lives in subtle and manifest ways."[14] And it will reflect the intensity of contemporary reality in all of its media-driven and consumerist-driven cacophony. It is poetry as Brecht—in one of his non-Stalinist moments—defined it: "a social function of a wholly contradictory and alterable kind, conditioned by history and in turn conditioning it. It is the difference between 'mirroring' and 'holding up a mirror.'"[15] This will not be a wholly new sort of poetry. As I have noted, the 1960s were rich in examples of it, though these examples represent a mode of writing that soon fell out of fashion. And it is not a kind of writing that necessarily links itself to an avant-gardist tradition. The kind of poem I refer to has no better example than Robert Lowell's "For the

Union Dead," which is among the greatest American poems of social engagement. In what follows, I want to discuss two poets—less familiar than Lowell—who have written the kind of poem I am speaking about. One is an esteemed older figure, Hayden Carruth, the other a poet of my own generation, Lawrence Joseph.

I want to focus on a single poem of Carruth's, likely written in the mid-1960s, probably within a year or two of Dylan's performance at Newport. It comes from one of his best individual collections, *From Snow, From Rock, From Chaos*. I suspect that one reason why Carruth has never been given the attention he deserves is that he has for the most part chosen to remove himself from the academy and the centers of the literary world. Carruth spent much of the 1960s on a farm in Vermont, and, like Frost before him, he was probably not a very competent farmer. In "Emergency Haying" the speaker's ineptitude at agriculture is made explicitly clear. America's war in Vietnam, which is raging as Carruth writes the poem, is not explicitly confronted, though certainly the poem must be read with the Vietnam conflict in mind. Carruth has always worked in a number of styles, and here he offers a plainspoken Frostian narrative. The poem's sentiments are ultimately very un-Frostian, however.

The tonal dissonance of the title hints at what is to come. "Haying" suggests a bucolic and pastoral approach, rural romanticism in the fashion of the Georgian poets or John Clare. But this is "emergency" haying, and a quality of alarm and urgency continually troubles Carruth's descriptions. Here are the poem's initial stanzas:

> Coming home with the last load I ride standing
> on the wagon tongue, behind the tractor
> in hot exhaust, lank with sweat,
>
> my arms strung
> awkwardly along the hayrack, cruciform.
> Almost 500 bales we've put up
>
> this afternoon, Marshall and I.
> And of course I think of another who hung
> like this on another cross. My hands are torn

by baling twine, not nails, and my side is pierced
by my ulcer, not a lance. The acid in my throat
is only hayseed. Yet exhaustion and the way

my body hangs from twisted shoulders, suspended
on two points of pain in the rising
monoxide, recall the greater suffering.

Well, I change grip and the image
fades. . . .[16]

Although Carruth's opening is cast in flat declarative sentences,
in an unadorned free verse with strong iambic underpinnings,
it's a striking verbal and symbolic tour de force. The dramatic
situation is established with unfussy authority, and the crucifixion imagery dexterously manages to pay homage to the ro-
coco excesses of the Metaphysicals—think of George Herbert's
"Good Friday" and its "Thy whips, Thy Nails, Thy wounds, Thy
woes"—while at the same time undercutting them. The speaker's sacrificial musings give way to laconic Vermontese: "Well, I
change grip and the image / fades. . . ." The lines which follow
are similarly reportorial, their gruffness made even more acute
thanks to the frequent use of caesura:

It's been an unlucky summer. Heavy rains
brought on the grass tremendously, a monster crop,

but wet, always wet. Haying was long delayed.
Now is our last chance to bring in
the winter's feed, and Marshall needs help.

We mow, rake, bale, and draw the bales
to the barn, those late, half green,
improperly cured bales; some weigh 150 pounds

or more, yet must be lugged by the twine
across the field, tossed on the load, and then
at the barn unloaded on the conveyer

and distributed in the loft. I help—
I, the desk worker, word worker—
and hold up my end pretty well too; but God,

the close of day. I fall down then. My hands
are sore, they flinch when I light my pipe.

In a 1976 essay, Carruth analyzes the kind of occasion for the lyric that this poem seems to draw from, intensely subjective on the one hand, a manifestation of the self-driven confrontation with the world that Carruth and others in his generation learned so meaningfully from the work of Lowell and the confessional poets. Yet certain occasions, certain crucial moments of insight, are seen by Carruth as transcending *mere* self-reckoning. Solipsism gives way to an acute perception of the communal. "Poets too have their moments of intensity, what the ancients call fury and which we translate as exultation. These moments are a spiritual happening. As for other people, I am neither mechanic or farmer, but at times I have worked in both trades in a half-professional capacity; and I know that personality can flourish, existence can flourish, in the engagement with machines and the land, though this is no longer permitted as an ordinary thing in our civilization. Every consciousness is a personality *en posse*."[17] *Exultation* and *fury*—note that the words are drawn from liturgical speech rather than from the jargon of psycho-babble. Yet such moments are not available to the priestly caste alone: exultation and fury may arise from artistic endeavor, but they may also arise in the course of hard physical work or the practice of a craft. The speaker of "Emergency Haying" experiences exactly this sort of epiphany—and, significantly, it occurs thanks to physical labor rather than from versifying. With no sort of transition, Carruth follows the lines I have quoted above with this:

I think of those who have done slave labor

Less able and less well-prepared than I.
Rose Marie in the rye fields of Saxony,
her father in the camps of Moldavia

and the Crimea, all clerks and housekeepers
herded to the gaunt fields of torture. Hands
too bloodied cannot bear

even the touch of air, even
the touch of love. I have a friend
whose grandmother cut cane with a machete

and cut and cut until one day
she snicked her hand off and took it
and threw it grandly at the sky.

The anecdote of the cane cutter amputating her own hand arrives as a terrific shock. Thanks to the poem's deadpan mode
of narration, the gesture does not strike us as melodramatic. In
a grimly ironic juxtaposition, beginning in the same line which
describes the hand thrown at the sky, Carruth now moves back
to the primary narrative of the poem, and brings us to his conclusion:

                                        Now

in September our New England mountains
under a clear sky for which we're thankful at last
begin to glow, maples, beeches, birches

in their first color. I look
beyond our famous hayfields to our famous hills,
to the notch where the sunset is beginning,

then in the other direction, eastward,
where a full new-risen moon like a pale
medallion hangs in a lavender cloud

beyond the barn. My eyes
sting with sweat and loveliness. And who
is the Christ now, who

if not I? It must be so. My strength
is legion. And I stand up high
on the wagon tongue in my whole bones to say

woe to you, watch out
you sons of bitches who would drive men and women
to the fields where they can only die.

Carruth's abrupt shift back to pastoral description is a risky
enough move, but his return to the crucifixion motif is even
more so. Risky, too, are the shifts between elevated diction and
the demotic ("woe to you, watch out / you sons of bitches"). Yet
all the elements of the poem's closure combine seamlessly to
make a statement of great rhetorical power, and a memorable il-
lustration of Carruth's notion that "every consciousness is a personality *en posse.*" The voice of the poem as it reaches its ending
manages to be personal and choral at once thanks to the subtle
insertion of the first person plural in the passage which begins
with "I look" and to the less subtle but even more resonant transformation of the speaker into an avenging savior who professes
to speak for all those who have faced torture and oppression. A
poem which in its opening promised to explore some straight-
forward (though by no means easy) problems—how its bookish
narrator could manage physical labor, how Marshall could bale
his hay in time—becomes as it unfolds a far more rangy and ambitious project, and a supremely successful example of what Mc-
Grath would call a "strategic" poem. And it goes without saying
that it is not the sort of poem one would encounter in your average graduate poetry workshop. Carruth is an adamantly eclectic
writer, temperamentally unwilling to work in a single identifi-
able style, and yet the empathy and ferocity of "Emergency Haying" can be found in many of his poems.

Lawrence Joseph is another kind of poet entirely, his landscape as urban as Carruth's is rural, a poet given to abstractions
in a manner that Carruth with his pastoral leanings would likely
find pretentious. And, whereas Carruth can be a wonderfully
mellifluous prosodist, whether working in free verse or received
form, Joseph over the course of his four collections seems to
have deliberately shed any desire for elegance, favoring instead
a hard-edged and even dissonant style, one designed to incorporate but not synthesize a long list of polarities. This list derives
in part from Joseph's biography: his grandparents came from

Lebanon, immigrating to Detroit, where several of his family members as well as the poet himself worked in the auto plants; the poems also allude to a rigidly Roman Catholic upbringing. Joseph later became a lawyer, and presently lives in New York City, where he is a professor of law at St. John's University. It is not surprising, given Joseph's background, that his early work is considerably influenced by Philip Levine, employing the older poet's short lines and working-class narratives. But by the time of Joseph's third collection, 1993's *Before Our Eyes,* Joseph leaves the stylistic influence of Levine behind. He retains, however, Levine's rueful awareness of how class struggle and commodification afflict American culture, and of how the immigrant dream of assimilation can be stymied or perverted. The world of the legal profession and the vocabulary of jurisprudence also figure significantly in Joseph's work, discussed not only in his poetry but also in a scathing memoir entitled *Lawyerland* (1997). In Joseph's earlier collections, this complicated background and its conflicting sets of loyalties are approached as subject matter, as the material for a skillfully rendered but familiar sort of personal lyric. But in Joseph's recently published collection, *Into It,* he leaves the personal lyric behind, though elements of it remain in the poems in a kind of vestigial and fragmented form. Now the dichotomies and ambivalence which fueled the previous poems are focused upon discourse itself, on language's seeming incapacity to authenticate contemporary experience.

Joseph's new mode as often as not seems to begin in the discursive—rhetorical questions posed in a manic perversion of the Socratic. ("How far to go—I have to, I know, / I promised. How, and when? / And where . . ." is how the book's opening poem commences, in a mode that is repeated in several of its other efforts.) Yet soon this method gives way to a kind of relentless collage—though it is not the formulaic reliance on lists and catalogues you encounter in certain of the Language writers. The antecedents instead seem to be *The Wasteland* and *The Bridge;* as with those poems, the yearning for lyric gravity always seems to devolve toward fragmentation. Above all, Joseph is concerned with how postmodern culture, especially in its more insidious forms of political discourse, debases language, a process which is seen as accelerating exponentially in the wake of 9/11 and the two Gulf Wars. This concern is of course a familiar one, but Joseph expresses it with a troubled intensity of vision that distinguishes it from theoretical cant. He alludes to Celan in the new collection, and seems to share with Celan the notion set forth in his famous Bremen speech of 1958, in which the lyric is seen as a desperate attempt at saving language from the ways in which the historical events of the last century have distorted it, perverted it, and put it to the service of violence. For Celan, survivor of the death camps and author of the most famous poem about the Holocaust, the task of the lyric is to set itself against what the Bremen address calls "deathbringing speech," and the lyric must confront such speech in all of its grim toxicity before emerging from this confrontation with a new linguistic precision and authority. Language must, he insists, "pass through" deathbringing speech.[18] Celan's metaphors suggest a process almost mythological, a kind of *katabasis* in which the lyric descends to the netherworld and emerges reborn or restored. For Celan, the goal of this re-emergence was a language of extraordinary concision, a form of verse alchemically refined through compression and neologism in order to make it once again capable of creating intimacy.

Joseph's new work shares Celan's goal of restoring language to its capacity for intimate speech, as well as his perception that language faces a kind of apocalyptic crisis. Yet Joseph rejects Celan's hermeticism and drive for refinement. The realities of contemporary existence demand from him linguistic dissonance and the presence of sometimes violently opposing modes of discourse within a single poem. Similarly, the new poems do not aspire to the narrative linearity of Joseph's early work. Their pace is often too rapid and their speaker's mediations too troubled to allow us to easily locate the poems in clear dramatic situations. Quotations from advertising slogans, sampled political jargon, and snippets of unattributed dialogue intrude to further intensify the poems' turbulence. The speaker seems to be desperately trying to bring order to his surroundings, but no fragments can be shorn against these ruins: the poems often sound like a radio playing on the scan mode. Yet references to two events are alluded to obsessively in the collection, and in a perverse fashion act as leitmotifs which give the individual poems and the book itself a cohesive form. As a consequence of the World Trade Center attacks and the second Iraq War, Joseph insists in the book's penultimate poem, "the game changed." The effects of this realignment are manifold, on levels both macrocosmic and microcosmic—as he tells us in these lines from "I Note in a Notebook":

> . . . A figure, in the factory
> behind the Jefferson Avenue Assembly, marking
> and filing the parts of the new model prototype
> Chryslers, standing at a window, smoking a Kool.
> Those with the masks of hyenas are the bosses,
> and those wearing mass produced shirts and pants,
> among them my father . . . Cavafy's poem, the one
> about how if he's wasted his life in this corner
> of the world he's wasted it everywhere. What
> is happening, what is done. Convicted
> of rape and murder, he leaves a piece of pie
> in his cell, believing he'll be able to eat it
> after he's electrocuted—the fact that a compound,
> 1, 3-diphenyl propane, forged from the fires'
> heat and pressure, combined with the Towers'
> collapse, has never been seen before.
> The technology to abolish truth is now available—
> not everyone can afford it, but it is available—
> when the cost comes down, as it will, then what? . . .[19]

An answer to the terrifying question posed at the end of this passage can to some extent be found in a poem I would like to discuss in more detail, "News Back Even Further Than That." It is not a consoling reply, yet the poem epitomizes the savage acuity of Joseph's vision. Here is the first of its three sections:

> I
> Dust, the dust of a dust storm;
> yellow, black, brown, haze, smoke;
> a baby photographed with half
> a head; the stolen thoroughbred
> the boy is riding bareback attacked
> by a lion; the palace, fixed up

as a forward command post—"This,"
says Air-War Commander Mosely,
"would make a pretty nice casino":
why is such a detailed
description necessary?
that smell in the air is the smell
of burned human flesh;
those low-flying A-10 Warthogs
are, each of them, firing
one hundred bullets a second.[20]

This is the sort of surrealist montage familiar to us from the
protest poetry of the Vietnam era—take away the Gulf War setting, and you may as well have a passage in Robert Bly's "The
Teeth Mother Naked at Last" or from certain of the poems of
Kinnell and Merwin. But whereas these writers deemed the surrealist catalogue alone sufficient to give the poem its purpose, Joseph's approach is more complex. In the poem's second section,
surrealism begins to commingle with a number of other modes,
but the effect is equally disruptive; Old Testament references,
political caricature, and a kind of mock-Elizabethan diction are
juxtaposed against the techno-babble of modern warfare:

II
The President refuses to answer a question
he wasn't asked. The President denies
his are the eyes of a lobster.
The map is being drawn: Mosul in the north,
Baghdad in the center, Basra in the south.
The news back even further than that:
"He Says He is the Prophet Ezekiel.
In the Great Mudflats by the River Chebar.
He Has seen, He proclaims, Four Angels,
Each with Six Wings, on a Fiery Wheel."
Collaborators cut into pieces and burned to death
in public, on spits, like lambs. In spray paint
across the armored personnel carrier:
"Crazy Train," "Rebel," "Got Oil? . . ." There,
on Sadoun Street, in a wheelbarrow, a coil
of wire, carpet, rolled, Persian, antique.

It is fitting that "the news back even further than that" supplies Joseph with the title of the poem: a confounding and seemingly oxymoronic line worthy of Gertrude Stein, jittery with spondees, it perfectly describes the poem's decentered mixture of satire, biblical language, and anachronism, all giving way as the passage ends to a kind of documentary panorama of a war-ravaged landscape. The grandiosity and chiliastic import of passages such as "He has seen, He proclaims, Four Angels," are set against the cartoonish slogans graffitied to the American armored personnel carriers. The dissonance is further intensified thanks to Joseph's refusal to identify the "He" in the passage in quotations—is it the president? God? someone else entirely?—and to the propulsive sonics of the lines; sentence fragments and caesuras abound. This caterwauling mixture all culminates in the final image of the Persian carpet in a wheelbarrow and its coil of wire. On the one hand, it suggests a refugee's cart. Yet the presence of the wire coil denotes something more ominous—the silken floral rosettes of the carpet may be hiding one of those "improvised explosive devices" the Pentagon likes to talk so endlessly about. As we come to the closing of the section, we are meant to hear the ticking of a bomb.

The final section of the poem introduces a new approach and a new voice. Told largely in the form of a monologue spoken by an unnamed woman, it begins with the sort of political rant which many of us on the Left heard from friends or delivered ourselves in the months following the second invasion of Iraq. Yet, slowly and inexorably, Joseph wrests from the exasperation and sense of helplessness which accompanies such speeches something entirely different and considerably more sinister:

> "I've just been to see her. It's made her
> mad—angry, yes, of course, but I mean mad,
> truly mad. She spoke quietly, quickly—
> maniacally. 'Wargame, they're using wargame
> as a verb, they didn't wargame the chaos—
> chaos? Do you think they care about
> the chaos? The chaos just makes it easier for them
> to get what they want. Wargame!
> What they've wargamed is the oil,

their possession of the oil, what they've wargamed
is the killing, the destruction,
what they've wargamed is their greed . . .'
Had I noticed that Lebanon has become
an abstract noun, as in 'the Lebanonization of'?
'It may just as well have been two or three
atomic bombs, the amount of depleted
uranium in their bombs, the bombs
in this war, the bombs in the war before this—
uranium's in the groundwater now,
uranium is throughout the entire
ecology by now, how many generations
are going to be
contaminated by it, die of it, be poisoned by it? . . .'

Was it just this morning that you yourself uttered the same
speech? We know who they are, and yet we don't know. It's the
Bush administration; it's the CIA; it's Halliburton; it's "I'm-not-
being-paranoid-but-it all-elides-together." That *they*, that terribly
real and terribly intangible *they*. They destroy the language in
order to justify the destruction of lives; they destroy the lives in
order to satisfy their greed, and their greed is never satisfied.
Deathbringing speech, Version 6.0—they've had seventy-odd
years to refine it. And on it goes. The woman's anger and dread
are our own. Yet as I read these lines I feel them to be more
than yet another expression of rage and futility. By this point
in the poem, the woman's rant has become something more
powerful—her words might even be termed prophetic. Because the woman is never identified, and because an unnamed
speaker—not necessarily the author himself, as the entire section is encased in quotation marks—has chronicled his visit to
her, we imbue the figure of the woman with a sense of mystery
and symbolic import. The speaker of the section has, after all,
made a kind of pilgrimage to the woman, a visit to an oracle. She
is not some tipsy woman at a party bitching about the Cheneys—
she is more akin to the sibyl, or to Clio, the muse of history,
regarded by the Greeks to be the sternest and most powerful
member of her sisterhood. And as the poem concludes, the
speaker himself seems emboldened; he is under her spell, and
the ending is a savage and unappeasable duet:

'War, a war time, without limits.
Technocapital war a part
of our bodies, of the body politic.
She quoted Pound—the *Pisan Cantos*—
she couldn't remember which—
there are no righteous wars.
'There is no righteous violence,'
she said, 'it's neurobiological
with people like this—
people who need to destroy and who need to kill
like this—and what we're seeing now
is nothing compared
to what we'll see in the future. . . .'"

An offering to Clio: the ending of Joseph's poem reminds us that such offerings must be composed out of our humbleness and our awe as we stand before Her. She demands that our witnessing against injustice make use of every resource of our craft, and She will not tolerate the tawdry sanctimoniousness which has come to dilute our thinking and our poetry. And surely Her famed sternness has grown even greater during an era when the forces of injustice have such powerful and insidious tools at their disposal. The game has changed in no small degree because the stakes have grown higher. As Adrienne Rich puts it, "the problem is not 'finding an imaginative interest in life,' but sustaining the blows of the material and imaginative challenges of our time."[21] And these blows fall down without ceasing. Reading the poems of *Into It* does not make me any more hopeful that the course this country is on will change; the crazed and entropic elements of our culture which Joseph's book so relentlessly rails against will never be altered in any crucial way by something of as little import as a poem, no more than a cut on a long-playing record album released by a skinny kid from Hibbing, Minnesota, to a quizzical public over forty years ago could. Yet I know that Joseph's poems are free of the cant and debased rhetoric from which our political discourse is formed; they are free as well of the similarly debased and cant-afflicted postures which pass for most political poetry today. They echo the spirit of "Maggie's Farm," in other words, and on this snowy morning in December, I too invoke that spirit, turning off the presidential news conference in favor of *Bringing It All Back Home.* I turn the speakers up; the drums and guitars and the nasally croon of twenty-five-year-old Bob Dylan commence. I turn the speakers up again. I want the lies drowned out, the self-aggrandizement and zealotry, the utter subservience to deathbringing speech. I want the songs to remind us that our strength is legion, that we again will say woe to you, you sons of bitches, and that we will find the words and the means to destroy the technology that would abolish truth. George W. Bush stands smirking at the podium. He is Maggie; he is Maggie's brother; he is Maggie's Ma and Maggie's Pa. And no more shall we work for him.

2006

Notes

1. Greil Marcus, *Like a Rolling Stone: Bob Dylan at the Crossroads* (New York: Public Affairs, 2005), p. 156.
2. Bob Dylan, *Lyrics: 1962–1985* (New York: Knopf, 1985), p. 166.
3. "Down on Penny's Farm," *Roots of Bob Dylan,* http://rootsofbobdylan.com/pennysfarm. June 6, 2014.
4. Morris Dickstein, *Gates of Eden: American Culture in the Sixties,* rev. ed (New York: Penguin Books, 1989), p. xix.
5. Todd Gitlin, *The Twilight of Common Dreams* (New York: Henry Holt, 1995), p. 33.
6. Piotr Gwiazda, "The Aesthetics of Politics/The Politics of Aesthetics: Amiri Baraka's 'Somebody Blew Up America,'" *Contemporary Literature* 45, no. 3 (2004): p. 483.
7. "Poets Against War," http://poetsagainstwar.com/poemsoftheweek.asp. Dec. 14, 2006.
8. Bruce Bawer, "A Plague of Poets," *Hudson Review* 56, no. 4 (Winter 2004): p. 285.
9. J. Bottum, "The Appalling Manners and Adolescent Partisanship of Our Antiwar Poets," *Weekly Standard,* Feb. 17, 2003. p. 9.
10. "Poets Against War," http://poetsagainstwar.com/displaypoem.asp?AuthorID=25151#453082072. Dec. 14, 2006.
11. "Poets Against War," http://poetsagainstwar.com/chapbook.asp#Dove. Dec. 14, 2006.
12. W. S. Di Piero, "Fat," *Poetry* 183, no. 1 (Oct. 2003): p. 49.

13. Quoted in W.S. Di Piero, *Shooting the Works: On Poetry and Pictures* (Evanston, IL: Northwestern University Press, 1996), p. 46.

14. Kevin Stein, *Private Poets, Worldly Acts: Public and Private History in Contemporary American Poetry* (Athens: Ohio University Press, 1996), p. xiv.

15. Bertolt Brecht, *Poems 1913–1956*, ed. John Willet and Ralph Manheim (London: Methuen, 1976), p. 483.

16. Hayden Carruth, *Collected Shorter Poems 1946–1991* (Port Townsend, WA: Copper Canyon Press, 1992), p. 88.

17. Hayden Carruth, *Selected Essays and Reviews* (Port Townsend, WA: Copper Canyon Press, 1996), p. 178.

18. Paul Celan, *Selected Poems and Prose*, trans. Joel Felstiner (New York: W. W. Norton, 2001), p. 395

19. Lawrence Joseph, *Into It* (New York: Farrar, Straus, and Giroux, 2005), p. 10.

20. Joseph, *Into It*, p. 38.

21. Adrienne Rich, *What Is Found There: Notebooks on Poetry and Politics* (New York: W. W. Norton, 1993), p. 108.

"Of Course I Would Have Saved Them If I Could"

On Capaciousness

In the summer of 1936, W. H. Auden took a trip to Iceland, a country which—then as now—cannot be called an especially popular tourist destination. Up until this time, the twenty-nine-year-old Auden seems to have had very little interest in that little piece of volcanic rock above the arctic circle, but he had decided to join a headmaster and some students of the Downs school, where he had recently taught, on a school field trip—mainly because he had a crush on one of those students, a young man named Michael Yates. Auden was at the height of his early fame, the best and best known of the young leftie poets who used to be called the Auden-Spender generation, and now are just called the Auden generation, Spender's reputation no longer being what it once was. Auden's esteem was such that he was quickly able to negotiate book contract with his publisher—the august Faber and Faber, which employed T. S. Eliot as its poetry editor— for a travel book about Iceland. He got Faber to agree to bring in his fellow poet Louis MacNeice as his co-author, and off he sailed to Reykjavik, MacNeice following a few weeks later. *Letters from Iceland,* the publication which resulted from these travels, remains one of the oddest travel books ever written. We do from time to time get some information about the land and its inhabitants, much of it condescending—Reykjavik is ugly and boring,; the geysers are over-hyped, and Icelandic cuisine is hardly a culinary delight. I can't attest to the veracity of these claims, but the descriptions of the stomach-turning food are pretty persuasive. Hakarl, for example, is "half-dry, half-rotten shark. This is white inside, with a prickly horn rind outside, as tough as an old boot.

Owing to the smell it has to be eaten out of doors. It is shaved off with a knife and eaten with brandy."[1] Auden likens its taste to boot-polish, but he finds the pickled sheep udders "surprisingly very nice."[2] For the most part, the book is only tangentially about its professed subject; Auden offers fragments from a kind an of epistolary novel involving members of a girls' school on a field trip to the Icelandic countryside, and interspersed throughout the volume are sections of Auden's long poem in rime royal, *Letter to Lord Byron*. It's one of his most brilliant technical performances, although its emphasis on topical satire badly dates the piece. MacNeice throws some of own versifying into the mix as well, none of it among his best. Paul Fussell, in his *Abroad: British Literary Traveling Between the Wars,* dismisses the book as "all just a bit of Camp," and I would be inclined to agree, were it not for a passage in the book that has haunted me for years.[3] Auden makes a visit to a whaling station in a place called Talknafjordur. He's writing from a bed and breakfast. Outside, the whalers are having a busy day:

> I wish I could describe things well, for a whale is the most beautiful animal I have ever seen. It combines the fascination of something alive, enormous, and gentle with the functional beauties of modern machinery. A 70 ton one was lying in the shipway like a large and very dignified duchess being got ready for the ball by beetles. To see it torn to pieces with steam winches and cranes is enough to make one a vegetarian for life.
>
> In the lounge the wireless was playing "I Want to Be Bad" and "Eat an Apple Every Day." Downstairs the steward's canary chirped incessantly. The sun was out; on the bay, surrounded by buoys and gulls, were the semi-submerged bodies of five dead whales; and down the slipway ran a constant stream of blood, staining the water a deep red for a distance of fifty yards. Someone whistled a tune. A bell suddenly rang, and everyone stuck their spades in the carcass and went off to lunch. The body remained alone in the sun, the flesh still steaming a little. It gave one an extraordinary vision of the cold, controlled ferocity of the human species.[4]

A vision indeed—no other term will do the scene justice, and we might even regard it as a vision of the prophetic sort. Here is the kind of "cold controlled ferocity" that very soon thereafter allowed the death camps to operate with such efficiency. Extermination becomes merely a problem of technique. You can stick your spade in the carcass and go off to lunch, satisfied that today's efforts will yield their quota of whale oil—or soap. We're reminded of Franz Kafka's "In the Penal Colony," with its similarly prophetic obsession with the nomenclature of extermination. The scene has the intensity, immediacy, and topsy-turvy mixture of the familiar and the strange that comes to us in dreams. Yet this dream originates beyond the self, much as it may also include the self. I am reminded of a passage in Carl Jung's *Memories, Dreams, and Reflections,* in which he Jung recounts a series of terrifying dreams that came to him in the months prior to the start of World War I. Their meaning is suddenly all-too-obvious: "On August 1 the world war broke out. Now my task was clear: I had to try to understand what had happened [to me] and to what extent my own experience coincided with that of mankind in general."[5] After Talknafjordur, Auden resolved to do much the same thing, though a bit less brazenly than the egomaniacal Jung. Auden biographer Richard Davenport-Hines offers several examples of how details from this event found their way into Auden's later poetry. He began to work them in more or less immediately. Here's a passage from "Letter to William Coldstream," one of several verse epistles which are interspersed in the Iceland book:

The saw is for cutting up jaw-bones.
The whole place was slippery with filth—with guts and
     decaying flesh—
          like an artist's palette.[6]

Compared to the prose, however, these lines are decidedly heavy-handed. (It's worth noting that Auden did not reprint it in any of his *Collected* volumes.) The woozy dactyls and the maddeningly reductive metaphor of the painter's palette have purged the descriptions of the immediacy and visionary resonance we find in the prose. Yet it is clear that this event *got to* Auden. He felt he had to return to this moment in order to get it right. The problem was that he got it right in the first place, recording the event *in situ,* almost improvisationally—and also cinematically. He's using techniques he had learned to employ a few years earlier as scriptwriter for documentary films. The most important thing is that he's able to describe the moment in all of its emotional complexity and contradiction—we see Auden's horror at the sight of the bloody carcasses reddening the bay, hear the canary's irritating chirp, and the songs on the wireless offering their blithely ironic soundtrack to the whole grim business. (Sixty years later Quentin Tarrantino will would make this sort of thing his trademark, though far less artfully, I think.)

It is the nature of visions to come out of nowhere. And, as often as not, they are violent. Saul was not *converted* on the road to Damascus, he was *struck down*, then blinded, and if you believe the narrative of the Caravaggio painting he gets thrown from his horse and lies on his back with hands in the air, writhing like an upturned beetle. But it is the nature of the artist to almost immediately transform the visionary into subject matter and challenges of craft. In a kind of medieval prefiguration of reality TV, St. Teresa of Avila for years kept a stenographer at her side—so that the chatter from her ecstasies would always be suitable for publication. And in *Goodbye to All That,* Robert Graves describes his reaction to a companion getting his skull blown off in during the Battle of the Somme: after watching the headless body stagger around the trench for a moment, Graves's first thought is horror. His next—"another caricature scene."[7]

Earlier, I mentioned that Auden peppered *Letters from Iceland* with sections of his poem, *Letter to Lord Byron,* a work he later published separately. If we can take what Auden tells us in the poem at face value, he'd never read Byron prior to his visit to Iceland, and a collection of Byron's writings seems to have been just about the only book which Auden carried with him on the trip. I bring this up because of a well-known letter of Byron's, so well known that any selection of this work would be likely to include it:

To John Murray
Venice, May 30, 1817

Dear Sir—,

The day before I left Rome I saw three robbers guillotined. The ceremony—including *masqued* priests; the half-naked executioners; the bandaged criminals; the black

Christ and his banner; the scaffold; the soldiery; the slow procession, and the quick rattle and heavy fall of the axe; the splash of the blood, and the ghastliness of the exposed heads—is altogether more impressive than the vulgar and ungentlemanly "new drop," and dog-like agony of infliction upon the sufferers of the English sentence. Two of these men behaved calmly enough, but the first of the three died with great terror and reluctance, which was very horrible. He would not lie down; then his neck was too large for the aperture, and the priest was obliged to drown his exclamations by still louder exhortations. The head was off before the eye could trace the blow; but from an attempt to draw back the head, notwithstanding it was held forward by the hair, the first head was cut off close to the ears; the other two were taken off more cleanly. It is better than the oriental way and (I should think) than the axe of our ancestors. The pain seems little; and yet the effect to the spectator, and the presentation to the criminal, are very striking and chilling. The first turned me quite hot and thirsty, and made me shake so that I could hardly hold the opera glass (I was close but determined to see, as one should see every thing, once, with attention); the second and third (which shows how dreadfully soon things grow indifferent), I am ashamed to say had no effect on me as a horror, though I would have saved them if I could.

It is some time since I heard from you—the 12th *April* I believe.

Yours ever truly, B.[8]

Here too we are presented with "an extraordinary vision." We can't be said to witness the "cold controlled" ferocity of human-kind here, for the Italians seem quite a bit less efficient at the niceties of extermination than their Icelandic counterparts. Indeed, the bungling of the first robber's execution, and his "great terror and reluctance" as he mounts the scaffold, increases both our sense of horror—it's a truly revolting spectacle—and our awareness of dramatic tension. Byron is of course both appalled and fascinated, and his bravura ability to capture that admixture never flags. The scene is evoked with a telegraphic precision: "the quick rattle and heavy fall of the axe; the splash of blood, and the ghastliness of the exposed heads. . . ." The rhythms are managed with special brio: the struggle to get the first robber to the chopping block comes to us largely in anapests, the triple feet teasing the scene out. But the fall of the blade that happens so suddenly is rendered in a rush of iambs—"the head was off before the eye could trace the blow." Auden, in a 1966 introduction to a selection of Byron's verse, notes that "Byron's genius is essentially a comic one," and comedic skill is all about timing. It is also about irreverence, which of course we see throughout the letter.[9] And it furthermore involves psychological insight. Shaken as the scene may leave him, Byron still peers through his opera glass, because "one should see every thing, once, with attention." This morning at the gym I put my time in on the treadmill, my iPod set to "*shuffle*," and two mute TVs above me. On one Rachel Ray prepared salmon, her studio audience wildly applauding; on the other CNN broadcast footage of a plane crash site in Thailand. A survivor swathed in bandages was talking, the caption below him reading "horrible, horrible, horrible." The soundtrack to this was the Louvin Brothers, their high reedy tenors at work on a murder ballad—"Knoxville Girl," to be precise—a song brought to Appalachia from England two or three hundred years ago. "She never spoke another word / I only beat her more." And this in turn was followed by Grover from Sesame Street, whose condition, he tells us, is "fuzzy and blue"—I'd mistakenly downloaded some of my kids' music from my computer to the iPod. Another ordinary morning in the 'burbs. "The second and third time (which shows how dreadfully soon things grow indifferent), I am ashamed to say had no effect on me as a horror." Sweat dripping from his brow and badly wanting a drink, his lorgnette pressed to the bridge of his nose, Bryon foresaw the state we're in today, just as surely as Jung saw the coming of a world at war. Horrible, horrible, horrible—yet the ending of the letter is a grimly ironic punch line: "though I would have saved them if I could." And then a kind of post-punch line: "it is some time since I heard from you."

Three final comments on this letter. First, could any of us, knowing that Auden had been devouring his Byron that summer, paging some elegant little pocket edition under the midnight sun, fail to see that Auden was under this letter's spell?

Consciously or unconsciously, he well may have had it in his mind at Talknafjorder, and it gave him the means to make sense, however provisionally, of his vision of our "cold and controlled ferocity." Literary influence is, after all, mysterious. Second, why is it that these two passages thrill and terrify me in a way that very few contemporary poems can? And how might we find the means to attain some of their energy and attentiveness, their protean ability to shift tone and diction—not to mention their sense of the artist's social responsibilities—into our own poetry? It's the second and third of these questions that I want to explore here.

Were we honest with ourselves, I think we would all agree that the qualities I am praising in these letters are ones which are not much in evidence in the poetry of our new century. The most striking quality of the letters is something we might label their capaciousness, their ability to incorporate, with an immediacy that is never less than artful, a large spectrum of human emotion, in all of its general messiness and contradiction. In some ways this is the poet's task as Keats defined it in his negative capability letter, written the same year as Byron's missive from the chopping block. We must be "capable of being in uncertainties, Mysteries, doubts, without any irritable reaching after facts and reason."[10] Yet there is something about this statement that has always seemed to me a bit effete and calculated. It sets the poet up as a kind of suave circus ringmaster of contradiction; despite the pressure of experiential paradox and dissonance, the poet will maintain his/her cool, and in some Hegelian way synthesize the contradictions, clean up the general mess, and alchemize it all into to a delicious concoction that is, well, Keatsian. I'm being unfair and a bit inaccurate, I know, but what I admire in the Auden and Byron letters is that they serve up their emotions raw—not, however, in that first-thought-best-thought manner that afflicts many contemporary poems and which seems to me one of the unintended legacies of Romanticism, but with the simple awareness that the contradictions don't get resolved, and that living with them ain't easy. I'm reminded of something Pasolini wrote after his disillusion with Marxism—"I no longer believe in dialectics and contradictions, but in pure opposition."[11]

This is not so much a rejection of Keats's notion as a kind of supercharging of it, an insistence that our uncertainties don't commingle as much as collide. There are glimmers of this sort of recognition in certain key Modernist poems—bringing this element out might be said to be the purpose of Pound's remorseless edits of *The Wasteland*. But it's with the middle-generation poets and the generation that followed them that the aesthetic of pure oppositions became crucial. And it emerges in various ways—in the relentless juxtapositions of public event and private experience that animates the best poems of Lowell's *Life Studies* and *For the Union Dead;* in the woozy shuffle between contemporary slang and mock-Elizabethan that characterizes the *Dream Songs;* in the grainy newsreel immediacy of Rich's *Leaflets* and *The Will to Change;* and in the terrifying emotional ricocheting between ecstasy and abjection which we see in James Wright. What Stanley Kunitz wrote of Wright could on some level apply to all of the poets on this list: "He is perpetually arriving at a crisis of style . . . . of which the meaning is that he is perpetually discovering a crisis of conscience. At that level of experience, things are capable of changing into their opposites, as suffering into joy, and despair into radiance."[12]

Since these writers made their key stylistic transformations in the 1960s, the prevailing period styles in American poetry have moved in other directions. For various reasons, some of them quite valid, a poetry based upon such urgency—upon states of emotional and stylistic crisis—came to seem a little quaint. The work of Ashbery and the Language Writers is about many things, but crisis and emotional reckoning seems not for the most part to be among them. And irony, a device which the middle generation and their successors wielded with a scalpel-like precision, has now become a less subtle tool, a kind of nine-pound hammer, less a stylistic device than a dogma. I am again being reductive here, I know, and I could stop and list several dozen exceptions to this trend—but it *is* a trend, and it worries me because it seems to so limit and enervate poetic expression. To continue in this reductive vein, let me here offer a poem from a recently published collection. It also happens to describe a public execution:

The Home of the Brave

   —after the Nick Berg decapitation video

The home of the brave is a small room.
At first, it mimics us.
Armed men stand side by side.
They are aware of their power.
They have concealed their identities.
Only their leader speaks,
and speaks at length,
reading from a prepared statement
foregrounding their intentions
with weak rhetoric,
belief in God.
His comrades fidget and remain silent.
When the screaming begins
the camera shakes
with a new honesty—
mimicry is done with now—
the men bear down,
and the home of the brave
is what we cannot understand,
what we cannot endure,
as long as we are free.[13]

A troubling subject, certainly, and the poem seems to indict both the moral repugnance of terrorist extremism and a world where acts of violence have become so commonplace and mediated that we respond to them with an apathetic shrug. The poem describes a download, not the killing of a hostage. It seems that the poem's author, Joe Wenderoth, wants to remind us of this point by framing it in the most listless language possible. The syntax and predictable endstopping are only varied at the moment when Berg's murder is described—"the camera shakes / with a new honesty— / mimicry is done with now." This in turn leads to the muddled statement offered in the final four lines, which are so maladroit that we are tempted to read them merely as parody, as something sampled from one of the more cheesy moments of a presidential address. But we can't quite be sure.

Wenderoth, like many younger poets, is a highly accomplished ironist. But here that very skill may have underscored his other limitations.

Rather than cite further examples of this sort of poetry, or offer further explanations about why it has become the prevailing period style, I want to conclude by discussing poems by three members of my own poetic generation who display the sort of capaciousness and unflappability which impresses me in Auden's poem and Byron's letter, a capaciousness which allows their poems to address and adapt to situations of emotional and moral crisis. They are writers, in short, who have found a way to live within the "mysteries and doubts" that have given way to "pure opposition," and who acknowledge their complexity and proliferation; furthermore, they have not succumbed to the nerve tic of mere irony as the primary method for confronting these states. They are, as I say, writers of my own generation, those of us born in the second explosion of the Baby Boom, in the years between the Eisenhower administration and the Kennedy assassination. I would not go as far as to label William Olsen, David Rivard, and Tom Sleigh as the most representative or typical figures of my generation, but they are among the best— best because their work reflects so well the literary, cultural, and historical forces which have shaped their era. Among these forces are Cold War childhoods—when your Wonder Years are lived among family bomb shelters and weekly duck and cover drills in elementary school, a sense of chiliastic dread colors your recollections of even the most bucolic and quotidian elements of suburban culture. And a youth spent during the Vietnam War, during one of the few historical moments in which it seemed that the values of a counter counterculture might endure and prevail, was also a crucial factor in shaping our worldview, thanks both to the promise of those values and to their subsequent betrayal. As poets, our early models were the middle-generation writers—Berryman and Lowell especially—and that extraordinary exfoliation of figures born in the mid- to late 1920s: Levine, Wright, Rich, Merwin, Kinnell. We of course admired the suppleness of their craft, their seemingly effortless ability to move between writing in free verse and in received forms, but we also gravitated to the tough and adversarial poetry which all of these writers came to practice as a consequence of Vietnam and the 1960s struggle for racial equality. But above all, we admired the sternly self-confrontational stance of these poets, their conviction that autobiography and historical and cultural force were inextricably linked. And we had the good fortune to begin to form our writing selves before the dumbing-down of the autobiographical imperative that began in the early 1980s, and the subsequent reaction against "confessional" poetry that was expressed so vocally in the 1990s. We were, thankfully, unaffected by a zeitgeist that often makes my own students sadly wary of relating personal experience in anything but its most oblique fashion; they don't want, as they keep saying again and again, to *sound too confessional.* About this my three generational peers do not much worry.

Let me begin with a poem from William Olsen's fourth collection, *Avenue of Vanishing.* Here is the poem's opening scene:

> *Bedside*
> Because it turns out the world really is a hospital,
> Because we had to have had before us a giant pair of scissors
> Before four bold wings can have newly ascended
> Before new doors can revolve, before new elevators
> Rise and fall empty and full, new numbers light.
> New floors with new doors both open and closed.
> Because there are nurses to sail both in and out of need,
> Because need walks the doctors somewhere or another,
> Because of elaborately adaptable need the bed . . .
> The bed could be wheeled right into traffic and snow
> Because so far there is only inside and outside
> And more of both than even creation could have concocted.
> Because the bed that bore us all and our desires
> And our exhaustions has become a contraption,
> Because the bed that keeps us coming back to it,
> The bed that once sailed to the ends of the earth—
> Now tied to trees dripping blood and sugar and sleep,
> Anchored where overhead a TV persists, such news
> As snows poor reception—because the reliable bed
> Is something even a family understands, the family
> Is how the world goes—a fool's dream of awareness—
> Grouped around this steel altar at its least and lowered
> Because the bed is a helpless, blameless invention,

All the same to it if it is made or not, empty or not,
Some fatiguing last probabilities, because there are
As many ways to die as people to find these ways
Because they surely are, because the tried is ever new,
Who can't lose their way anew among so many alive?[14]

This is a passage of dizzying relentlessness, not merely because
it reminds us of how unsettling hospitals can be, but because its
tone seems to waver between authority and incomprehension.
The line Olsen employs is a fairly strict hexameter, yet Olsen's
syntax, laden with asides and oddball locutions ("because the
reliable bed / Is something even a family understands, the family / Is how the world goes—a fool's dream of awareness—")
seems to deliberately undercut prosodic fluency. And Olsen's
percussive repetition of "because" is an unexpected use of
anaphora, that oldest of poetic devices. Rather than evoke the
liturgical language of the psalms or *The Book of Common Prayer*,
here repetition is used to frame a kind of rant. Longinus in
his "On the Sublime," disdained anaphora, seeing it as method
befitting of barristers rather than poets. In fact, Olsen sounds
quite a bit like one of those lawyers Longinus complains about:
"By his manner, his looks, his voice, he strikes you with insult,
when he strikes you like an enemy, when he strikes you with his
knuckles, when he strikes you like a slave . . . . he belabors the
minds of the jury and assaults them again and again."[15] And yet
at the very same time that Olsen beats us up, he offers passages
of a kind of childlike simplicity: "The bed that once sailed to
the ends of the earth / Now tied to trees dripping blood and
sugar and sleep." The opening two-thirds of "Bedside" is such
a tour de force that it takes us awhile to ask the obvious question: What is so distressing the speaker? He is surely bothered
by something greater than having a crummy HMO. The answer
comes in the poem's final passage, which manages to be both
horrific and majestic:

Because who hasn't made their own bed, because
Who hasn't slept who hasn't been led by night there,
My mother's hands playing the fabric of the spread
As if it were a piano, tongue-tied, isolate fingers

She's ghost-smoking, working on an invisible crochet
"Hate Hate Hate Hate Hate . . . . I want to die"—
"Wake up!" Machado said the Gospels reduced to
But not now, not until you have what you want—
Any belief in love itself is what I'd have you want—
Look me in the eye with that sort of love that looks
Through me as if grief were so much tissue paper,
With a love which doesn't stop with me or you, that
Doesn't stop when there's no more world to fear
Because there's no need to wheel the bed outside,
Because a hospital melts like a snowflake, because
The walls and windows and even the bed liquefy,
Even the things she's seen that aren't there vanish
Because how much energy there is in emptiness,
Take everything away, there's still something there.

Surely we are surprised to be brought to the deathbed of the speaker's mother; more surprising still is how Olsen evokes this scene; the tone is coolly objective, the details grotesque. Olsen devotes only four lines to overt description of the mother, and her actions—the "ghost-smoking," the hands "playing the fabric of the spread / As if it were a piano"—are a kind of acrid parody of domesticity. Her single line of dialogue is shocking and artful at once. The five repetitions of "hate" with their rush of spondees, followed by the two strict iambs of "I want to die" may be seen as a grimly ironic allusion to Lear's grief over the dead Cordelia ("Why should a dog, a horse, a rat, have life, / And thou no breath at all? Thou'lt come no more, / Never, never, never, never, never. / Pray you, undo this button. . . ."). Yet as soon as we feel we can situate ourselves within this deathbed scene, Olsen changes tack again. He offers Machado's theological observation but then immediately questions it, and rather than directly address the mother—the gesture we are apt to expect at this point—Olsen's focus is more ambiguous: "Look me in the eye with that sort of love which looks / Through me as if grief were so much tissue paper / With a love that which doesn't stop with me and you. . . . ." This may be an injunction to the mother, but we suspect that it is instead the reader who is addressed, a notion that's confirmed a few lines later, when the mother is referred to in the third person. Olsen's plea is elaborated in the poem's final six lines, where the speaker's agitation gives way to a grave and stately music. Like so many of our meditations on mortality, its desire for the peace which passeth all understanding is predicated upon an understanding of the limitations of human love. And while the poem may not take a strict position on the existence of divine love, it adamantly refuses to regard oblivion as our only possible fate: "Take everything away, there's still something there."

Like Olsen's poem, David Rivard's "We Either Do or We Don't, but the Problem Evolves Anyway," which appears in his 2006 collection *Sugartown*, presents us with a speaker whom Longinus would detest: he begins his poem in the manner of a trial lawyer giving a closing argument. His voice is more jittery and arch than Olsen's, but he employs many of the same rhetorician's tricks:

> It isn't that hard, they say.
>
> It doesn't amount to more than an ache, really.
>
> Give yourself some space they say—
>
> as if the self were a cozy little back room, a small hall
> strung with incandescent streamers,
>
> and all that needed to be done, all that was ever required,
> was to tear a few down.
>
> But the problem is, friends,
>   the problem is
> there are a great many top-of-the-line things
>
> that each and every one of us
> has gone around saying we'd die for,
>
> items of an apparently
> absolute power
> and perfection, in a variety of impenetrable styles—

"That's a color hair I'd die for," she says,
    speaking sometime in the afterglow of a dark haircut
    flickering by,

a bleak thing to say,

but so human, so sadly and completely full of the silliness
of wanting.

that for once it sends
all the clarity suspended in the chlorinated sunlight
straight over the edge—

it haywires and clouds with lightning,
and the incurable sluices flood.[16]

Like Vallejo, a poet who seems to have significantly influenced
him, Rivard is often given to a sort of secular sermonizing, one in
which the sternest forms of social criticism can unexpectedly—
and almost involuntarily—give way to empathy. There's a cranky
conviction to these lines, and this, combined with Rivard's edgy,
caffeinated approach to free verse, allows for some rather astonishing shifts in tone and approach within a mere twenty-four
lines. The opening lines present us with a sort of post-punk Sa-
vonarola, but just when we think he's about to torch his Bonfire
of the Vanities, the railing against consumerism morphs into the
more focused scene of the woman "speaking sometime in the af-
terglow of a dark haircut / flickering by." Although this scene in-
jects some specificity into a poem that had hitherto been purely
rhetorical, it is a strangely unsettling specificity, vivid but almost
oxymoronic. It's not simply that the meaning of the woman's
seemingly innocent aside is reconfigured by Rivard; it's as if reality itself has begun to arrange and alter itself around her com-
ment. Soon the remark "haywires and clouds with lightning."
This process of distortion and disruption continues, even as the
poem coalesces around a more specific setting. Here is the poem's conclusion:

And what do you do then?

What do you do
when you've been set down
on the cool aluminum bleacher seats of the aquarium
at the beginning of the sea lion show
you're asked point blank
if you think it's true—
this thing you call acceptance—
and what would acceptance feel like
if you were one of those other children & adults
each & every one of whom
is a paraplegic
whose wheelchair has been parked
by the rim of the pool?

Because the sea lions are sleek things,
full of resistant veering powers.

And the wish to be given back
the child you were once won't work

And the dominos the laughing sisters
threw far across the grass
have been stolen now by rooks.

So don't speak too soon of acceptance.

That the sun stands apart
from all that it abuts,
unwilling to judge it,
may be our only real hope.

Here too Rivard refuses to limit the poem to a prevailing strategy. Just as we begin to feel that we have finally found ourselves within a clear dramatic situation—we're in the audience of the sea lion show at a place like Sea World, a locale which, after Rivard's anti-consumer diatribe, can't be seen as merely another quaint example of Americana—Rivard defies our expectations once again. Partly this is because the you's identity is ambiguous—it may be the speaker, it may be the woman who wants to die for her new 'do; but increasingly, as the poem unfolds, we suspect that it may be the reader. Partly this is because the sea lion show seems to shift from a realistic scene to an allegorical one. The "resistant veering powers" of the sea lions might well describe the shifts which the poem makes as it struggles to understand the intricacies of longing and acceptance. And of course the poem continues to morph in its final lines, first to the fabular— "and the dominos the laughing sisters / threw far across that the grass / have now been stolen now by rooks"—and then to the eccentric moralizing of the conclusion. The conclusion's homage to the impersonality of the universe is not a gesture of sophistry in the way it so often appears to be in your average Hardy or Robinson Jeffers poem, perhaps because Rivard has made his insight seem like a hard-won reckoning. As with Olsen's poem, a conclusion that should strike us as bleak comes across as oddly bracing.

Let me finish with Tom Sleigh's "Airport Economy Inn," which concludes his 2007 collection, *Spacewalk*. Sleigh's poem is one of the most recent examples of a small but significant sub-genre of American poetry which turns the broodings of an insomniac self into an emblem of the human condition. It follows in the tradition of Lowell's "Night Sweat," Kees's "For My Daughter," Galway Kinnell's "In the Hotel of Lost Light" section from *The Book of Nightmares,* and Delmore Schwartz's "In the Naked Bed, In Plato's Cave," among others. Indeed, in many ways it seeks to enact the bittersweet epiphany which concludes Schwartz's poem, with its insistence upon the isolate self's almost involuntary link to the social world and to history: "So, so / O son of man, the ignorant night, the travail / Of early morning, the mystery of beginning / Again and again, while History is unforgiven."[17] Sleigh's poem may enact this reckoning, but for him the stakes are higher than they were for Schwartz, the unforgiven forces of history more immediately and urgently asserting themselves. Writing from the relative innocence of the 1930s, Schwartz lies awake because some carpenters have been at work down the street and he has heard a milkman "straining up the stair." Contrast this with a nocturne of the new century, where you can't so easily shut history out. The beginning of the poem finds Sleigh's speaker engaging in what must be the second most popular activity conducted in a cheap hotel room— he's channel surfing:

No one speaking, nothing moving

except the way the snow keeps falling,
its falling a kind of talking in the dark
while all across the valley we keep on sleeping

in the separate conditions of our dreaming.

His face all overgrown with concern

the newsman's mouth says whatever it's saying
explosions going off, sound turned down, wind
ripping at some twanging strip of metal.[18]

This opening creates a mood of claustrophobic tension that will characterize the entire poem. The majority of the lines end with trochaic participles, creating a falling rhythm that suggests agitated movement within a closed space. The speaker seems not to be lying on the bed, but pacing the room, channel selector in hand, and he orbits the television screen with the same astonished fascination of Byron circling his Roman guillotine—or of Rilke's panther padding back and forth within his bars. Yet the scene before the speaker is static and shorn of meaning: the newsman's mouth is "overgrown with concern," his gestures so ritualized and the footage of the explosions so sadly familiar that their effect is merely benumbing. And although the TV's sound is turned down, the scene is cacophonous; outside, the wind is "ripping /at some twanging strip of metal." Sleigh's stanza form—a regular but decidedly inelegant pattern of single-lined stanzas encasing tercets—further contributes to the passage's unsettling effect. I can't imagine that Sleigh would in any way characterize himself as a concrete poet, yet the form mimics the appearance of a television screen, once again suggesting pattern without meaningful continuity. The random noises, the drab setting, and the speaker's racing thoughts appear innocent enough, but they soon seem to conspire toward some private apocalypse:

My friend's voice keeps murmuring in my head,

murmuring she's stressed by going out

with two men at once, worrying they'll cross
and she'll lose them both, she's starting
to drink and smoke too much, love's

her liar, a chimney head, an alky.

No one speaking, nothing moving but snow

falling, falling, burying this motel
with its takeout menu, *New Standard Bible,*
checkout time 11 a.m.,

smily face envelope to leave the maid a tip:

out in the hall someone's pounding

on the ice machine, one hand beating rhythm to
fuck it fuck it fuck it fuck it . . .
Reveries of living here year after year

scalloped walls, cottage cheese ceiling,

plaster hands praying on the checkout counter,

complimentary donuts hoarded in the ice bucket
DO NOT DISTURB credit card imprint
Room 401's one of our regulars

The villanelle-like repetition of "no one speaking, nothing
moving" and the tawdry catalogue of details seem to simultaneously isolate the speaker and link him to what Transtromer—
in a poem which is also set in a shabby motel—calls "society's
mechanical self-reproaches." This sense of crisis only intensifies
as the poem moves toward its conclusion, fueled in no small
measure by the war footage which continues to flicker from the
television:

. . . . food, god, death, money, a TV clicker

to push the world back and bring it closer,

fantasies of lust so ridiculous and charmed
you need two king beds and a mirrored ceiling.
No one speaking, nothing moving

but for the screen lighting up with bombs falling

through shifting fortunes of the soldier

on a stretcher, body gone limp,
lost in glare spilling off a Humvee's side
that keeps hearse-like pace with the stretcher moving

above the stretcher's shadow.

No one speaking, nothing moving,

my eyes close, I drift and doze,
dissolving to jags, chunks, splinters,
flake piling on flake erasing diamond-cut angles

of every crystal swirling through streetlights

before fading back to parking lot gloom as these lines stretch
    out

and return to the margin
as if nothing can stop this pattern
from repeating, words

telling it in irregular shifts of rhythm

while the crawl keeps crawling at the bottom of the screen.

This is a pitiless and unsettling closure, but not a wholly
bleak one, if only because it is so resonant with implication.
The description of the snowfall, with "flake piling on flake erasing diamond-cut angles," invariably recalls the ending of James

Joyce's "The Dead," and its vision of the interdependence of the dead and the living. Yet for Sleigh the closure's symbolic import is anything but tidy; we're presented with a kind of mash-up; the snow covering the parking lot is identified not only with the captioning that "keeps crawling at the bottom of the screen," but also with the act of writing itself, a process which Sleigh sets in opposition to the isolation, carnage, and drive toward oblivion which are the predominating *but not prevailing* elements of his poem. This is not the radical reversal of "suffering into joy, despair into radiance" which Stanley Kunitz observed in James Wright, but Sleigh does find the means to shore some fragments against his ruins. You may not get a good night's sleep at the Airport Economy Inn, but at least you'll check out in the morning.

The crawl keeps crawling on the bottom of the screen: Charles Bernstein says somewhere that the problem is not that our poetry should be at least as well written as prose, but that it needs to be at least as interesting as television. And much of the time, indeed most of the time, it isn't. But I keep returning to Byron's letter: perhaps what poetry can do for us, and do as well or better than any other art form, is to force us to again and again confront the bewildering intricacies of experience as though for the first time. Let it speak against our television souls, those parts of us which serve only to suggest "how dreadfully soon one things grows indifferent." True, we may need to understand indifference before we can arrive at wisdom. But poetry—if it tells us anything—tells us that indifference, the indifference which permits the cold controlled ferocity of the human species and allows it to thrive, should not be our condition or our fate. The lines stretch out and return; they keep filling the whiteness of the page, the shimmer of the laptop screen, even as the crawl keeps crawling.

2007

Notes

1. W. H. Auden and Louis MacNeice, *Letters from Iceland* (New York:, Random House, 1937), p. 44.

2. Auden and MacNeice, *Letters from Iceland*, p. 44.

3. Paul Fussell, *Abroad: British Literary Travel Between the Wars* (New York:, Oxford University Press, 1980), p. 219.

4. Auden and MacNeice, *Letters from Iceland*, p.149.

5. C. J. Jung, *Memories, Dreams, Reflections* (New York: Vintage, 1969), p. 175.

6. Auden and MacNeice, *Letters from Iceland*, p. 224

7. Quoted in Randall Jarrell, *The Third Book of Criticism* (New York: Farrar, Straus & Giroux, 1969), p. 85.

8. Peter Quennell, Eed., *Byron: A Self Portrait* (New York: Oxford University Press, 1950), p. 408.

9. W. H. Auden, introduction to *The Selected Poetry and Prose of Byron* (New York: Meridian Books, 1966), p. xi.

10. Robert Gittings, ed., *The Letters of John Keats* (New York: Oxford University Press, 1970), p. 43.

11. Barth David Schwartz, *Pasolini Requiem* (New York: Pantheon, 1992), p. 370.

12. Stanley Kunitz, *A Kind of Order, A Kind of Folly: Essays and Conversations* (Boston: Atlantic-Little, Brown, 1978), p. 256.

13. Joe Wenderoth, *No Real Light* (Seattle, Wave Books, 2007), p. 61.

14. William Olsen, *Avenue of Vanishing* (Evanston, IL: Northwestern University Press, 2007), p. 81.

15. Longinus, "On the Sublime," in *Criticism: The Major Texts*, ed. W. J. Bate, ed. (San Diego, CA: Harcourt, Brace, Jovanovich, 1970), p. 74.

16. David Rivard, *Sugartown* (St. Paul, MN: Graywolf Press, 2006), p. 28.

17. Delmore Schwatrz, *Selected Poems 1938–58: Summer Knowledge* (New York: New Directions, 1967), p. 25.

18. Tom Sleigh, *Spacewalk* (Boston: Houghton Mifflin, 2007), p. 96.

"Tell Me if It Is Too Far for You"
On Sympathy

> We are moving in opposite directions, I and the child,
> though on the same path. He has not yet captured his
> individual soul out of the universe about him. His self is
> outside him, his energy distributed among the beasts and
> the birds whose life he shares, among leaves, grass, clouds,
> thunder, whose existence he can be at home in because
> they hold, each of them, some particle of his spirit. He
> has no notion of the otherness of things.
> —David Malouf, *An Imaginary Life*

It's all downhill from Santa Fe to the White Sand Missile Range,
a three-and-a-half-hour drive where you slowly descend from
five thousand feet above sea level to inhospitable desert bro-
ken here and there by creosote and little else. "My" desert, the
otherworldly and majestic saguaro forests of southern Arizona,
where I lived for a time, looks nothing like this lunar landscape,
its sand the glossy blazing white of cheap printer paper. We are
driving to a hole in the ground, but this is a pilgrimage of sorts.
My friend the poet Matt Donovan is taking me to the Trinity
Site, which on two mornings a year, once in April and once in
October, is opened to the public. I've been teaching for a week
at Matt's school, the College of Santa Fe, and our trip to White
Sands marks the end of my visit, a stay that has been more than
a little melancholy, since the college has gone bankrupt and will
close at the end of the spring term. Matt and his colleagues will
be out of jobs; the students will transfer to other colleges. On
this particular morning Matt is understandably tired of talking
about the school's fate, and so we first talk po-biz, the sort of

shop-talk that so often happens when poets get together, and which outsiders have every right to think of as trivial and dull; then the talk goes literary and becomes more interesting to us both. For some reason, we devote a lot of time to the relative virtues of recent translations of Dante, and since this is a sort of pilgrimage, and an unsettling one, I'm wondering to myself who of the two of us is Dante, and who is Virgil. I'm the older one and I'm in the passenger seat with the map, but I'm hardly the most capable of guides, having taken us off on the wrong exit for a thirty-mile detour. But we're on our way, we "undertake that deep and savage road," as Robert Pinsky puts it in the closing of his translation of Canto II. Past a military checkpoint at the gates of the missile range, past a fork in the road where a jeep, a Hummer, and several MPs point you in the right direction, the deep and savage road ends in an asphalt parking lot in the middle of the middle of nowhere; there's space for a thousand or so cars and a score or so of tour buses. Another MP points us to our parking space, and we've moved from the Circle of This, to the Circle of That, the transition signaled by vendors of Fat Boy Burgers, and Little Man Dogs with the Works; there's a souvenir and book stand sponsored by the missile range, and some additional stands that hawk things that the Official Government Vendors seem to find too tacky—t-shirts emblazoned with mushroom clouds, metal paperweight facsimiles of Fat Man and Little Boy, and so forth.

You pass several signs warning you that pocketing of Trinitite—the substance formed when the heat of the Trinity blast fused sand into pebbles—is strictly forbidden. But even if I tried, I'm not sure I could distinguish the still mildly radioactive Trinitite from regular stones. From here you walk a quarter-mile alley—girded in a cyclone fence—to Ground Zero, which is circled by a still larger cyclone fence. The Main Attraction, the Center of Circle Nine, the "melancholy hole" formed on the banks of this American Cocytus, is a small depression in the sand, marked by a stone obelisk.

Members of a motorcycle club and some Japanese tourists are having their pictures taken around the structure. A sort of photo gallery has been hung on the insides of the surrounding fence—they probably tack the pictures up the day before each public viewing, taking them down and placing them in storage again when it's over. You could draw some metaphors from this, I suppose. Here's the semi that pulled the device from Los Alamos; here's the wooden tower they erected for exploding it; here are two shirtless GIs posing beside the bomb as it creaks from chains, cigarettes dangling from their lips; here's Oppenheimer with his famous fedora and pipe. People are taking photos of the photos; someone's Scotty lifts his leg to pee beneath an image of a mushroom cloud; his owner wears an iPod, and I'm trying to imagine what his soundtrack for all of this might be like—another metaphor that fails me, and would probably have failed Dante as well.

Back at the parking lot, we can board buses that take us a couple of miles further down the road to the McDonald Ranch. In 1944 the government sent the McDonalds and their thousand head of sheep to points unknown, and it became a kind of base camp, first for the ten thousand tons of TNT that were exploded at Ground Zero to see what sort of damage that amount of explosive might inflict; and then a few months later it became the staging point for the more significant explosion. Although the government "restored" the ranch back in the 1970s, the cruelty of the desert elements has brought it back to the state of dilapidation it must have been in during 1945. The wooden sheep pens are half-fallen; the windmill tower looks ready to topple; the cistern where GIs cooled off during the scorching summer days is empty and caving in. The ranch house itself is five small rooms, and as Matt and I approach it another bus unloads several dozen boy scouts and scoutmasters—soon they're surrounding us. On each of their caps is a symbol of an atom, and beneath it embroidered in cursive is *Nuclear Energy*. We stand in the ranch house living room; this is where plastic sheets were placed upon the doorways and windows so that the final assembly of the bomb could be done dust free. Above the door someone's written in chalk the words that were also etched there in the summer of '45—not "NO THINGS WERE / BEFORE ME NOT ETERNAL; ETERNAL I REMAIN"; not "ABANDON HOPE ALL YE WHO ENTER HERE." No, this gateway, portal, or hell-mouth bears script that's more prosaic—REMEMBER! WIPE YOUR FEET!

Remarkably, no photos seem to have been taken to record the

bomb's final assembly, so there's nothing on the walls to com- memorate the event save a small explanatory sign. The scouts crowd in and immediately crowd out, but Matt and I stand here a good long while, both sensing that here is the true Ground Zero, the place where the Manhattan Project's bewildering con- coction of science, bureaucracy, money, and hubris came to its irrevocable end. And it seems to have been a prosaic end. Here the University of California's Dr. Robert Bacher, before begin- ning the final assembly, asked an army official to sign a *receipt* for the plutonium inside the core. Officially, it belonged to the uni- versity, not to the government, and Bacher wanted to be sure his school would be properly reimbursed for its materials.[1] A shitty little room, smaller than my study at home. Rooms have auras, Matt will later say. And this one surely does, a hue of pulsing and compounded darkness. Yet also the place where the curtain be- gan to part, and a light famously brighter than a thousand suns would be unleashed. This very room, with its peeling paint and floorboards that must have groaned beneath the weight of the infinitely calibrated metals, and the plutonium core spewing its toxicity against its lead casing like some cosmic rattlesnake shut tight and writhing in a box.

We walk back to the bus. Some of the scouts have wandered off past the no trespassing signs to the remains of the sheep pens. The scoutmasters call after them, wanting to know why they're too damn dense to read the signs. Back to the bus now, back to the parking lot. We pass the bunker, S10,000, where the scientists and soldiers gathered to witness the blast, where in Op- penheimer's words, "A few people laughed, a few people cried, most people were silent." The place where Oppie waxed poetic, "There floated through my mind a line from *The Bhagavad-Gita* in which Krishna is trying to persuade the Prince that he must do his duty: 'I am become death, the shatterer of worlds.'" The place where Oppenheimer's colleague Max Bainbridge put things in a more practical perspective. "Oppie," he said, "now we're all sons of bitches."[2] It's all been too much, we decide to bypass the bunker, and until we hit a burger joint an hour or so down the road—a place that was much favored by the Los Alamos scientists—we're mostly silent. Of course, after a beer or two we revive, and we talk about whether we each will write about this day.

It's an oddly complicated discussion—is it an act of hubris to exploit the story of history's greatest act of hubris? And what about the manifold ironies and sheer surreal lunacy of this day—the Little Boy Burgers, the Fat Man paperweights, the tourists from Kyoto asking a tattooed biker with a storm trooper helmet to affix their memory forever at Ground Zero—is it a similar act of hubris to exploit them? And what's the rule on tarting everything up with metaphors—to comparing a plutonium core to a rattler shoved into a box, to conjuring some demonic Ground Zero Playlist on somebody's iPod? And what of Dante, literature's greatest master of metaphor, whom Mandelstam spoke of in awe as he described "the innumerable conductorial flights of his baton"?[3] If you throw the august Florentine into the mix, you can gain some authority, right? But doesn't that gesture seem hollow and disingenuous, like Iggy Pop's claim that his favorite music is by Anton Werbern, not "I Wanna Be Your Dog" or "96 Tears"? And one further cold and terrible fact—and it IS a fact—also pertains. As Robert Hass puts it at end of his great poem "Heroic Simile," "There are limits to the imagination." Some events beggar that intricate matrix of guile, observation, awe, invention, and judgment that we call an imaginative act. Some events are beyond the blandishments of metaphor. Some events should refuse our attempts to shape them into satire—or to attempt the opposite of satire and imbue them with empathy.

I can sense your unease, dear Reader. About the satire part you will probably not disagree with me. But what about empathy? Isn't empathy the most noble and lordly goal of the poet? As Keats so memorably put it, "If a sparrow come before my window I take part in its existence and pick about the gravel." But wait—the brain of a sparrow has the weight of a couple packets of artificial sweetener. Taking part in its existence seems within the realm of possibility. But how do you project yourself into the consciousness of Dr. Bachman and his compatriots as they ease the plutonium core into the bomb, the assembly complete? And when the mushroom cloud looms up, whose head is easier to enter—Oppenheimer's as he thinks of Hindu scripture, or

Bainbridge's as he curses us all? But the fact is that both abilities are beyond us. Yes, we can pick about the gravel with the sparrow, but can we really claim to enter the consciousness of even a twelve year-old Second-Class Scout, running around a sheep pen and getting yelled at by his leader?

To say some distances can't be bridged or even narrowed flies against several different conventional wisdoms. *Othering* is a term that crops up repeatedly in post-colonial culture theory. And we in the West are supposedly masters of it. Through our magnificently honed skills at Othering, we can dismiss, demean, and dehumanize those are Aren't Like Us. Being Not Like Us means, too, that you pose a danger that must be stopped and punished. What Dante does to Muhammad is especially telling in this respect: he's way way down in Circle Eight, and for all eternity a demon keeps cutting him in two with a gigantic scimitar. All of Dante's genius with metaphor and his creepy delight in the scatological are brought to bear upon his description. Let's Go to the Video Tape, courtesy of Pinsky:

> No barrel staved-in
> And missing its end piece ever gaped as wide
> As the man I saw split open from his chin
>
> Down to the farting-place, and from the splayed
> Trunk the spilled entrails dangled between his thighs.
> I saw his organs, and the sack that makes the bread
>
> We swallow turn to shit. . . .[4]

We do no Othering like *that* anymore, you might argue. We study the Koran in comparative religion classes, correct? But that defense may be as dubious as a certain chief executive pounding the podium with its Presidential Seal while insisting that We Do Not Torture. If you're of a literary bent, the photographs from Abu Ghraib could easily have summoned up Dante, and I for one must confess to being reminded of Muhammad's punishment on the day that Saddam Hussein was hung. There's at least a scatological connection: a rumor on the Internet had it that the dangling Saddam shit himself.

Pound upon your laptop, Dear Reader, and say aloud that We Do Not Other. But it's not as easy as that. The cave painters of Neolithic Europe rendered mastodons and aurochs and hairy rhinos with uncanny realistic precision. Human forms are almost absent in their artistry, and on those rare occasions when they do occur, they seem crude and childlike. One of the earliest such representations is the famous Killed Man on the walls of Cougnac, c. 15,000 b.p. He's a stick figure, bristling with spears—captured from another clan, perhaps, then tortured before he was killed.[5] The mastodons and aurochs and rhinos are likely the evidence of some sort of ritual magic, of some long-lost religious ceremony. But the killed man seems outside of ceremony. He's the Neolithic equivalent of newsreel footage, not even worth an effort at verisimilitude. I became a Unitarian in no small measure because it is a religion that insists upon a paradoxical but imperative belief in the spiritual unity of all people on the one hand, and a respect for their vast diversity on the other. I became a poet and a teacher for similar reasons. But how do we become the sparrow when something in us—something, perhaps, in our very genetic makeup, in survival instincts that inhabit and fan out from the primitive areas of thought, from the thalamus and medulla, from the so-called reptile brain—first wants to kill the sparrow, second to eat it raw, spitting out the feathers and the bones, and then to flee when we hear the footsteps of a predator upon the leaves of the jungle floor?

Let me step back here, and do what one is supposed to do in an essay with a title such as this, and try to provisionally define those two related words, empathy and sympathy. It's not as easy as you might think. *The Princeton Encyclopedia of Poetry and Poetics* states that empathy is "the projection of ourselves into, or the identification of ourselves with objects either animate or inanimate."[6] The term derives from the German word *enfuhlang*, coined by a nineteenth-century German critic, Hermann Lotz. Sympathy, by contrast, "is a fellow feeling with the ideas and emotions of other human beings, or with animals to whom we attribute human ideas and emotions." Interestingly enough, neither *The Princeton Encyclopedia* nor its cousin *The Longman Dictionary of Poetic Terms* offers actual entries for sympathy. Look up sympathy in the *Princeton* and you're referred back to empathy; the *Longman* doesn't even bother to do that. Empathy is the Top Banana; sympathy seems always to play second fiddle. I employ these dead metaphors for a reason, since both dictionaries imply that empathy is not merely a stance of significant importance to imaginative writing, but is in fact, as the *Longman* maintains, "the basis for devices such as METAPHOR, PERSONIFICATION, and other stratagems of identity and substitution."[7] Empathy makes the world go round; the implication is that it is more desirable to fuse with another person, animal, or object than it is to project "fellow feeling." Yes, I'm being reductive here, but only to a small degree. At least since the Romantics, we seem to take for granted that it is empathy which creates the most memorable metaphors, and that ideas are as often as not the metaphors' by-product, the plutonium produced by the yellowcake uranium. One of the first poems I ever loved, James Wright's "A Blessing," does just that with the "two Indian ponies" who have come to "greet" the speaker and his friend after they have stopped their car on a roadside. "They ripple tensely, they can hardly contain their happiness / That we have come. / They bow shyly as wet swans. They love each other. / There is no loneliness like theirs."[8] Thanks to his comparison of the ponies to the wet swans, Wright assumes that he also understands that (a) the ponies feel love for each other, and (b) their solitariness is absolutely unique. Even the *Princeton Encyclopedia* acknowledges that this sort of syllogistic thinking—find the right metaphor, and you achieve both empathy with the thing you describe and some new insight about life in general—can be carried to absurdity. The editors cite an effort by Coleridge that you will not find in many anthologies:

> In his *To a Young Ass,* Coleridge laid himself open to ridicule by sympathetically regarding the likenesses and defying the differences between himself and an underprivileged donkey: "Innocent foal! Thou poor despis'd forlorn! / I hail thee *Brother*—spite of the fool's scorn! / And fain would take thee with me, in the Dell / Where high-soul'd Pantisocracy shall dwell!"[9]

Brother ass: perhaps in poor Coleridge's case it's just the laudanum talking. And perhaps there's something in our nature that wants us to identify with equine species. Poets seem to want to be like horses (or in Coleridge's case, donkeys) almost as much as they want to be like birds. I myself have attempted the bird metamorphosis once or twice, and would have probably tried to do so again in a poem or two had I not a few years ago taught a poetry workshop with my colleague Mary Ruefle. At one point in the class Mary wondered aloud why so many poets want to be birds in their poems—yet you never hear of a bird wanting to be a poet. There are limits to the imagination, limits to empathy as a poetic strategy, and limits to the usefulness of metaphor. As George Lakoff and Mark Johnson state in their problematic but important study of the uses of metaphor, "when we say that a concept is structured by a metaphor, we mean that it is partially structured and that it can be extended in some ways but not in others."[10]

But after we have knocked empathy off its pedestal, after we have offered further evidence of the limitation of metaphor by offering up yet another dead one, what then are we left with? It is more realistic to Other Coleridge's Young Ass than to recognize him as our long-lost brother—but can there be *any* potential in a poem which proceeds from that premise? And what about the limitations of figurative language, the fact that metaphors can "be extended in some ways but not others"—isn't that in some perverse way an invitation to employ metaphor in new and surprising ways? Shortly after my return home from New Mexico, I started looking over poems about the Bomb, the Nuclear Era, and the Cold War. There are certainly a great many such poems; there's even an anthology, *Atomic Ghost,* devoted to them. I don't know what I was looking for in this project, but it returned me to a poem by Thom Gunn that's always been a favorite of mine:

A Drive to Los Alamos

Past mesas in yellow ruin,
breaking up like everything,

upward to the wide plateau
where the novelist went to school,
at the Ranch School for Boys
in 1929. And that was
All there had been up there.

(His face "borrowed flesh,"
his imagination disguised
in an implacable suit)
Somebody asked: were you
Considered a sissy?
No, he said
in his quiet voice, I was neither
popular nor unpopular.

(The twenty-five boys
of that expensive spartan school
laconic on horses
hunted among the burnt-out furnaces
of the wilderness. Where
a rock fell it stayed.)

One building remained, massive
and made of good brown wood,
surrounded now by shoddy
prefab suburb—a street
named after Oppenheimer,
another Trinity Drive.

In the science museum
we looked through a brochure
for the extinct school.
That was Mr. So-and-so, he said.
That was the infirmary, that was
where the lucky boys went.
(Aware, quietly, of what the past
becomes, golden in ruin.)
Those were the sleeping porches.
Yes, they were cold.
Another picture showed a healthy boy
after a hunt, with a dead deer.
That was Jack Matthews.
(I make up the name,
since I do not remember it,
but he did.)[11]

This poem, which appeared in Gunn's best individual collection, 1982's *The Passages of Joy*, epitomizes the later Gunn at his

best. It's not for nothing he uses the word "laconic" to describe the appearance of the schoolboys on horseback in stanza two, peering out from what we presume to be a group photograph—the eloquence of old photographs is always predicated on their laconic qualities; they fascinate us in no small measure because they are at once transparent and utterly mysterious for what they withhold. As Roland Barthes puts it in *Camera Lucida,* his magisterial meditation on photography, " a specific photograph reaches me; it animates me, and I animate it. . . . I must name the attraction which makes it exist, *an animation.* . . . The photograph itself is in no way animated, but it animates me: this is what creates every adventure."[12] The speaker of "A Drive to Los Alamos" treats his day with the elderly novelist much in the way Barthes describes the curiously transactional nature of how we view photographs. He must animate the novelist's story, but he also must be careful not to betray the mute authenticity of that story by presuming too much, or by in any way embellishing it. In adopting this stance, Gunn must operate from the assumption that the distance between the novelist's memories and the speaker's own impressions of his subject can be lessened but never bridged. For Gunn's speaker, the novelist must remain, in Barthes's words, *inanimate.*

But in that fact lies much of the poem's power. Although the tone of the poem initially seems detached and objective, by stanza three—when Gunn first encloses a passage in parenthesis—we no longer can assume that Gunn's stance is merely reportorial. The parentheticals create a deliberate ambiguity, partly because they suggest a hushed, *sotto voce* commentary on the action that seems sometimes to be the thoughts of the speaker, sometimes those of the novelist, and sometimes neither or both. By withholding the pronoun reference in one of the poem's most eloquent passages ("Aware, quietly, of what the past / becomes, golden in ruin"), Gunn prevents us from determining whether this revelation is arrived at by the speaker, is projected upon the consciousness of the novelist, or whether it is a generalization which both arrive at simultaneously. As readers we may not know whom to attribute this epiphany to, but the lines have an immediate and strongly visceral effect. We're drawn both to the hesitant stutter of the caesuras and enjambment at the start of the passage and to the exquisite sonics of "golden in ruin." The point of view of the poem seems to continually morph and hover, and these shifts are often signaled by Gunn's asides and indirect dialogue. Of the poem's forty-three lines, fourteen are encased in parentheticals, and an additional nine may be read as indirect dialogue we can attribute to the novelist.

My main point, however, is that the poem resists what we might call the empathic fallacy. Gunn cannot and will not give himself over completely to the consciousness of the novelist. It is a poem of sympathy, not empathy; it strives for "fellow feeling," but acknowledges the immense difficulty of such endeavor, and all the quietly pyrotechnical devices which the poem employs are offered as evidence of that difficulty. The final sentence of the poem ("I make up the name, / Since I do not remember it, / But he did") is diffident but powerfully resonant. The distance between the speaker and the novelist is narrowed. For both (and by extension, for all of us) the past lies "golden in ruin." But those ruins are as different as the pyramids of Yucatan are from the ziggurats of Sumer, as a Neolithic menhir in Cornwall is from the kitschy little obelisk at Trinity.

Gunn was always a poet on the outside looking in. The reasons for this are to some degree biographical. His decision in the 1950s to leave his native Britain for San Francisco, where he lived until his death in 2004, made him seem too American for many of his British readers—and yet to American readers he was always a Brit. He never abandoned the received forms with which he first made his mark on the literary world, and yet he could also, as "A Drive to Los Alamos" so well illustrates, write in a uniquely nuanced free verse. And, as a gay man who came out long before it was socially acceptable, and who wrote of what some straight readers would regard as the seamier side of gay life—portraits of street hustlers, skateboard punks, and meth heads, of trysts in leather bars, and so on—he had no patience with PC pieties. His reckonings with the intricacies and perils of desire could never be constrained by well-intentioned moral codes. A few years before Gunn's death, I watched a good percentage of a Chicago audience walk out during his reading of an uncollected series of poems about the serial killer/cannibal Jeffrey Dahmer. Gunn seemed saddened, even a little hurt, by his listeners' departure. I suspect that this was because, for Gunn, sympathy always trumped sensationalism, even in the case of someone as monstrous as Dahmer. And sympathy, for Gunn, always carried a measure of self-doubt. The elegies which comprise his 1992 collection, *The Man with Night Sweats*, may well be the most enduring testament of the AIDS pandemic. But you can't be sympathetic, Gunn suggests, without questioning your own motives. In a poem entitled "In a Time of Plague," Gunn finds himself conversing with two "fiercely attractive" junkies on a park bench. They're shooting up, and invite the speaker to share their needle:

> I seek
> to enter their minds. Am I a fool,
> and they direct and right, properly
> testing themselves against risk,
> as a human must, and does,
> or are they the fools, the alert faces
> mere death's heads lighted glamorously?
> I weigh possibilities
> till I am afraid of the strength
> of my own health
> and of their evident health.[13]

I seek to enter their minds. The pull of empathy at this moment seems as powerful to the speaker as the allure of drugs or sex; and yet, albeit with some reluctance, he resists all three. This is certainly not a "just say no" decision, yet it allows the poem to end on a note of sad fellow feeling. Gunn watches the pair amble off, "restless at last with my indecision." They look for other companions on "the moving concourse of people / who are boisterous and bright, / carrying in faces and throughout their bodies / the news of life and death."

Let me offer two provisional premises regarding sympathy, then. Sympathy cannot exist without some form of resistance and self-doubt ("Am I a fool, / and they direct and right"), and fellow feeling cannot be maintained for long. When the speaker of "A Drive To Los Alamos" makes up the name of Jack Matthews, he is motivated above all by fellow feeling and sympathy, but as soon as he does so he is also acknowledging a distance between himself and the novelist that can never be overcome. It is the obverse of Bishop's famous revelation near the close of "In the Waiting Room," where the speaker simultaneously understands her connection with humanity and her isolation from others. "You are an *I,* / you are an *Elizabeth.* / You are one of *them.* / *Why* should you be one too? / I scarcely dared to look / to see what it was I was."[14] You awaken on a cave floor as the fire your mother kept all night dies down. You know you are alone as well as that you are a member of your clan. Later that day, as you hunt deer with your brothers, you come upon a group of strangers. You and your brothers have daubed your bodies with red ochre; they've daubed theirs with something blue. You are wary as they approach, and their words are strange to you. Therefore you speak with them in sign language. The vestiges of that sign language exist to this day, and the term we use for it is poetry.

Here's a little poem by James Schuyler which also struggles with these issues. They're implicit even in its title, "Self-Pity Is a Kind of Lying Too":

It's
snowing defective
vision days and
X-
mas is coming, like
a plow. And in the
meat the snow. Strange,
it reminds me
of an old lady I
once saw shivering
naked beside a black
polluted stream. You
felt terrible—but
the train didn't
stop—so. And the
white which is
some other color or
its absence—it
spins on itself
snd so do the *Who
At Leeds* I'm playing

to drown the carols
blatting from the
Presbyterian church
steeple which is
the same as fight-
ing fire with oil.
Naked people—old,
cold—one day we'll
just have snow
to wear too.[15]

The limpidity of Schuyler's poems, their ability to make difficult reckonings and revelatory description seem almost
improvisational—much in the way that Bishop does in her best
work—makes his writing defy conventional analysis. The poem
is just *there*.

But indulge me for a moment. The poem's first two sentences,
engaging as they may be, seem a species of throat-clearing. They
surely suggest the tone of lamentation Schuyler calls forth in his
title, and thanks to devices such as the line break after the first
syllable of "X- / mas," they possess a certain quirky prosodic authority. But—let's face it—they're gibberish. But then Schuyler
conjures the "old lady / . . . shivering / naked beside a black /
polluted stream." Just as soon as we share in the speaker's shock
at this vision, the scene is over: "You / Felt terrible—but / The
train didn't / Stop—so." Can you imagine a more piercing statement about the world's cruelty? Yet Schuyler pointedly leaves it
undeveloped. We shift to a few lines devoted to the nature of
whiteness—not whiteness as some Melvillean symbol of the in-
scrutability of the universe, but whiteness as further evidence of
the speaker's uncertain mental state and solipsism. Then we shift
once again to the comic scene of the Who versus the carols "blatting" from the Presbyterian church. This is *writing as erasure*, but
not in the toxically cant-ridden sense in which that term is employed by literary theorists. Schuyler seems to want to write the
vision of the old woman by the stream out of memory, through
deflection, through denial, through wisecracks. But the closing
of the poem is quietly triumphant because Schuyler finally allows her to return: *one day we'll just have snow to wear too*. We are

one with the woman; we will all share her fate. The gesture is all the more moving because it is made with such reluctance, almost involuntarily. (I'm once again reminded of Bishop, and that zinger—*Write it!*—in the final line of "One Art.") And need I add that the poem's closing is a gesture of sympathy? Schuyler very empathically does not want to *become* this woman. But he makes her hover hauntingly before us—she is one of the shades; shivering, certainly, but also beckoning from the other shore of the Styx.

I'm reminded of Federico Garcia Lorca's brilliant but famously impenetrable essay on the Duende, in which he insists that the most enduring art is created through our collaboration with one of a trio of emblematic figures, the Angel, the Muse, and the Duende. The Angel and the Muse are different from the Duende for two important reasons—they are *external* forces; they visit themselves upon the artist, who is the subject of their mysterious largesse: "The Angel dazzles, but hovers in mid-air, shedding his grace and the man, without any effort whatever, realizes his work, his fellow feeling, or his dance. . . . The Muse dictates, and in certain instances, prompts." The Duende, however, is far more fickle, far less benign, and arises from within: "it must come to life from the innermost recesses of the blood. . . . The true struggle is with the Duende."[16] And, perhaps because it derives from our physical essence, from reckonings with our own corporeality, encounters with the Duende always involve a profound sense of our mortality in ways which encounters with the muse and the angel do not. "When the Muse sees death on the way," says Lorca, "she closes the door." "When the Angel sees death on the way, he flies in slow circles and weaves in tears of narcissus and ice the elegy we see trembling in the hands of Keats."[17] Admittedly, Lorca's entessalated bombast and his rhapsodic necrophilia are sometimes a little hard to take. Still, the conclusion of Schuyler's poem strikes me as a powerful argument for existence of the Duende, especially when we are told that he

will not approach at all if he does not see the possibility of death, if he is not convinced he will circle death's house, if there is not every assurance he can rustle the branches, borne aloft by us all, that neither have, nor may ever have, the power to console.[18]

This leads me to wonder if the poem of sympathy may require a third essential, one even more challenging to contend with than an acknowledgment of the distances it must lessen and the self-doubts it must confront. I hesitate to insist that it must struggle with the Duende, but I suspect that true fellow feeling cannot be arrived at without some sort of deep and visceral understanding that what most unites us with another is a sense of our mutual mortality. For each of us, even those memories which lie golden in ruin will someday be completely swept from the earth. And once we are stripped down to nothing but the snow we have to wear, we will have no recourse but to lie down together and sleep. Sadly, perhaps Lorca is right: when confronted with such realities, not even poetry has "the power to console."

The following poem by Milosz, "Elegy for N.N.," arrives at sympathy through a vast and almost cosmic struggle. But sympathy cannot change the past, nor mitigate our essential hopelessness. Written during the poet's years of California exile, and long before the international acclaim that followed his receipt of the Nobel Prize, it employs all of the characteristic motifs of what might be called Milosz's Golden State Period: regret and survivor guilt predominate. Here, as in other poems of the California years, he employs the grand and majestic catalogues which he learned from Whitman and Jeffers, but in a manner that is singularly un-Whitmanic. The vatic gestures and incantations invariably pull at their leash and are violently reined in. The Golden State poems arise from a condition of spiritual house arrest. The setting is comfortable, but the Monitoring Device has been clamped snugly to your leg, and it continually beams your location to Exile Central. You can't even start up the Saab and make a trip to Trader Joe's without first getting the okay from the History Police, or the Federal Bureau of Memory Investigation. Here are the poem's opening stanzas:

Elegy for N.N.
Tell me if it is too far for you.
You could have run over the small waves of the Baltic

and past the fields of Denmark, past a beech wood
could have turned toward the ocean, and there, very soon
Labrador, white at this season.
And if you, who dreamed about a lonely island,
were frightened of cities and of lights flashing along the
    highway
you had a path straight through the wilderness
over blue-black melting waters, with tracks of deer and
    caribou
as far as the Sierras and abandoned gold mines.
The Sacramento River could have led you
between hills overgrown with prickly oaks.
Then, just a eucalyptus grove, and you had found me.

True, when the manzanita is in bloom
And the bay is clear on spring mornings
I think reluctantly of the house between the lakes
And of nets drawn in beneath the Lithuanian sky.
The bath cabin where you used to leave your dress
Has turned into an abstract crystal.
Honey-like darkness is there, near the verandah,
And comic young owls, and the scent of leather.

How could one live at that time, I really can't say.
Styles and dresses flicker, indistinct,
not self-sufficient, tending toward a finale.
Does it matter that we long for things as they are in
    themselves?
The knowledge of fiery years has scorched the horses
    standing at the forge,
the little columns in the marketplace,
the wooden stairs, and the wig of Mama Fliegeltaub.

We learned so much, this you know well:
How, gradually, what could be taken away
is taken. People, countrysides.
And the heart does not die when one thinks it should,
we smile, there is tea and bread on the table.
And only remorse that we did not love
the poor ashes of Sachsenhausen
with absolute love, beyond human power.[19]

Milosz cannot visit the dead beloved—her spirit must instead undertake a protracted journey to him. It is a hejira from the deepest recesses of memory, from the Lithuania of the couple's childhood. She must soar fearfully across the Atlantic and traverse North America, arriving finally before the expatriated Milosz in Berkeley. This summoning triggers a flood of memories for the speaker. But they are vexed recollections, vivid with specifics but shorn of their intended significance—"the bath cabin where you used to leave your dress / has turned into an abstract crystal." Milosz labors mightily to harness the emotional agents of memory, to exploit its olfactory and gustatory triggers and to lend to his visual representations a photographic precision— "the scent of leather," "the tea and bread on the table," the "comic owls," and the similarly comic "wig of Mama Fliegaltaub." He seeks to *please* the shade of N.N. through vividly rendering their shared memories. Successful as these efforts may be, Milosz comes to see them merely as an exercise in nostalgia. "Does it matter that we long for things as they are in themselves?" Milosz asks. His answer is yes, but this knowledge provides only a very partial consolation. Shades are hard to please, and our personal losses pale beside the immensity of historical tragedy. Milosz comes to accept that what he and N.N. most truly share is a kind of psychic lassitude—call it the stunned aftermath of PTSD. It is the torpor that comes to those who have endured too great a percentage of a horrid century's upheavals:

> You get used to new, wet winters,
> to a villa where the blood of the German owner
> was washed from the wall, and he never returned.
> I too accepted but what was possible, cities and countries.
> One cannot step twice into the same lake
> on rotting alder leaves,
> breaking a narrow sunstreak.
>
> Guilt, yours and mine? Not a great guilt.
> Secrets, yours and mine? Not great secrets.
> Not when they bind the jaw with a kerchief, put a little cross
>   between the fingers,
> and somewhere a dog barks, and the first star flares up.

No, it was not because it was too far
you failed to visit me that day or night.
From year to year it grows in us until it takes hold.
I understood as you did: indifference.

"And how dieth the wise man?" asks Ecclesiastes. "*As* the
fool." Yet Milosz's summoning of N.N. attests that if value does
not come from wisdom in the abstract, then at least it arises from
the pair's mutual understanding, their *collective* wisdom. Only
together may they "summon what was possible." Only together
can they bear the sorrowful knowledge of Ecclesiastes's great
contemporary Heraclitus: "One cannot step twice into the same
lake / on rotting alder leaves, / breaking a narrow sunstreak."
Milosz takes this hoariest of metaphors and reshapes it, particu-
larizes it, and his effort results at least in a partial consolation,
for it reminds both Milosz and his beloved that the beauty of the
past is as unbearable as its traumas. Sympathy should never be
easy, Milosz insists. He would abhor a jargon term such as this,
but sympathy is fundamentally a species of *tough love.*

Tell me if this is too far for you, Gentle Reader. We're all sons of
bitches now. Our pasts lies golden in ruin, and that ain't much.
Someday we'll all have snow to wear, too. I do not want to leave
you like this, but I will leave you in the snow. I speak of a snow-
storm that has been raging for days, and it is Christmas Eve,
1989. The figures under house arrest number four—among us
are the great Slovenian poet Tomaz Saluman, and the similarly
estimable Australian novelist and poet David Malouf. Also here
is Lynda Hull, whose death is still several years away. And I'm
here too, Dear Reader. We're the only guests at Yaddo, the writers' colony in upstate New York, alone in a vast mansion that
was once was the home of the incomprehensibly wealthy Trask
family. None of us planned to be here. A blizzard has closed the
airports. Tomaz cannot return to Ljubljana; nor David make his
connecting flight to Sydney. Lynda and I have tickets to Minneapolis, where my mother lies dying. My companions are writers
of the highest order. In the coming years I will never be far from
the extravagantly surreal and yet somehow delicate and tragic

poems of Tomaz. I'll teach them often to my students. And I will read—several times, for it's a work of incomparable invention and beauty—David's novel of Ovid's Black Sea exile, *An Imaginary Life*. In it, Ovid, the humbled cosmopolitan, doomed to end his life among the barbarians of Tomis—who wear animal furs, who consider squirrel meat the finest of delicacies—undertakes one final project, one grander and even more challenging than *The Fasti* or *The Metamorphoses*. His barbarian captors have encountered a feral child; they have netted him and caged him, and brought him to their village as a kind of curiosity or untrainable pet. Yet Ovid, for reasons he at first does not quite understand, endeavors to teach the boy. The task at first seems impossible, for the child "has no notion of the otherness of things." The teaching is slow and fitful, but in the process both Ovid and the boy are irrevocably changed:

> I have come to a decision. The language I shall teach the Child is the language of these people I have come among, and not after all my own. And in that decision, I know I have made another. I shall never go back to Rome. . . . When I try to articulate what I know, I stumble suddenly on what, till this moment, I did not know. There are times when it comes strongly upon me that *he* is the teacher, and that whatever comes new to the occasion is being led, slowly, painfully, out of *me*.[20]

And Lynda? Earlier this week she showed me her most recent poem, finally finished here at Yaddo after months of tinkering. It is called "*Utsuroi,*" a Japanese word meaning "transience," but of a subtle and particular sort, in which we recognize beauty only as we become aware of its passing. As Lynda puts it,

> I have always loved

> these moments of delicate transition:
> Waking alone in a borrowed house

> to a slim meridian of dawn barring
> the pillow before the cool breeze,

a curtain of rain on the iron steps, rain
laving lawn chairs arranged

for a conversation finished days ago.
The Japanese call this *utsuroi,*

a way of finding beauty at the point
it is altered, so it is not the beauty

of the rose, but its evanescence
which tenders the greater joy.[21]

But have I mentioned the snow? It's fallen for days, nearly a
foot of it since yesterday alone. The staff has all gone home, having first thawed a turkey for our foursome to cook. We're in the
"little" kitchen, where the servants prepared their own meals.
And together, although none of us has much expertise when it
comes to cooking, we're made a decent Christmas Eve repast,
ending with instant pudding, topped with green cherries. And
now, in the library—the *little* library, not the big one where the
Trasks kept their signed editions of Dickens and their elephant
folio of *Birds of America*—we play Scrabble, three games, with an
almost hypnagogic concentration. Tomaz remarks that he would
love to be able to write poems with this same degree of attentiveness and conviction. Three games: Lynda wins them all, beating
David in the final one by a mere three points. And now the clock
strikes midnight. We have saved a bottle of champagne to open;
we've lit some candles. We each make a toast; and as he sips from
his plastic glass, David surveys the bookshelves and makes an
odd request, an absolutely *baffling* request, given the evening's
circumstances. "Would you mind hearing," he asks, "a poem
by Thomas Hardy?" I'm thinking to myself that there could be
nothing in the world that would make this bittersweet evening
more bittersweet than a reading from this most mirthless of poets, but David already has the behemoth *Complete Poems* in his
hands. He opens it to a poem that in the coming years will grow
to be not simply a poem that illustrates sympathy better than almost any other I can think of, but a poem that will become one
of those *you can't imagine living without,* a poem whose grave and

utter pathos grows with its every reading. "You've probably never read this one," David tells us. "It's not very well known." He takes a sip from his glass; the candles flicker.

At the Railway Station, Upway

"There is not much that I can do,
   For I've no money that's quite my own!"
   Spoke up the pitying child—
A little boy with a violin
At the station before the train came in,—
"But I can play my fiddle to you,
And a nice one 'tis, and good in tone!"

   The man in the handcuffs smiled;
The constable looked, and he smiled, too,
   As the fiddle began to twang;
And the man in the handcuffs suddenly sang
      With grimful glee:
      "This life so free
      Is the thing for me!"
And the constable smiled, and said no word,
As if unconscious of what he heard;
And so they went on till the train came in.
The convict, and boy with the violin.[22]

   —For Matthew Donovan

2009

Notes

1. Richard Rhodes, *The Making of the Atomic Bomb* (New York: Simon and Schuster, 1986), p. 659.

2. Peter Goodchild, *J. Robert Oppenheimer: "Shatterer of Worlds"* (London: British Broadcasting Corporation, 1980), p. 162.

3. Osip Mandelstam, "Conversation about Dante," in *The Poets' Dante,* ed. Peter S. Hawkins and Rachel Jacoff (New York: Farrar, Straus and Giroux, 2001), p. 51.

4. Robert Pinsky, trans., *The Inferno of Dante* (New York: Farrar, Straus and Giroux, 1994), p. 395.

5. Gregory Curtis, *The Cave Painters* (New York: Knopf, 2006), p. 233.

6. "Empathy," in *The Princeton Encyclopedia of Poetry and Poetics: Enlarged Edition,* ed. Alex Preminger (Princeton, NJ: Princeton University Press, 1974), p. 221.

7. "Empathy," in *The Longman Dictionary of Poetic Terms,* ed. Jack Myers and Michael Simms (White Plains, NY: Longman, 1989), p. 96.

8. James Wright, *Above the River: The Complete Poems* (New York: Farrar, Straus, and Giroux, 1990), p. 144.

9. *Princeton Encyclopedia of Poetry and Poetics,* p. 222.

10. George Lakoff and Mark Johnson, *Metaphors We Live By* (Chicago: University of Chicago Press, 1980), p. 13.

11. Thom Gunn, *Collected Poems* (New York: Farrar, Straus, and Giroux, 1994), p. 372. (In an endnote to the collection, Gunn identifies the novelist as William S. Burroughs.)

12. Roland Barthes, *Camera Lucida: Reflections on Photography,* trans. Richard Howard (New York: Farrar, Straus, and Giroux, 1981), p. 20.

13. Gunn, *Collected Poems,* pp. 463–64.

14. Elizabeth Bishop, *The Complete Poems, 1927–1979* (New York: Farrar, Straus, and Giroux, 1983), p. 140.

15. James Schuyler, *Collected Poems* (New York: Farrar, Straus, and Giroux, 1993), p. 48.

16. Federico Garcia Lorca, "The Duende: Theory and Divertissement," in *The Poet's Work: 29 Masters of 20th Century Poetry on the Origins and Practice of Their Art,* ed. Reginald Gibbons (Boston: Houghton-Mifflin, 1979), p. 32.

17. Lorca, "Duende," p. 36.

18. Lorca, "Duende," p. 36.

19. Czeslaw Milosz, *New and Collected Poems (1931–2001)* (New York: Ecco/Harper Collins, 1981), p. 266.

20. David Malouf, *An Imaginary Life* (New York: George Braziller, 1978), pp. 94–95.

21. Lynda Hull, *Collected Poems* (St. Paul, MN: Graywolf Press, 2006), p. 114.

22. Thomas Hardy, *The Complete Poems* (London: Macmillan, 1976), p. 607.

"In All Them Time Henry
Could Not Make Good"

Reintroducing John Berryman

I.

"The high ones die, die. They die. You look up and who's there?"—so writes Berryman's alter ego, Henry, at the start of "Dream Song #36," a poem which is ostensibly an elegy for William Faulkner. Berryman is writing in the early 1960s, when the High Ones, all the heroes of literary Modernism as well as a sadly large percentage of the poets of the generations following them, were passing fast and furiously. This makes parts of Berryman's masterwork seem less like a poem suffused with elegy than an obit page with its syntax roughened up and fashioned into six-line stanzas. Henry makes note of every death, and he has to work hard to keep up: Frost is eulogized in the "Dream Song" that follows, and later Williams and Eliot. And soon the bodies of Berryman's contemporaries start to pile up: Sylvia Plath, Theodore Roethke, Louis MacNeice, and most notably his friends Delmore Schwartz and Randall Jarrell. And though they are High Ones, they tend to die pointlessly and ingloriously. Plath gets her gas jet going; Jarrell springs in front of a passing sedan; Roethke's heart stops during a boozy dive into his neighbor's swimming pool, and Schwartz's in a flophouse hallway, his body unidentified for days. Die, die, die: Berryman's repetitions not only underscore the benumbing frequency of the High Ones' demises but also remind us that poets are often bestowed with the dubious blessing of dying more than once, just as Henry does, several times, over the course of *The Dream Songs'* 385 sections. Crucial poets are supposed to be immortal, but we've known for quite some time that they're not. Reputations ebb and flow; the patient goes into cardiac arrest, and it takes a while for the ICU staff to hustle the paddles out and administer the electrical current. Sometimes it seems that the patient will never revive. John Donne was a dead horse for three hundred years, and there was a time—a fairly long time, given the relative short-ness of American literary history—when Dickinson and Whit-man were regarded as quaint eccentrics, by no means among the crucial poets. And on the ICU for Literary Reputations, John Berryman has languished for a couple of decades. Some of his ward-mates have already been wheeled to the morgue. Big Shots of yesteryear, ranging from Conrad Aiken to Anne Sexton and Richard Hugo, are all lying cold on the slabs downstairs. Several of Berryman's pals are down there too, among them Schwartz and Jarrell. True, there have been some surprising recoveries—who would have thought that Amy Lowell and Edna St. Vincent Millay were anything but goners? Yet now they're both up and about, subjects of new biographies and selections bearing the august imprint of the Library of America. Berryman, however, does not look to be leaving soon. His breathing is labored, his vitals weak.

I find myself thinking of "Dream Song #36" on a chilly Janu-ary afternoon, thirty-three years—almost to the day—after John Berryman, the literal John Berryman, leapt to his death from the Washington Avenue Bridge on the University of Minnesota campus. A thick wet snow is falling outside my office window, and because this is Virginia, where an inch or two of snow is a cause for a panic that seems comical to this Minnesota na-tive, I'm reading with bemusement an email from my dean, an-nouncing that the university where I teach will close today at three. An hour before, I'd been trying to say something about the importance of inventive syntax to one of my students, who'd come into my office for a conference about his recent poems. To illustrate my point, I'd pulled from my shelf a very tattered copy of *The Dream Songs,* and opened it to that glorious first stanza of #29. Is there any other passage in American poetry which so acutely renders despair and weariness, and yet at the same time does so with such bedazzling panache?

There sat down, once, a thing upon Henry's heart
só heavy, if he had a hundred years,
& more, & weeping, sleepless, in all them time
Henry could not make good.
Starts again always in Henry's ears
the little cough somewhere, an odour, a chime.[1]

My student, who'd taken a British poetry survey the previous
semester, immediately likens the passage to Hopkins. I add that
the stylized vernacular and rhythms also owe much to the blues,
an art form which Berryman deeply revered. At this point I am
poised to launch into one of those monologues fueled in equal
parts by rapture and pedantry that English professors can indulge in when discussing a work they dearly love, but two things
stop me short. The first has to do with the student: I ask him
if he's ever read Berryman. He's an intelligent kid, one of the
better-read undergraduates I've worked with. But he replies by
shaking his head. Wait a second, he adds, didn't Berryman shoot
himself or something? "And besides," he tells me as he wraps
himself in his scarf, "this stuff is just too weird for me to do anything with." He leaves my office, promising to work more on
his syntax. The second thing which has taken me aback has to
do with the copy of *The Dream Songs* from which I'd read to the
student. I have a number of copies of the book floating around:
one at home and a couple at school, desk copies accumulated
from teaching Berryman over the years. But in this copy there's
a flurry of notes on the margins of #29, and they seem to be in
three distinct hands, one set in blue ink, one set in green, one
in a faded pencil, and I'm puzzled for a moment because I can't
recognize the handwriting. Who has done this? Did I long ago
buy a used copy of the book that someone had scribbled in?
Had I loaned it to a student who had no qualms about writing
all over someone else's book? With the student safely out of the
office, I ponder these questions, and it takes me several minutes to realize that one of these mysterious hands is that of my
eighteen- or nineteen-year-old self, his handwriting so different
from mine that it seems a stranger's. The second must be my—
what?—thirty- or thirty-five-year-old self's, looking equally alien

but whose notes are more pedantic. I must have been preparing a class in a hurry, writing so fast that my comments are unrecognizable to me today. And the hand in the green ink, so entwined in this jumbled marginalia that it too was at first mysterious, is that of Lynda Hull, my late wife, whose poetry possessed something of Berryman's extravagantly quirky music. They die, they die, they die. I am sifting through archaeological strata, staring at pentimento and grave goods, layered like Troy or Mycenae or Jericho: two dead poets as well as two dead selves. I begin to page through some recent anthologies, wondering how Berryman is faring these days. Although at the time of his death he was perhaps the most highly esteemed poet of his generation, eclipsing figures such as Bishop and his friend Adrienne Rich, and even giving the Heavyweight Champ of the era, Robert Lowell, some very serious competition, you wouldn't know it today. Bishop and Rich each have close to thirty pages devoted to their work in the new *Norton Anthology of Contemporary Poetry*; Berryman has seven and a half. All but one of the selections are from *The Dream Songs*. The poet's early efforts in the High Modernist vein are ignored, and so are *Homage to Mistress Bradstreet* and his sonnets, the key long works which prepare him for the *Songs*. *20th Century American Poetry,* a new anthology from Simon and Schuster designed to compete with the *Norton,* allots Berryman five poems, and notes how precipitously the poet's reputation has fallen in recent years. The book gives more space to Weldon Kees, born the same year as Berryman and a figure of utter obscurity during the time of Berryman's literary triumph. This I note with a certain ambivalence, having played a small role in Kees's revival. Today, though, my satisfaction at seeing Kees moved off the ICU is accompanied by something akin to guilt. By championing Kees, have I been unwittingly disloyal to Berryman?

It's indiscreet, I know, to cast all of these speculations in such personal terms. Berryman was never a mentor for me in the way he was for figures such as W. S. Merwin and Philip Levine, both of whom have written movingly about Berryman's teaching. Though my first semester as an undergraduate at the University of Minnesota coincided with Berryman's final months of teaching, I never studied with him. More than once I'd catch a glimpse of him around the campus, however, and once or twice

I snuck into one of his lectures. (Interestingly enough, he taught for the Humanities Department; English didn't want him.) Of these lectures I remember nothing, yet I have an oddly vivid recollection of spying Berryman through the window of Gray's Drugs, which sat on the edge of the university campus, and had an old-fashioned lunch counter. There was Berryman on a stool, thin and frail beneath the leonine beard, bent over a plate of runny eggs, a trembling fork poised above them. I'm tempted to remember that egg yolk ran down the legendary beard, but that would be embroidery. I knew it was Berryman, though, and I'd read some of his poems; unfortunately, it hadn't been the significant work, only a gathering of pretty minor fare entitled *Short Poems*, which his publisher had issued after the immense success of *The Dream Songs*. I didn't think much of the book. If Berryman was never a mentor for me, and if my memories of him are so trivial, why then do I feel the need to talk about him in the first person, and why does my lunch counter glimpse of him remain lodged in my mind with all the intensity of a vision? The answer lies not in what is, strictly speaking, an encounter with Berryman, but in a coincidence, a coincidence that came to be of significant importance in the baffling and circuitous process that turns someone into a poet.

But how could my utterly unremarkable eighteen-year-old self ever become a *poet?* I was all tabula rasa and acne, my life revolving around the classes I sleepwalked through at the university, the pot I smoked each morning, and the Grateful Dead records I listened to each night. I use "sleepwalking" in a more or less literal sense, as I also had a job, a job ideally suited for a hippie slacker. I worked as a night watchman in a large medical building, nothing much to do but read and walk the hallways a couple of times a night checking to see if the office doors were locked. I'd punch out at six in the morning, and ride the bus from St. Paul to campus, where my sleepless nights and the weed would catch up to me, and I'd snooze through the lectures I attended. That was me at the start of January 1972. The winter quarter had just begun, and as uneventfully as the fall quarter had.

The bearded poet's winter quarter could not be said to have begun so uneventfully. Berryman, who seems to have lived his adult life in a perpetual state of crisis, is undergoing yet another period of deep depression and emotional agony. He's labored mightily these past two years to stay sober, but now he's slipped. His third marriage is failing, with Berryman's much younger wife at long last rebelling against her role as caretaker. He's finished a new book of poetry which his friends regard as inferior and have counseled him not to publish, and he has abandoned a novel about his struggle with alcoholism. He has come to question as well the religious conversion that figures so strongly in his final two collections of verse. On January 5, he considers checking into a hotel where he will stab himself to death, but he reconsiders, and later that day writes his last attempt at verse. It hews to the stanzaic arrangement of *The Dream Songs*, a form he could never quite get out of his system. It begins,

> I didn't. And I didn't. Sharp the Spanish blade
> to gash my throat after I'd climbed across
> the high railing of the bridge
> to tilt out, with the knife in my right hand. . . .[2]

It's not an entirely hopeless missive, though it's surely pathetic; Berryman then speculates that perhaps his wife won't let him out of the house, thus allowing him to avoid the terrible fate he's planned. And maybe the university police will see him on his way to this grisly rendezvous, and "clap . . . him in for observation." Despair, debasement, the stagger from Yeatsian music to blunt abjection: all the elements of Berryman's mature style are there, but the charm, erudition, and wry genius which could bring these improbable ingredients together into memorable verse are absent. And by this point Berryman's detractors are saying that his peculiar genius left him some time ago. He crumples the poem and tosses it into his wastebasket, where it will be found on the day of his death. On January 7, a Friday, Berryman leaves his home for school. He walks to the Washington Avenue Bridge, which spans the Mississippi and divides the university into east and west bank campuses. He stands for a moment on the railing before he leaps. Witnesses will later report that he waved. It is 9 in the morning. At 9:10 or 9:15 I start across the bridge myself, having slept through a psychology lecture that began at 8, on my way to a Spanish class. The Washington Avenue Bridge was in those days an ugly piece of work; there are lanes for cars on its lower tier; pedestrians can cross on the top. On a bone-chilling day like this one, you wouldn't want to walk along the railings as Berryman had; you'd instead choose the enclosed walkway, and it's through this I would have ambled that morning, picking up a copy of the student newspaper from a kiosk, or greeting the girl who sat in the row before me during the psych lecture. Below me, the police cruisers would have already gathered on the west bank shore, where Berryman had landed, having first hit one of the bridge pilings, missing the iced-over river entirely. And as I yammered my pathetically Midwestern-accented Spanish or choked my quiz on irregular verbs, the cops would by now have identified the body as Berryman's. He'd carried no wallet, but in his pocket was a blank check, and his name was engraved inside the rim of his glasses, which, though shattered, had remained on his face through the fall.[3]

It took me a couple of days to hear of Berryman's death. And of course, because I was eighteen and knew less than nothing, I greeted the news with a grotesque mixture of emotions. Suicide, from a bridge of all things: now *there* was a career move. And remember, the 1960s were scarcely over; these were the waning days of existentialism, of live-fast-and-die-young, when suicide and early death possessed a cachet that they hadn't had since the days of the Romantics. Jim Hendrix, Janis Joplin, Jim Morrison, James Dean, and Plath: they were the new Chattertons and Young Werthers. Self-destruction was hip, and it even had its protocols, not as elaborate as those for hari-kari, but nearly as ritualized. Anne Sexton, who would end her own life shortly after Berryman, reacted to the death of Plath with a horrifying competitiveness. As Sexton biographer Diane Middlebrook writes,

> Sexton was frank about her anger at Plath for having "stolen" the finale Sexton planned for her own career. "*That* death was mine!" Sexton told her doctor. Suicide was a *glamourous* death, for an artist; the world would now pay more serious attention to Plath's poetry than was otherwise conceivable. . . . More, Sexton knew that her own suicide, whenever it occurred, would seem like a copycat act. This seemed unfair to Sexton, since she was older than Plath.[4]

If someone as smart as Sexton—who, despite her mental anguish, should have known better—could endorse such idiocy, than surely a callous eighteen-year-old from Mahtomedi, Minnesota, could easily have been duped into thinking Berryman's death was somehow classy. Berryman may not have been beautiful and young like Jimi or Janis, but in my dumbfuck adolescent brain I'd conflated Berryman's hundred-foot fall into a slab of cement with Hendrix torching his guitar during Monterey Pop. And so, like those kids in my poetry writing classes of today with black eye shadow and pale makeup, who've just made the not-very-long leap from goth rock singers to the poems of *Ariel,* from Nine Inch Nails to Lady Lazarus, I'd found my Suicide Hero. Not only that, but I was *right there* in the audience when the flames licked the Stratocaster—or almost there. Five minutes earlier, I thought, and I could have been the one he waved to, Henry's final benediction mine alone.

And thus began my apprenticeship to John Berryman. A few days later I purchased *The Dream Songs,* and all that winter and spring I read and reread its poems. They were utterly entrancing. Yes, they were difficult, never friendly in the manner of the Brautigan and Snyder poems I favored, but instead were militantly obtuse and allusive, recalling the Stevens and Eliot poems I'd dipped into and never much liked. Yet they were at once much funnier and much sadder, and there was a quality in the mixture of voices and emotions and dictions which seemed to me even more intimate, somehow, than the Zen-Lite clarities of Snyder. I reveled in Henry's picaresque bluster, and I loved the poems' breakneck shifts in person, their manic antiphonal slither. I even found that I could put up with the blackface dialect that ensued when Henry's unnamed companion entered, his fruitless effort to console or admonish this improbable hero. Berryman seemed almost as good to me as the other great bard who'd passed through Minneapolis, Bob Dylan. And though I knew even then that *The Dream Songs* went on too long, that its self-important division into seven books couldn't mask the fact that the collection was cobbled together and cohered in only the vaguest of ways, the book never left my bedside. And Henry, Berryman's supreme creation, part Falstaff and part Hamlet, agonized and cornball by turns, mostly Berryman but also the loose and bobbing mask that allows this brooding Achilles to leave his tent and wearily lampoon himself, was simply the most astonishing literary creation I knew of save for the lyrics of *Highway 61 Revisited*. I cherished the book, and knew that to understand it better I needed to also school myself in its allusions and influences, and so through it I learned a good deal of what I know about literature, albeit in an ass-backward sort of fashion. Because Berryman was a Shakespeare scholar, and I knew in an inchoate way that Shakespearean allusions abounded in the poems, I enrolled in Shakespeare classes. Because Berryman loved Yeats and Hopkins, I studied Yeats and Hopkins. Because of Berryman's Schwartz and Jarrell elegies, I went to their work. Like all obsessions, certain of its effects were comic. I read two biographies of Adlai Stevenson, simply because, in a minor "Dream Song," Henry expresses admiration for him. I listened over and over again to Bessie Smith, since "Dream Song #1" references her "Empty Bed Blues." And I remember staying up until 2 a.m. one night, waiting excitedly to watch a crummy B-movie on "The Late Show"—*The Prisoner of Shark Island,* starring Paul Muni, alluded to in "Dream Song #7." I even became something of a stalker, should such a thing be possible when the prey is already deceased. I'd walk every couple of weeks past 33 Arthur Avenue SE, Berryman's home, and more than once drove my VW microbus out to Resurrection Cemetery in Mendota Heights to visit Berryman's grave. More inane pilgrimages followed: I found out where Berryman's campus office had been, and was a bit enraged that the university hadn't set a plaque or a marker there. Around this time Minnesota lowered the drinking age to eighteen, and my bar of choice became the one where Berryman hung out, though I could never see the point of the martinis Berryman favored. But what a thrill it was to down a Pabst beneath a framed photo of Berryman, knowing these were the booths where he'd composed several "Dream Songs"—on cocktail napkins, no less. How mighty Berryman seemed, and how puny was I. When, at nineteen, I was able to grow a beard for the first time, my girlfriend told me I looked like Kenny Loggins, paying me what she thought was a terrific compliment. I was crushed when she hadn't recognized my real model. Hadn't I read her all those "Dream Songs" by candlelight?

The odd thing about this phase was that my obsession with Berryman never prompted me to try to write like him. Clumsy tyro versifying was coming out of me all the time, but perhaps my student was right in his claim that Berryman, at least the Berryman of *The Dream Songs,* is just too weird to get anything from. You can't write in the form of *The Dream Songs*, or begin to imitate the lurching shifts in diction and tone, with their wrenched syntax and jarring neologisms, without coming up with something that sounds like pastiche or parody. It's an idiom that more than one critic has likened to Esperanto, but that metaphor is imprecise. If Esperanto (along with Shakespeare, Milton, and Whitman, among others) is a universal language, then Berryman-speak is a kind of pidgin, the creole spoken by a tribe of one on an isolated island; he's half a world away from where the mother tongue is spoken, but he has access to a good library, a decent record collection, and plenty of time to mull over every one of his life's mistakes, indiscretions, traumas, and humiliations. (Onanism figures in this mix as well, in the form of Henry's endlessly lascivious and stereotypical sexual fantasies—but as an eighteen-year-old I could relate to that.) When this Crusoe creates a Friday, he fashions a kind of dialect within a dialect, for the speech of Henry's imaginary companion, "who addresses him as Mr. Bones and variants thereof," derived from the stylized vernacular of blackface minstrelsy. Is it possible to imagine a more oddball or unlikely means to great poetry? For poetic models, I stuck to James Wright—the middle-period Wright, not the considerably more complex figure of the late poetry—and Robert Bly, whose crimped surrealist ecstasies in cornfields were far less difficult to imitate. They were metaphor-driven poets in a way that Berryman was not, and it required little training to concoct the sort of pseudo-profound and atavistic similes that abound in *Silence in the Snowy Fields*. From Wright and Bly I learned of Neruda, who was *exceedingly* easy to parrot. I cared for these writers in part because I learned how steal from them, to make the more facile elements of their method part of my young poet's toolkit. But Berryman, in his vast eccentricity, remained a figure of awe. And to some degree he remains this way for me today. True, I once was able to write a reasonably credible poem in the form and style of *The Dream Songs*, but I only could do so within the context of a much longer sequence of poems, and only by casting the poem as a monologue spoken by Berryman/Henry.

The point of all this is that Berryman has left almost no heirs, and surely this has something to do with the decline in his reputation. Compare this situation to that of Bishop and Lowell, Berryman's most important generational peers. Bishop impersonations have for twenty-some years been a graduate workshop staple, and the influence of Lowell's *Life Studies*, despite the hits Lowell's reputation has taken in recent decades, remains considerable enough to enable poets who've never even read Lowell to adopt many of his strategies. Bishop and Lowell are still fashioning the lingua franca. But Berryman? The charter flights aren't even stopping on his island anymore.

II.

Yet on the very January afternoon during which I watched my student leave Berryman prostrate, abandoning Henry to yet another of his many demises, I found evidence that something of a Berryman revival may be in the works. This isn't a triumphant return. Lazarus is not rising easily or grandly; as in the Giotto fresco, his time underground has left him quite a bit worse for the wear. He rises in the way in which Henry rises in "Dream Song #91," in the last of a series of self-elegies entitled "Opus Posthumous":

> Noises underground made gibber some
> others collected & dug Henry up
> saying 'You *are* a sight.'
> Chilly, he muttered for a double rum
> waving the mikes away, putting a stop
> to rumors, pushing his fright
>
> off with now accumulated taxes
> accustomed in his way to solitude
> and no bills. Wives came forward, claiming a new Axis,
> fearful for their insurance, though, now, glued
> to disencumbered Henry's many ills.[5]

Those who have gathered to exhume Henry are the Library of America and poet Kevin Young, editor of *John Berryman: Selected Poems,* a review copy of which I discovered in my office mailbox, before I made my way home in that dusting of snow that had so paralyzed the drivers of Richmond. Although the Library's imprint suggests that Berryman remains canonical, there are some strings attached here. The Berryman volume is issued not as one of those Big Tomes in Glossy Black Jackets where the Library features the likes of Stevens, Frost, and Pound (and even Francis Parkman), but in a newer series called "The American Poets Project," designed to provide "a compact national library of American poetry." It's a pocket-sized book, not much bigger than a wallet or an iPod, its dust jacket printed in mauve and yellow, a color scheme that doesn't exactly suit the author of *The Dream Songs.* The good news is that Berryman's held his place in the canon; the bad news is that he's now relegated to one of the farm clubs of Parnassus, the double-A leagues of minor-major figures; his teammates also include John Greenleaf Whittier, Edgar Allen Poe, "The American Wits," Edna St. Vincent Millay, Amy Lowell, and (I kid you not) Yvor Winters, all of whom are represented in the compact series. Berryman is not, however, the only Major-Major Figure sent down to the Minor-Majors: Dr. Williams is also on the farm club team, as are two once-formidable presences from Berryman's own generation, Theodore Roethke and Muriel Rukeyser, both uneven writers, whose claims to importance are strengthened thanks to the judicious selections required by the compact format. And it must be said that Berryman profits from this format too.

Curiously, a comprehensive selection of Berryman's poetry has never been available in this country before; Berryman's misleadingly titled *Collected Poems* contains all the short lyrics, as well as the sonnets and *Mistress Bradstreet,* but nothing from *The Dream Songs,* which Berryman's publisher has always issued as a separate volume, and always in its entirety. This makes for some obvious problems: the second-rate "Dream Songs," especially those from *His Toy, His Dream, His Rest,* the longer but weaker second volume of the sequence, tend to distract the reader from the most innovate songs, most of which appear in the volume's first installment, which were published in 1964 as *77 Dream Songs.* In the *Collected*, the poetry of his unusually long apprenticeship, burdened with its Yeats affectations and haughty Modernist detachment, threatens to distort the significance of Berryman's far more engaging sonnets and the *Bradstreet* sequence. Yet these latter two works are themselves problematic, marred for differing reasons by a kind of self-indulgence which Berryman overcame (though precariously) in *The Dream Songs*. Sadly, the self-indulgence returns as a kind of tsunami in Berryman's final two books, *Love & Fame* and *Delusions Etc.*, where Berryman strips off the Henry mask and speaks in a guilelessly direct autobiographical poetry that is usually flat and uninteresting, or indulges in devotional verse that is for the most part banal. Finally, to make the messiness of this very messy oeuvre just a bit more turbid, there are the hundreds of unpublished "Dream Songs" that exist in Berryman's literary remains, some of which were gathered by his biographer John Haffenden in a long-unavailable volume entitled *Henry's Fate*. Yet a small number of these poems (not the efforts that were famously composed on cocktail napkins after a couple of stiff ones) are of the first order. Berryman himself seemed in the end to have realized what the sprawling unevenness of his poetry could have done to his legacy; one of the last projects he completed was a selection of his poems, including the best of *The Dream Songs*, which he compiled for his British publisher, Faber and Faber, and which was issued there not long after his death. Although Berryman's muse may have been lost, sloshed, or badly hung-over during his final years, Berryman's discernment as a critic of his own work seems in this case not to have failed him: it's an impeccable selection of 170 pages; most of the essential Berryman can be found in the book, and I've always wondered why the volume never was reprinted in the States. Had *this* book been the introduction to Berryman that American readers encountered during the decades since his death, I doubt if his reputation would still be languishing on the ICU. Kevin Young appears to use the Faber book as his starting place, but he also makes a discerning selection from Berryman's flawed last books, showcases the sonnets in a more convincing way than Berryman himself did, and even brings to the table some early work that does not appear in the *Collected*; in the context of a volume which aims to show Berryman's evolution rather than simply to be comprehensive, this work too looks surprisingly interesting. Berryman once entitled a poem "The Poet's Final Instructions," and with Young's selection it might be said that Berryman's will has finally been executed.

Young is well suited for this task, being one of the few contemporary poets of consequence who can be said to have been influenced by Berryman. He favors long poetic sequences that carry something of the flavor of *The Dream Songs;* they make use of a Henryesque mixture of high-culture references with pop-culture subjects, and they are characterized by the same nervy willingness to over-indulge that is both the bane and the glory of Berryman's writing. In his introduction, Young praises a variety of Modernist and post-modernist long poems which he characterizes as "over-reaching, under planned, unruly, wonderful messes that do not aspire to formal perfection but which delight in their sense of surprise, of *personality*."[6] It's a characterization which echoes the qualities which Berryman glorified in a seminal essay on Whitman, whose example, more than any other, allowed the poet to make a definitive break with the cult of impersonality promulgated by the Modernists and New Critics who were his early models. (It's worth noting that the arid symmetries of these writers have been unwittingly revived in certain strains of post-modernism, most notably in Language writing, methods which Young, in his turn, has also rebelled against.) Furthermore, Young is a writer of color, and his guardedly sympathetic reading of the minstrelsy and dialect motifs of *The Dream Songs* finally sets this can of worms to rest. Young notes that "for Berryman, as for many white rock-and-roll artists, black dialect (however imaginary), provides a gateway to a wider sense of American language, not a sign of cultural decay but of cultural vitality. The fearlessness through which Berryman breaks through the polite diction of academic poetry into a liberating variety of idioms is a major part of his legacy."[7] For aficionados of Henry, there will be something a bit sorrowful about Young's very sensible desire to re-introduce Berryman, to state the claims for his place in American poetry, and to defend his excesses and infelicities, but you can't quibble with the judgments of Young's introduction. It is now possible for the first time to get a clear picture of Berryman's very curious development, and to ascertain at long last how the best of Berryman will endure.

The conventional wisdom that the early work is weak is still borne out in Young's selection, but in it we read the early poems with a new understanding of just how radical was the shift from the dutiful Modernism of the apprentice work to the weird mastery of *The Dream Songs.* It's mostly the voice of Yeats we hear, but all the Usual Suspects among the Modernists haunt the work, so much so that an individual poem can partake of several of their voices at once: an elegy for Crane starts in the manner of *White Buildings,* but shifts to undigested Audenisms ("Impermanence in place, he will not walk / Again the swift contemporary sky"). But there are glimmers of the work to come even here: a series of monologues entitled "The Nervous Songs" prefigures the staccato dictional shifts and emotional extremity of *The Dream Songs,* and in them he even arrives at the form of the later poem.

The first poems which suggest that Berryman could ever be a poet of the stature of his friends Jarrell, Lowell, and Schwartz come in the form of the 117 sonnets Berryman wrote in a kind of frenzy in 1947 but didn't publish until twenty years later. Chronicling an extramarital affair with a woman the poet calls "Chris," and taking place during Berryman's stint of teaching at Princeton, they are a wacko mixture of Elizabethan contrivance, heaped-on literary allusion, and bald self-disclosure, erudite and horny by turns. The sequence has little to offer by way of plot: the couple has a few secretive trysts, in places such as parked cars; the beloved leaves town on vacation, and the speaker pines for her. Eventually they part. The final lines of the sequence are telling: "Presently the sun / yellowed the pines & my lady came not / in blue jeans & a sweater. I sat down and wrote." As Adam Kirsch witheringly observes, "it is hard to say which Berryman found more desirable, Chris herself or the poems she inspired."[8] Yet in the sequence we see the first inklings of Berryman's originality. William Meredith refers to the sonnets as a "puppyish tour de force," and for the first time in Berryman's career he seems *capable* of a tour de force.[9] His stance toward his influences has changed; he no longer seems a dutiful graduate student aspiring to Shakespeare scholarship nor a slavish disciple of Yeats, Eliot, and Auden. Now Berryman has arrived at something of the passive-aggressive stance toward the tradition which figures so strongly in *The Dream Songs*. He appropriates his masters while at the same time doing violence toward them. He likens Chris to Petrarch's Laura, but only to contrast Petrarch's chaste devotion to his muse with the speaker's own erotic ardor; he revels in the illicitness of the affair while at the same time infusing it with buffoonery: to " 'your face, bright and dark, back, as we screw/Our lives together,' he writes in sonnet #67." Again and again, he sets himself against the rarefied allusive vocabulary, impersonality, and formal precision of Modernism: sonnets these may be, but they're improvisational and frequently sloppy; the rhymes often seem calculatingly bad, designed to provoke us. Thus we have "softest crotch" paired with "Morning-after botch," and "kibitzer's mouth" with "curiosity's truth." And while the invariable references to Dido and Aeneas, Lancelot and Guinevere, and Tristan and Isolde appear in the sequence, so does Groucho Marx. Combine this mixture with the poems' local color and journalistic specifics—Princeton streets and watering holes get mentioned, along with the poet's quotidian tasks—and you might as well be reading a heterosexual version of O'Hara's *Lunch Poems*. Young reprints a far greater number of the sonnets than Berryman himself did in his Faber selection, and while many of these efforts are excruciating, Young allows us to see the arc of the collection, to view it, as Berryman seems to have when he allowed the book to at last be published, as a kind of *roman a clef.*

Homage to Mistress Bradstreet, Berryman's other large project prior to *The Dream Songs,* garnered him the praise of his contemporaries which he seems to have so deeply craved. It is Berryman's submission to the Big Modernist Long Poem sweepstakes, and it has all the requisite bells and whistles: an immensely difficult style comprised of inverted syntax and archaisms, an appropriately literary subject in its examination the life of the early American poet Anne Bradstreet, and a quirky, elliptical structure along the lines of *The Wasteland* or *The Bridge.* The poem was received ecstatically when it first appeared in the *Partisan Review* in 1953, and yet again when it appeared in book form a few years later. *Bradstreet* still has its admirers, though I am not one of them. Like Lowell's *The Mills of the Kavanaghs,* published not long before it, the poem is notable largely for its dubious ability to take the baroque and mannerist strains of Modernism to their most bizarre extremes. (Stanley Kunitz, in a review of the book, allows that he has read the poem six times and still doesn't understand it—the implication being that if the poem is *that* obscure, it's got to be a kind of masterwork.)[10]

But, as with Lowell in *Kavanaghs, Bradstreet* was a book Berryman seems to have needed to get off his chest before his real work could begin. And, as with his sonnets, *Bradstreet* employs some devices Berryman will use to greater success in *The Dream Songs,* most notably in the passages of imaginary dialogue between the poet-narrator and Bradstreet—who speaks sometimes in monologue, but sometimes is evoked in the third person. These shifts in diction and person prefigure the quirky eclogue form that we'll later see in the exchanges between Henry and his blackface companion. Young reprints *Homage to Mistress Bradstreet* in its entirety, as he should, despite the poem's flaws.

So now we arrive at *The Dream Songs.* After slogging through its 6,160 lines, and after hearing the many anecdotes of Berryman's facility at writing the later songs, readers tend to draw the mistaken assumption that the book came easily. In fact, as we know from the Haffenden and Mariani biographies, the book evolved in slow and costly fashion; the first volume, begun in 1955, took Berryman eight years to complete, and it arose above all from a combination of personal crises and intense self-assessment. He made his initial plans for the book shortly after his arrival in Minneapolis, his formerly bright teaching career in a shambles. He'd just been fired from a position in Iowa because of his drinking, and his friends Allen Tate and Saul Bellow had to pull a good many strings to convince the administration at Minnesota to hire him. His first marriage had ended, and he spends much of his first year in Minnesota undertaking a preposterously obsessive project of dream analysis, apparently because he is too broke to afford a shrink. He is "busy and literally out of the world," he reports to his mother, "dealing solely with dreams."[11] Painful memories haunt this project, revolving most significantly around the suicide of Berryman's father when the poet was twelve. At the same time, he commences an agonizing exchange of letters to his mother, in which he queries her about his father's death. (The circumstances of his father's suicide are cloudy, and there has always been speculation that he was murdered by the poet's mother and future stepfather.) This is the "irreversible loss" which Berryman alludes to in his prefatory note to the poem, the "departure" mentioned in "Dream Song #1." When Berryman finally snaps out of the trance of his self-analysis, he begins to plan a new work, longer and more ambitious than anything he has composed before. Mariani does a masterful job of summing up Berryman's design for the poem:

> In a note written late in [1955] he considered the form of the new poems. Like his earlier Nervous Songs, the Dream Songs would use the three 6-line rhyming stanzas, though he wanted them to be "*much* 'rougher' and more 'brilliant'" than anything he'd yet done; he wanted a coarse demotic language to fit into the music of the poem without calling too much attention to itself. And he wanted the poem to deal with the human condition, but channeled through the life of one man. Each poem would have at least "one stroke of some damned serious humor." He wanted a "gravity of matter," but he wanted it wedded to a "gaiety of manner." He would avoid sentimentality at all costs, letting the poems arise naturally out of the situations in the poems themselves. . . . He also meant to get all the sexual longing and lust into his poems he could. . . . He would begin the sequence with memories of his childhood and end with a poem about his daughter, when that event should finally happen. He would use the old iambic norm, but jazz it up and make it freer, mixing it with "rocking meter, anapests, spondees, iambs, trochees, dactyls" until he drove the prosodists "right out of their heads" with his weird riffs and sweet new music. He would rely on Christian symbols to grid the sequence, though he meant Henry to be closer to the picaresque hero in Apuleius' *Golden Ass* than to Christ. He would leave the door ajar on the off-chance that some change of heart might yet someday visit Henry.[12]

Within a few years Berryman was able to gain some momentum for this outlandish project, and need it be added that it resembles nothing else in American poetry? Yet the poem at its best is far more than the sum of its vastly idiosyncratic parts.

True, the poem has little of the austere and sobering introspection that haunts Lowell's *Life Studies,* which was begun at the same time. Nor is Berryman interested in the sorts of visionary spiritual reckonings which preoccupy Bishop in many of the poems of her *Questions of Travel,* much of which was also written in the late 1950s. When compared to Bishop and Lowell, the Berryman of *The Dream Songs* seems all performance and bluster. But I wonder if this contrast has more to do with choices of strategy than with depth. Lowell arrives at the new candor of *Life Studies* through modeling his poems on memoir and realist fiction— *The Education of Henry Adams* was his favorite book.[13] Bishop's most enduring models are the lyrics of Herbert and Hopkins. In differing ways, Lowell and Bishop seek a classicizing purity and economy in their mature styles. Berryman, by contrast, devises *The Dream Songs* as a dramatic poem, a performance piece. Although Henry is its only real character, he is rendered through stagecraft, in monologues and dialogue which ultimately derive from the Marlowe and Shakespeare plays which Berryman knew quite nearly by heart. His method allows for a vastly greater variety of tone and diction than anything which Bishop and Lowell would permit themselves, and although this tonal and dramatic complexity withers into mere diary notes in the later "Dream Songs," the first ninety-one sections—everything up to the end of its "Opus Posthumous" series—are remarkably accomplished, all of them good, and about a dozen of them unquestionably great. Young would probably not completely agree with my claim, as he reprints less than half of *77 Dream Songs,* and perhaps too many of the efforts of *His Toy, His Dream, His Rest,* where—as Lewis Hyde pointed out a number of years ago in a controversial essay—Berryman seems to have written a large percentage of the poems while completely sloshed.

Reading the new collection, I find myself also wondering whether the decline in Berryman's reputation has something to do with the fundamental laziness and conformity of anthologists, who seem to have conspired to make #s 4, 14, and 29 just about all readers know of Berryman. #29 may indeed be the most characteristic poem in the series, but #14 strikes me as mostly shtick, its tone merely antic, showing little evidence of the tragicomic sensibility that inhabits the best of the songs. #4 is a bit more striking thanks to the chilling irony of its closing, but it is by no means the sequence's best or most representative effort. Young of course prints this trio, but his selection also showcases poems which have largely been ignored by anthologists, and many of them are overlooked gems, not just because they are fresher than the anthology fare, but because they are better. Here, for example, is #51:

Our wounds to time, from all the other times,
sea-times slow, the time of galaxies
fleeing, the dwarfs' dead time,
lessen so little that if here in his crude rhymes
Henry them mentions, do not hold it, please,
for a putting of man down.

Ol' Marster, being bound you do your best
versus we coons spare now a cagey John
a whilom bits that whip:
who'll tell your fortune, when you have confessed
whose & whose woundings—against the innocent stars
& remorseless seas.

—Are you radioactive, pal? Pal, radioactive.
—Has you the night sweats & the day sweats, pal?
—Pal, I do.
—Did your gal leave you?—What do *you* think, pal?
—Is that thing in front of your head what it seems to be, pal?
—Yes, pal.[14]

What a strange radio is Henry, set—as he so often is—on some curious scan-mode that straddles centuries and cultures, picking up everything from Campion to Charley Patton. One moment he's Prometheus bound; the next he's Amos 'n' Andy; the effect is at once mellifluous and cacophonous. As I type the poem out, my spell-as-you-go function goes into overdrive when faced with the neologisms and archaisms, red-lining madly. There is "whilom," an outmoded term for "formerly"; there is "Marster" and "woundings" and of course the problematic "we coons." There are lines of utterly strict pentameter interlaced with Hopkinsian concoctions made entirely of trochees and spondees. And, as in so many of the "Dream Songs," some passages continue to baffle, even after repeated readings. The "we coons" chorus of stanza two—if it *is* them and not Henry speaking—appears to be comparing Henry's plight to their own condition of servitude, but we can't exactly be sure. Stanza two may be murky and egregious, but one and three are astounding. Take away the nebulae and white dwarfs, and the poem's opening stanza could be a lost speech by Hamlet. Yet the final stanza seems a combination of blues lament and dialogue from a Beckett play. But for all the authority and range of reference in the poem, it, like "Dream Song #14," avoids pretension in part because it questions the very ability of "valiant art" to offer solace: don't hold Henry's "crude rhymes" against him, Berryman begs. They do not help to make us any less insignificant as we stand under the night sky or on the shores of the "remorseless seas." Henry's only means of consoling us and himself is to bemoan his sorrow, to build his own version of Rilke's "lament heaven." (Never mind that one of the Dream Songs insists that "Rilke was a *jerk.* ") The bluesy keening of the poem's final stanza is not merely Henry weeping because his "gal" left him; it is deeper than that. It is the gut-wrenching chiliastic dread of Robert Johnson's "Stones in my Passway," or St. Louis Jimmy's "Goin' Down Slow." And though the dialogue of the concluding stanza veers toward slapstick, "that thing in front" of Henry's head is unmistakably the same .32 caliber automatic pistol used by Berryman's father—as "Dream Song #384" grimly puts it—to shoot "his heart out in a Florida dawn." Berryman favored the New Testament over the Old, but as I read him I am reminded of the terrible conundrum which concludes the opening chapter of Ecclesiastes: "For in much wisdom *is* much grief, and he that increaseth knowledge increaseth sorrow."

The author of Ecclesiastes, in his brutally dithyrambic nihilism, seems echoed by Berryman in a final "Dream Song" I'd like to discuss. Anthologists and critics have largely ignored the theological strain in Berryman's writing, but he seems to me one of the most absorbing and convincing religious poets of our time. The case for this claim can't be made, however, in the poems of frigid piety that followed his religious conversion during the writing of *Love & Fame.* Young includes portions of the two most ambitious efforts from this phase, *Fame's* "11 Addresses to the Lord" and "Opus Dei," which appeared in the posthumously published *Delusions Etc.* In them, Berryman is trying to be a good Catholic and a good Twelve-Stepper, and although we wish him well in these efforts, the result is a tepid poetry. The "searching and fearless personal inventory" which AA asks of its practitioners becomes his goal here, but it infuses the poems with a cloying tone of regret and remorse. As Douglas Dunn writes, "his religious poems in *Love & Fame* are intended to 'criticize backwards' [the book's] earlier, scandalous sections; and, presumably, the carnality, comedy, and religious doubts of *The Dream Songs.* "[15] But it is in the pugnacious agnosticism of *The Dream Songs* where Berryman's concerns as a religious poet are most memorably expressed, through an irreverence that never overshadows their longing. "I was always a religious bitch," said Billie Holiday, in a quote Berryman might well have known. So it is with Henry as well. Witness "Dream Song #46":

I am, outside. Incredible panic rules.
People are blowing and beating each other without mercy.
Drinks are boiling. Iced
drinks are boiling. The worse anyone feels, the worse
treated he is. Fools elect fools.
A harmless man at an intersection said, under his breath:
    "Christ!"

That word, so spoken, affected the vision
of, when they trod to work next day, shopkeepers
who went & were fitted with glasses.
Enjoyed they then an appearance of love & law.
Millennia whift & waft—one, one, er, er . . .
Their glasses were taken from them, & they saw.

Man has undertaken the top job of all,
son fin. Good luck.
I myself walked at the funeral of tenderness.
Followed other deaths. Among the last,
like the memory of a lovely fuck,
was: *Do, ut des.*[16]

There's of course the familiar hodge-podge of allusion and diction. One commentator has claimed that the opening line alludes to a passage in *Sadism and Masochism* by the German psychoanalyst Wilhelm Stekel, but I suspect Berryman instead had in mind a passage in one of Hopkins's "terrible" sonnets, in which the melancholy Jesuit bemoans an exile both physical and spiritual: "I am in Ireland now; now I am at a third / Remove. Not but in all removes I can / Kind love both give and get."[17] Henry starts the poem, as he does so many others, in the outer dark, the "third remove," of isolation and alienation, brought on not just by himself but also by the ruthlessness of mankind—whose folly seems to grow greater as the poem goes on. We have a street person becoming a Christ figure, and shopkeepers who seem to be enacting a perverse version of the Supper at Emmaus— but these disciples do not recognize their god. And when Henry notes that "Man has undertaken the top job of all," he seems no more happy about the ascendancy of secular humanism than is the Christian right. But the poem isn't entirely pessimistic. "The funeral of tenderness" may have taken place, but the closing of the poem may be (*may* be, for the ending is finally ambiguous) cautiously hopeful. Charity may persist, though in an imperiled state, lingering "like the memory of a glorious fuck." And it is a classic Berryman gesture to juxtapose the earthiness of the f-word with a high-sounding passage in Latin—*Do, ut des*: "I give, that you might give," a term deriving from Roman law, and describing the principle of reciprocity, an ancient equivalent to the golden rule. Yet the words seem at the same time to evoke the liturgy—"this is my body that is given to you." But then again, "to do" someone is a synonym for "fuck." A cheap trans-lingual punch line? Definitely. But also something more far profound than that, which is the Berryman M.O. Has any other American poet had the chutzpah (or hubris) to attempt to play Lear as well as his Fool—both together, in the same performance? Lowell, his friend and most ruthless competitor, wrote a review of *77 Dream Songs* that seems to have tested their friendship. To the hypersensitive Berryman, Lowell's listing of the book's shortcomings in an otherwise awestruck appraisal—Lowell spoke of "the threat of mannerism, and worse—disintegration"—had damned the book with faint praise. But the end of the review suggests that even Lowell had been humbled by the invention and pathos of the collection. "All is risk and variety here. This great Pierrot's universe is more tearful and funny than we can easily bear."[18]

III.

On that January morning, it must have started to snow. This was Minnesota, after all. I would have ridden the Lake Street bus toward the commune I shared with a shifting cast of some dozen others. Nondescript commercial Lake Street—"Lake Street where the used cars live," as Berryman had it in a poem, whose body by this point was cooling in a cubicle at the Hennepin County morgue, a place at least as chilly as the river he had missed in his leap. I'd been up all night, at school all day. The mercury would likely have been dropping, and after I walked into the house I must have smoked a joint with my roommates, and listened attentively with them to something that today would make me cringe, Led Zep or Pink Floyd, Black Sabbath or T Rex. By then I could sleep, waking at midnight, perhaps, to a clear sharp sky outside my window, for now it was too cold to snow. Did I fall asleep a green untutored child, but waken as a writer? Hardly. This is a vain poetry—that day exists as a few stray neurons burnt down to embers, a bundle of synapses barely connecting; it lives through guesswork, reconstruction, speculation. I knew nothing then of who I was, and of who I was then I still know next to nothing. But there is one thing I am sure of: on that day one of the High Ones died.

2005

Notes

1. John Berryman, *The Dream Songs* (New York: Farrar, Straus and Giroux, 1969), p. 33.

2. John Berryman, *Henry's Fate and Other Poems* (New York: Farrar, Straus and Giroux, 1977), p. 93.

3. John Haffenden, *The Life of John Berryman* (Boston: Routledge & Kegan Paul, 1982), p. 419.

4. Diane Middlebrook, *Her Husband: Hughes and Plath—A Marriage* (New York: Viking, 2003), p. 217.

5. Berryman, *Dream Songs*, p. 106.

6. Kevin Young, introduction to *John Berryman: Selected Poems* (New York: Library of America, 2004), p. xx.

7. Young, introduction, p. xxiv.

8. Adam Kirsch, *The Wounded Surgeon: Confession and Transformation in Six American Poets* (New York: W.W. Norton, 2005), p. 110.

9. William Meredith, "A Bright Surviving Actual Scene: Berryman's Sonnets," in *Henry's Understanding: Reflections on the Poetry of John Berryman,* ed. Harry Thomas (Boston: Northeastern University Press, 1988), p. 97.

10. "Stanley Kunitz, "No Middle Flight," in Thomas, *Henry's Understanding,* p. 112.

11. John Berryman, *We Dream of Honor: John Berryman's Letters to His Mother,* ed. Richard J. Kelly (New York: W.W. Norton, 1988), p. 291.

12. Paul Mariani, *Dream Song: The Life of John Berryman* (New York: William Morrow, 1990), p. 301.

13. Robert Lowell, *The Letters of Robert Lowell,* ed. Saskia Hamilton (New York: Farrar, Straus and Giroux, 2005), p. 225.

14. Berryman, *Dream Songs*, p. 55.

15. Douglas Dunn, "Gaiety & Lamentation: The Defeat of John Berryman," in Thomas, *Henry's Understanding,* p. 150.

16. Berryman, *Dream Songs,* p. 50.

17. Cary Nelson, ed., *Anthology of Modern American Poetry* (New York: Oxford University Press, 2000), p. 726; *Gerard Manley Hopkins: Poems and Prose,* ed. W .H. Gardner (London: Penguin, 1953), p. 62.

18. Robert Lowell, *Collected Prose,* ed. Robert Giroux (New York: Farrar, Straus and Giroux, 1987), p. 111.

"To the Betrayed World"

Darth Howard, Ashurbanipal,
and a Defense of Poetry

Nearly twenty-five years ago, I served as the poet Howard Nemerov's assistant during the Breadloaf Writers' Conference. I can't say this was a particularly pleasant experience, for the Nemerov that I saw during those weeks was embittered and misanthropic. The charitable characterization would be curmudgeonly, and in some respects Howard was expected to act this way—he was the conference's elder poet, trying to fill the shoes of Frost, that most curmudgeonly of curmudgeons, and his great Breadloaf predecessor. It was a character actor's role, designed for someone too far on the other side of fifty to play a leading man, demanding a performance sly and aloof, avuncular and imperious by turns; he was doing the Grand Old Man of American Letters, or at least of Northern Vermont during the month of August. And, although his work had even at that point fallen out of fashion, Howard had the requisite credentials—he'd won both the National Book Award and the Pulitzer; he'd served as the US poet laureate. He'd written criticism and fiction as well as verse, and he was a versifying fiend. His *Collected Poems,* issued a few years earlier, ran to over five hundred pages. And I suppose it is testament to Howard's earnestness about playing this part to add that he was only sixty-three at the time, not even old enough to collect social security, yet somehow he seemed much older. My own role was a much smaller one, and straight out of central casting. I was Snarky Young Poet—ambitious in some respects, but also a sycophant and a careerist. I had just turned thirty; my first book had just been published, and I did whatever I could, literary and extra-literary, to advance my career. I wrote the poems, of course, but I also edited poetry for a literary journal, and I wrote reviews, most of which today make me cringe. They were of two sorts: the type that sucked up to the poets I liked—and who, coincidentally, might read them and somehow be inclined to later help my career along—and the kind that gave no quarter to the sorts of poets who seemed irrelevant to me. These latter reviews could be merciless, but they always focused on the stragglers from the herd. A few years ago one of these reviews was mentioned in a biography of the poet John Ciardi—a figure of Howard's generation and quite similar to him in several key respects—and the author of the book seemed to believe that my review of a Ciardi *Selected,* published in *Poetry* (which then, as now, set the industry standard for the snarky review), may have hastened his death.

Breadloaf was in those days a decidedly hierarchical place, modeled on the military. The director, the poet Robert Pack, lorded over the place like a five-star general, and the staff, poets such as Marvin Bell and Galway Kinnell, were brigadier generals; the associate staff, poets of somewhat lesser reputation who assisted the staff poets, were colonels or majors. I was there as a fellow, a distinction reserved for poets with one or two books published. They weren't paid in the way that the staff and associate staff were, but they were given food and lodging; their only responsibility was to be the workshop assistants to the staff. The fellows were like first lieutenants or captains, different from the enlisted men and women, who paid big money to attend the conference. And, most important of all, we had the privilege of admission to the Officers Club, a place called Tremen Lodge, where there was always a daily cocktail hour before lunch, another before dinner, and yet another after the evening reading. A great career opportunity. But obviously I had been weighed against my fellow fellows and somehow found lacking, for I got stuck with Howard Nemerov. My graduate school teacher Steve Orlen had been Howard's fellow a few years earlier, and he'd warned me about what to expect: he'll treat you like his houseboy, Steve had warned. All you'll be doing is fetching his coffee and going down to the Middlebury ABC store to buy him his fifths. (Although I never saw Howard drunk, he had a reputation as a tippler.)

Steve's prediction was mostly accurate. Howard's workshop was a disaster. Partly this was because no one in the class seemed to have any affinity with Howard's aesthetic. This was still the era of Deep Image writing and confessional poetry, and Howard was a formalist, schooled in the haughty impersonality of Eliot and the New Critics, deeply read in the tradition, and favoring even in his most densely meditative poetry a kind of wit and intelligence that seemed almost Augustan. He had written a scathing review of the influential Stephen Berg and Robert Mezey anthology *Naked Poetry,* which had been a kind of Bible of subjectivist poetry in open form. He must have wanted his wit and disdain for poetic fashion to be on display in the workshop, too, but the sorts of gestures that might have worked in one of Howard's satirical epigrams came across as boorish when practiced on human subjects rather than upon a readership. "My dear," he said to a young woman after he had sat in silence for a few minutes of discussion about her poem, "I think you should divide this poem into two parts—and then you should throw them both away." He'd rarely speak during the discussions, save to add a disdainful zinger of two toward their conclusions. These sorts of comments, I found out later, were being uttered by rote. During one of the mandatory cocktail hours I mentioned Howard's divide-the-poem-into-two-parts line to a poet who had previously assisted Howard. "Oh that one," she said. "He trots it out every time he teaches a workshop." I tried once or twice to respectfully disagree with Howard about a student poem. This was not a wise strategy. Someone had submitted a very small and to my mind rather unambitious poem about shooting baskets with his pals. Howard for once spoke enthusiastically about the poem, but I insisted it could be longer and more—I think this was the word I used—"searching." "David," said Howard, "I won't say I disagree with you; I'll just say you're *wrong.*" He phrased this with the sort of weary comic exasperation you get from Bill Maher talking about Republican presidential candidates who don't believe in evolution.

I look back at this experience with a greater degree of charity toward Howard than I ever could have possessed in my snarky days. Clearly, it pained him to see students so wrong-headed and so ill-read, to have to teach people who had no knowledge of poetry written before about 1970 and who were enduring him because the workshops of the fashionable stars of the conference like Kinnell and Matthews had already been filled. One day Howard spoke of an interview a young woman journalist had recently done with him. "Who's your favorite poet?" she had asked, to which Howard replied, "George Herbert." "Oh," said the woman, "where does he teach?" Howard thought this anecdote funny enough to be worth telling twice during the workshop, as though it were the definitive indication of just how clueless these young "creative writers" were about our art and sullen craft. And yet Howard came back to Breadloaf year after year, dutifully trying to fill the shoes of Frost. Of course, what I now see as one of the less egregious forms of writerly vanity I then saw as a kind of deep effrontery toward Howard's students and his colleagues. He was famous for never attending the readings or lectures of the other staffers, and I had pretty much made up my mind to skip Howard's lecture. But Howard saw to it that this wouldn't happen.

His lecture was scheduled to take place fifteen minutes after a session of the workshop ended. As the students were packing up their things, ready to move off to the chapel where the lecture would take place, one of them asked Howard about what he would be discussing. For once, what seemed like a blank look came over him. "Why don't you come and see?" he told her. And then he turned to me: "David, would you please go over to the library"—rustic as the mountaintop cabins and lodges of Breadloaf may have been, the campus still had a small library—"and bring the 'P' volume of the Britannica to me in the chapel?" By the time I had done this, Howard was already standing—empty handed—at the podium. He took the heavy volume from me, flipped through it for a moment, and then began to intone, in that manner he affected in workshop—stentorian one minute, regular-guy casual the next—"Poetry is a vast subject, as old as history and older, present wherever religion is present, possibly, under some conditions—the primal and primary form of languages themselves." Howard might have seemed to many of us to be old and in the way, might have seemed far less bardic than Galway Kinnell doing his Whitman shtick, or Bill Matthews with his wordplay and pyrotechnics, but he was giving the tyros and poetasters of Breadloaf their comeuppance. For Howard had, in a more or less literal sense, written the book on poetry, or at least the essay that the editors of Britannica saw fit to serve as its definition. And what better way to let us know he was king of the cats? The essay was nuanced, elegant, sly. It began with an attempt to define poetry ("the other way of using language"); moved on to discuss the differences between poetry and prose; tried to define poetic diction and say something about the experience of reading poetry. It made reference to poetic form; defined the old bugbear about the relationship between form and content by saying that "the poem is a much simplified model for the mind"; engaged in a lengthy parable for poetic expression drawn from Menelaus's encounter with the shape-shifter Proteus in the *Odyssey*; and ended—and here Howard's New Critical credentials were being displayed—with a discussion of the poem's unified effect, drawing upon quotes from John Crowe Ransom and I. A. Richards just to make sure you got the point. But the essay's most telling moment came shortly before this. He quoted Shakespeare's Sonnet 30, then commenced his discussion of the poem with this:

> The poem, acknowledged to be a masterpiece by so many generations of readers, may stand as an epitome and emblem for the art altogether, about which it raises a question that must be put, although it cannot be satisfactorily or unequivocally answered: the question of whether poetry is a sacrament or a confidence game or both or neither. To reply that poetry is not religion and must not promise what religion does is to preserve a useful distinction; nevertheless, the religions of the world, if they have nothing else in common, seem to be based on collections of sacred poems. Nor, at the other extreme, can any guarantee that poetry is not a confidence game be found in the often-heard appeal to the poem's "sincerity." One will never know if Shakespeare wept all over the page while writing the 30th sonnet, though one inclines to doubt it, nor would it be to his credit if he did, nor to the reader's that he should know it or care to know it."[1]

I won't quote the rest of Howard's discussion of the poem, save to say that even Shakespeare wouldn't have fared all that well in a Nemerov workshop. The sonnet is "full of artifice, and even the artifice degenerates here and there into being artsy."

I can't say that hearing Howard's essay did much to piece my snarky armor. The stunt of having an underling deliver the "P" to the podium at the very last minute before his lecture must have been something he'd tried during previous Breadloafs. The lecture of course attested to Howard's brilliance, and it evidenced the position Howard so often put forth in his own poetry—Wyatt Prunty characterizes Nemerov as "a skeptic in dialogue with hope."[2] But Howard's ill-mannered posturing at the conference led me to conclude that the skeptic had by this point in his life won the dialogue. (Never mind that Howard's actions were far less damaging and compulsive than the behavior of most of the rest of us attending the conference, for whom it was a clinic for narcissism and various sorts of bad behavior.) I saw Howard as a figure akin to the disillusioned priest in Ingmar Bergman's *Winter Light*, or like the speaker in any number of Thomas Hardy poems. The problem was not that the sacramental could no longer speak to you, but that you were deeply pissed off, positively enraged, that the sacramental had let you down. And thus the con game was all you had left. Walking back to the library with that fat leather-bound "P" in my hands, I resolved to do two things—never to be the kind of teacher that Howard became, and never to read his work again.

But I am now closer to Howard's age on that day than I am to the snarky young thing I was. And it recently came to pass that I broke both of these vows. Not that I realized it at the time, mostly I was just plain exasperated by an undergraduate writing class that seemed even by undergraduate standards to be lackadaisical, self-involved, and completely unread; even that raw talent that's supposed to be there in abundance in every creative writing class was absent. Workshop discussions seemed to be conducted with Haldol or Thorazine listlessness. They'd only get a little involved in conversations when they complained about the poets I was having them read. Poor Tomas Transtromer, a figure I admire immensely, became mostly the butt of some Swedish jokes—PC coverage doesn't seem to extend to Scandinavia. The only thing more boring than Transtromer, piped up one young woman, would be owning a Volvo. Far be it from me to admit that my own Volvo was at the very moment sitting in the parking lot. This was certainly a different kind of workshop, and I hoped it didn't signal a trend among undergraduates. But there was cause for me to worry. As any teacher of creative writing knows, the prevailing subject matter among undergraduates is bad love, Dorm Love 101, you might say. Breakups with boyfriends and girlfriends that make you a little pensive, but which you characterize as the cause for suicidal thoughts so that the poem seems a little less wimpy. Cute guys at bars who got away, boyfriends who stay around long enough so that you get fed up with the way they hold their fork or scratch inside their ears at restaurants, and so forth. There's variation within the theme, but not much. This group, tellingly, seemed more interested in masturbation. Usually it was the male students who discoursed on this subject, and it led you to conclude that they spend a lot of time in front of TV or computer screens, but the female students made their contribution, too. After a few weeks of this, I began to hear the voice of Howard Nemerov in my head when I taught. Not Howard's poems, mind you, since I hadn't read them, but Howard as a sort of weary and glib tempter, a yawning Satan. "Why not give 'em the line about dividing the poem into two parts?" Old Nick was saying. "Don't say you disagree with them, just say they're wrong." Slowly, inexorably, I was Going Over to the Dark Side. Darth Howard was at my shoulder, telling me to feel how the Dark Side guided the hand that held my laser sword.

By the middle of March, after a round of conferences that further persuaded me that the students in my class were beyond hope of salvation, I found myself in the university library returning books, and a sudden urge came upon me: perhaps Howard's Britannica article might explain something to me, might help me to feel more charitable to my hapless students—or, conversely, bring me over for good to the Dark Side. Clearly Howard must have reprinted the article in one of his essay collections. But if you wanted further evidence of the decline of Howard's reputation, my school's very large library said it. The big self-indulgent collected was there, but only one of his six books of criticism, and none of his novels or collections of short stories. So I went off to the reference stacks, an action which during the era of Wikipedia seemed even more retro than Howard's poems.

Do they even *publish* print encyclopedias anymore? But there, in the 2007 edition of Britannica, sat Howard's essay, knocked down a couple of notches, insofar as it was now a section of an entry entitled (I kid you not) "Literature, the Art of." But I dutifully Xeroxed the essay, and in my office placed an Amazon order for Daniel Anderson's recent edition of Howard's *Selected Poems*, a mercifully lean and mean volume of 150 pages.

What did I hope to learn from Darth Howard? I suppose the simple (or simplistic) explanation is that I was looking for a decent answer to the question of *why?* Why write poetry if we are never to know the answer to the question of whether our craft is to be characterized as a sacrament or as a con game? Or, worse yet, why should skepticism so often seem more truthful than sacrament? Literary naysayers of the Larkin ilk have never been among my favorite poets, but the week during which I went on my library prowl for Howard Nemerov was a troubling one, and it made me wonder if the skeptics and the con-gamers were onto something I wasn't permitting myself to admit. A deranged creative writing major had murdered thirty-three students and teachers up the road from me on the campus of Virginia Tech. The place was fresh in my mind from a poetry reading I had given there a few weeks earlier, and the director of Tech's writing program, the estimable Lucinda Roy, had been my host. Now she was on all the morning news shows and on CNN, telling the wrenching story of how she had repeatedly and unsuccessfully brought the disturbing writing and behavior of the murderer to the attention of Tech's administration and mental health professionals. Poetry is supposed to bring us solace when we are confronted with events such as these, but somehow during this week it instead seemed trivial or even culpable. I kept coming back to a passage from an interview with novelist Don DeLillo that I'd come across not long after 9/11:

> a writer can be deeply influential, but in a society that's filled with glut and repetition and endless consumption, the act of terror may be the only meaningful act. . . . People who are powerless make an open theater of violence. True terror is a language and a vision. There is a deep narrative structure to terrorist acts and they infiltrate and alter consciousness in ways that writers used to aspire to.[3]

Anyone with passing knowledge of DeLillo's work knows that he likes his apocalypse straight with no chaser, and often he seems to be consuming immoderate amounts of it. But the links DeLillo makes between terrorist acts and the act of writing—whether they are prompted by ideological and religious fanaticism or a disordered brain—suddenly seemed too uncomfortable to be easily dismissed. Not that poetry was to *blame* for anything, but surely it was not acting sacerdotal; it was not ritual magic, and it was not memorable. Another Tech professor, Nikki Giovanni, was seen on all the news coverage as well, chanting an execrable poem at a memorial service that may have brought some consolation to the grief-stricken students of Tech and the families of the slain, but it did no justice to poetry.

A day or so later I found myself in my poetry workshop, teaching a poem by Herbert, in this case Zbigniew and not George, having decided with a sort of Quixotic lunacy that perhaps one way to address my crisis of faith was to assign my students the task of writing an ars poetica. When in doubt, I must have reasoned, just recite the catechism. I trotted out Horace's version from the *Epistles;* I subjected them to Lowell's great epilogue to *Day by Day,* but the biggest bloc of poems came from Poland. I tried to explain to them something about the grandly desperate irony which pervades several generations of twentieth-century Polish verse, reminding them of the many historical upheavals and crises experienced by that nation, and speculating that such conditions may have been the cause of a near-mania for the ars poetica among Poland's leading poets. When the usefulness of literature is constantly assailed by the forces of repression and violence—and I reminded them that Milosz, Swir, and Herbert all fought in the anti-Nazi underground—is it surprising that poets see fit to defend themselves, not just against their critics, not just against the Stalinist party hacks and purveyors of social realism, but against their own self-doubts, which seem curiously to both deepen and to recede as a poem is composed? There was Milosz's consternated and diffident contribution to the genre with those famously maddening lines, "The purpose of poetry is to remind us / how difficult it is to remain just one person, / for our house is open, there are no keys in the doors, / and invisible guests come in and out at will." There was Szymborska's terse and slippery anti-poem "Some Like Poetry." And above all Herbert's "Five Men," a work I remember reading to students during the aftermath of 9/11. It is not a feel-good poem, at least not initially. Its opening section mourns the insufficiency not just of verse, but of language and human memory itself:

> They take them out in the morning
> to the stone courtyard
> and put them against the wall
>
> five men
> two of them very young
> the others middle aged
>
> nothing more
> can be said about them[4]

Although Herbert refutes this last statement by beginning a second section, things go from bad to worse. The descriptions arrive clinically; the effect is altogether Zola-esque:

> before the bullet reaches its destination
> the eye will perceive the flight of the projectile
> the ear record a steely rustle
>
> the nostrils will be filled with biting smoke
> a petal of blood will brush the palate
> the touch will shrink and then slacken
>
> now they lie on the ground
> covered up to their eyes with shadow
> the platoon walks away
> their buttons straps
> and steel helmets
> are more alive
> than those lying beside the wall.

I have always found the third and final section of the poem to be one of the most resonant justifications of the poetic endeavor that I know of, a justification that does not arrive without soul-searching and self-criticism, and whose argument is deepened by those selfsame uncertainties:

I did not learn this today
I learned it before yesterday

so why have I been writing
unimportant poems on flowers

what did the five talk of
the night before the execution
of prophetic dreams
of an escapade in a brothel
of automobile parts
of a sea voyage
of how when he had spades
he ought not to have opened
of how vodka is best
after wine you get a headache
of girls
of fruit
of life

thus one can use in poetry
names of Greek shepherds
one can attempt to catch the color of the morning sky
write of love
and also
once again
in dead earnest
offer to the betrayed world
a rose

The closing gesture of the poem is majestic, and it is accomplished in part thanks to Herbert's insistence that we separate the motives for poetry from the subjects of poetry. The quietly triumphant conclusion is dependent upon the five partisans it elegizes, but the poem is not *about* them. Their death is not just any death; if we were to see it as so we would be no different from the executioners who would turn them into mere dead flesh, less alive than the buttons, straps, and steel helmets of the firing squads. If we are to recognize this, if we are to assert as well that our craft is sufficiently capable, then the poem may be at once about what the five dead men spoke of on the night of their execution and also about a whole panoply of subjects which may include Greek shepherds and the color of the morning sky. If we have sufficient faith and sufficient style—and they are not necessarily mutually exclusive; Geoffrey Hill maintains that for the poet style *is* faith—then the radius of the poem expands to contain what can only be called the universal. Not "universal truths," perhaps, but a model of the world itself, one in which the loquacious shepherds of Virgil's *Georgics* rub shoulders with a card game among some condemned men circa 1943, a distributor cap, a sea cruise to Estonia, and the mole on the face of a Madame who ran a sporting house in Krakow. Should the poem find the means to contain this vast and unruly sort of mixture, then perhaps it can, in the end, make the proper offering to the betrayed world. A rose such as this is no mere garland, bauble, or gaud. And Herbert, whose work so often insisted upon a sense of the tragic which is built upon a knowledge of classical literature—one of his best-known poems is entitled "Why Read the Classics?" and we should also recall his chilling allegory about the relationship between art and politics based on the myth of Apollo's flaying of the satyr Marsyas—is no doubt alluding to the fact that the Greek word for a gathering of poems derives from the term used to describe a garland of flowers, the words from which we derive the English *anthology*. The gift of the rose and the gift of the poem are one—though the world to which these offerings are made is no less betrayed as a result of this transaction.

Or so I would like to think, and I had hoped that this view was so indubitably conveyed in Herbert's poem that my students might have been awakened from their trances for a moment and seen the poem for the grave and haunting accomplishment that I thought it to be. Two of them found the poem quite stirring—one of whom later told me that she'd lost a high school friend in the Tech slayings, and the poem helped her to make sense of her grieving. But most of them were unmoved and skeptical. The most strongly voiced contention, and it came from the class's brightest student, was that the poem's final section seemed like a desperate and clumsy response to the argument of the second—a deus ex machina, with poetry saving the day like the cavalry galloping to a wagon train attacked by Comanches. All the closing meant was fuzzy and wishful thinking on the part of Herbert. And so the bell rang; they left the room; they would busy themselves during the next week with their defenses of an art which they probably didn't think important enough to protect. And except for that one student who would open up the poem again in a dorm room or a coffee shop and think of her dead friend as she went over its lines, "Five Men" and its author had been given the delete button in fourteen brains, allowing more memory space for contemplating the next illegal download, Friday night's first Long Island iced tea, and whatever combination of overworked hormones were concocting another sticky fantasy. Zbigniew Herbert, where does he teach?

I was being too hard on them, I know, and too hard on myself. I wanted the sacramental to have the last word, but when poets discuss their craft and their motives for poems, such an outcome is rarely assured. Things get in the way, various failures of craft, failures of character, or a legitimate reluctance to see the process as solemnly as I had come to see it. Witness the example of one of the earliest lyric poets that we know of, a poet who preceded even Sappho. I speak of the Assyrian monarch Ashurbanipal, who reigned in the seventh century BC. Assyrian kings were notably bloodthirsty, but Ashurbanipal had a sensitive side, which may explain why another despot with literary ambitions, Saddam Hussein, regarded him with such admiration. Most depictions of Ashurbanipal show him doing manly things such as drawing the string of a massive bow, tooling around in his war chariot, or killing lions—you've probably seen the reliefs from his Nineveh Palace on display at the British Museum. And even the depictions of Ashurbanipal at leisure suggest he had something of a mean streak. The renowned "garden party" relief from Nineveh shows Ashurbanipal reclining on a sofa under a date palm while a harpist serenades him and attendants fan him and lavish him with plates of food. In the background you can also see the severed head of Teumman, a rival king; it hangs from a tree upside down, suspended by a rope through its jaw. But Ashurbanipal was also a great patron of the arts, and thanks to the enormous library he amassed at Nineveh, we have in our possession a treasure trove of ancient Near Eastern literature, not least the most complete copy of the *Epic of Gilgamesh*. Unlike other Assyrian kings, Ashurbanipal was literate, which was no mean feat when your mode of writing is impossibly complex cuneiform script, written not in your native tongue, but in Akkadian, a language already ancient in Ashurbanipal's day, about as distant from his own speech as Old English is from ours. Here, in an autobiographical annal, Ashurbanipal struts his stuff: "Marduk, master of the gods, granted me as a gift a receptive mind and ample power of thought. Nabu, the universal scribe, made me a present of his wisdom. . . . I have read the artistic script of Sumer and the obscure Akkadian, which is hard to master, taking pleasure in reading from the stones from before the Flood." Nabu was the god of writing, and a poem of Ashurbanipal's which addresses him is characterized by some of the same ambivalence about the value of poetic effort that we encounter in Herbert's "Five Men." The poem begins with an almost Wordsworthian memory of Ashurbanipal's childhood training as a scribe: "In my childhood I longed for the assembly, to sit in the tablet house." But somehow the language of his former heart cannot be recaptured. Ashurbanipal begins to contemplate suicide; he wants to hurl himself from a high tower and starts to sound as though he's writing a Nineveh-an version of one of the "Dream Songs":

> Often I go up to the roof in order to plunge down,
> but my life is too precious, it turns me back.
> I would hearten myself, but what heart do I have to give?
> I would make up my mind, but what mind to I have to make
>   up?
> O Nabu, where is your forgiveness,
> O son of Bel, where is your guidance?[5]

It is a poem which touches upon all the familiar motifs—the insufficiency of writing, and the crisis of self which deepens this sense of doubt for the speaker. "Why have I been writing unimportant poems about flowers?" Perhaps Ashurbanipal would more typically refrain from odes to nasturtiums and instead write of littering the plain with bodies of his conquered and scattering their testicles like summer cucumber seeds, but you get the point—it's just no fun anymore, and is the problem with Nabu's wondrous gift of stylus and cuneiform, or is it with Ashurbanipal himself? What came first, the testicle or the king? The solution comes in an answer poem in which Nabu sends Ashurbanipal an implausibly reassuring dream vision:

> Your ill-wishers, Ashurbanipal, will fly away
> like [pollen] on the surface of the water
> They will be squashed beneath your feet
> like [mayflies] in the spring!
> You, Ashurbanipal, you will stand before the great gods
> and praise Nabu.[6]

This is precisely the sort of sophistry that my students felt they had detected in Herbert's poem; a more or less literal deus ex machina pertains, in fact. When in doubt, call in the deity, and let him puff you up in his monologue. Who wouldn't want a jacket blurb from God? David Damrosch, from whose highly readable book on the rediscovery of the Gilgamesh epic I draw these examples, regards Ashurbanipal as a pretty good poet—for a monarch. Damrosch thinks him at least the equal of Elizabeth I and Hadrian. Is he, however, a sacramental poet or a con artist? I suppose it depends on whatever judgment we might make on the dream-vision offered by Nabu. You're laying claim to some very powerful mojo if you can channel a god. But I suspect that Ashurbanipal was using Nabu to serve his own vanity, to treat his despair with a purposeful dose of hubris. "The poet is a little God," says the Chilean futurist poet Vicente Huidobro. To this contention Ashurbanipal would no doubt reply—"Why just be a *little* god?"

I suppose, as I surveyed the genre of the ars poetica in response to the consternating events of the spring, I could draw two very provisional conclusions about the form. First, there are certainly a lot of examples of it, occurring throughout literary history. Second, far too many of them, perhaps the majority, seem afflicted with the sort of arrogance and/or cluelessness that we encounter in Ashurbanipal's versifying. Their confidence is dauntingly glib, and I do not except some of the more storied examples of the form. Horace is great fun, but his famous contribution to the genre seems just a little too busy for my taste; he's funny and serious by turns, with a downright mania to entertain us. He's Kenneth Koch in a toga, and he seems much more interested in the sort of tour de force which he is so obviously capable of than he is in probing the deeper and more unsettling implications of poetic utterance. And this stance also seems very much the prevailing one after the advent of Modernism. The most notable examples strive above all to be cagey—Moore's "Poetry," MacLeish's "Ars Poetica," Thomas's "My Craft or Sullen Art," Frost's "Directive," and any number of poems by Stevens. And among European and Latin American poets, the genre often becomes an opportunity for mere surrealist obliquity—Neruda's "The Art of Poetry" has a lot of striking imagery, but it's all smoke and mirrors—when I'm told that poetry is, among other things, "a humiliated scullion, the fug of a deserted house," I'm not inclined to argue, though I don't find such definitions particularly useful. Sure, there are exceptions to this tendency toward archness, but they as often as not eschew the sacramental in favor of an excessively hard-boiled approach: Auden deadpanning that "poetry makes nothing happen."; "It is difficult / to get the news from poems / but men die miserably every day, / for the lack of what is found there." This famous passage from Williams's "Asphodel, That Greeny Flower," seems truthful to me but bleak, more akin to something that would emerge from the pen of Raymond Chandler. Why organizations like the Academy of American Poets would glom onto these lines for their ad campaigns has always puzzled me. Seeing them emblazoned on a coffee cup only makes my Starbucks taste more bitter. When we enter the age of post-modernism the ars poetica seems only to exist as some weird and highly specialized evolutionary adaptation, like eyeless fish in caves. You can't find many Shelleyan defenses of poesy in an age so enraptured of irony. The anthologists who seem to endlessly reprint Strand's "Eating Poetry" surely know this. And the Language poet Bob Perelman, in a brilliant but maddening essay-poem called "The Marginalization of Poetry," is much better at explaining why contemporary verse is afflicted with such an "abject object status" than he is at offering any sort of solution to this condition.[7] Where, among all this fiddle, in the poetasting of all these Ashurbanipal wannabes, is something like humility? Something like earnestness? But to utter a word like earnestness only further convinced me of how retro and hapless my desires had become. Sure, there's probably some deftly sketched little noodling about the art of poetry in the corpus of Mary Oliver, but I was not so desperate as to read something by her. And of course there's plenty of earnestness in that great generation of American poets born between the mid-1920s and mid-1930s, the generation of Levine, Rich, Merwin, Bidart, Williams, Valentine, and the two Wrights. But somehow these poets weren't helping me out of my crisis, either—perhaps because their work exuded a kind of confidence and sense of purpose that I at this point in my writing life did not possess. Like Herbert and Herbert (for I was dipping into a lot of George as well as Zbigniew during these months), their writing was leaving me awestruck but unsolaced: they were just too damn daunting. So my stewing continued unabated—when I was able to write, my poems were indifferent, and now there were all those half-assed student ars poeticae to wade through, a burden for which I had only myself to blame. The funk I was in was hardly a Dark Night of the Soul, and surely my response to this mid-life crisis was better and cheaper than going out and buying a Porsche to replace the Volvo my students were ridiculing, or taking up hang-gliding in the way that one of our friends had done. My questions were simple ones, and they shouldn't have seemed as abject as they did to me at the time. Why write? How do I write better? And, finally, as W. S. Graham put it, what is the language using us for?

I suppose in some ways my answer to this dilemma was to follow the example of any number of rock singers who are long in the tooth and seem well past their creative prime. They all, at one point or another, record an album that purports to go "back to their roots." But where was I rooted? I had no interest in reliving my Snarky Young Poet years. But as the days wore on I found that I was going back to some of my early poetic loves, writers I hadn't read with any seriousness for decades. This company included James Schuyler, Randall Jarrell, John Logan, Robert Penn Warren, and Richard Hugo, figures whom anthologists have put on starvation diets or killed off entirely, figures whom even my brightest graduate students have probably never heard of, let alone read. Furthermore, I soon found I was gravitating ever more intensely to the poetry of two figures who are even more neglected. Yet when I was a young poet, I couldn't live without their work. I speak of Jon Anderson and James L. White. My students won't have heard their names, either, but their work was very sustaining for me at one point in my life. And as I re-read their poems last spring, they were sustaining to me once again. I want to close with a brief discussion of two of their poems, partly because they are each a variant on the ars poetica, a genre which both writers particularly favor. And they are crafty and authentic approaches to the form, untainted by Ashurbani-palism: neither of them writes glibly, and neither acts as though they have in their possession the unlisted phone number of Nabu. They are poets of subtle lyrical effects, and troubling revelations, yet their skepticism often gives way to gestures of quiet transcendence. Furthermore, I want to pay homage to these writers because they were also my teachers, my literary mentors. They were both a dozen years older than I, a small distance in years that seemed huge to me in my younger days. I studied formally with Anderson; he was my graduate thesis advisor. As for James L. White, the older poet took me under his wing for no reason save that, somehow, he recognized in me some promise that wasn't in evidence to anyone else. And for years I took him almost everything I wrote. Because many of the questions which brought me to topic of this essay also involve teaching, to end with Anderson and White seems especially fitting.

Though only one of his books remains in print, and Anderson had mostly lapsed into poetic silence in the two decades before his death this year at the age of sixty-six, there are a good many writers of my own generation who hold him in the highest regard. If you were a poet coming of age in the late 1970s and early 1980s, you went to Anderson in no small measure because his poems were untainted by the sort of egotistical gigantism and imagistic overkill that marked the period style. Anderson may have been a very introspective writer, and often a very bitter one—his poems are peppered with lines such as "The secret of poetry is cruelty"; "We who have changed and have no hope of change / must now love the passing of time"; and "These are the raptures of falling in space forever"—but his stance seemed radically different from the benumbing solipsism of confessional verse. Anderson had a penchant for abrupt shifts in tone, and similarly surprising shifts in diction, always moving from the demotic to an old-fangled formality and back again. He favored statement over image, but employed it in a fashion that seemed urgent and provisional at once, freshly minted evidence of a writer's ongoing quarrel with the world. At his best he could sound like a more terse version of Ashbery—and shorn of Ashbery's annoying campy natter. At other times, the work recalled Donald Justice, but it was mercifully free of Justice's humid nostalgia. The poems seemed intimate yet quirky (an adjective Jon often used when teaching, and usually as a form of high praise). Or perhaps it's more accurate to characterize them as intimate *because* of their quirkiness. Here's a characteristic effort, drawn from the new poems section of his 1982 selected volume, *The Milky Way*. It is not his best poem, but it's a poem about writing that avoids the usual chest-thumping:

Tucson: A Poem About Wood

Jesus, the wind blew, hard, for the first time in ten hot days
    tonight.
We opened windows & doors. I tried to read.
I wished my son, 3, was awake, so we could have perfectly
    talked.

I don't start to talk or read the way I start to write.

My best friend, who I'm gladdened to live alongside,
& three young men are enclosing his porch next door;
four upright beams, then a window or space for it—

Wood. I would like to have helped that fragile, gathering
    shape,
especially to have hammered the frame that will hold glass.
But then I wouldn't have seen it, or my friends, working.

I write for something to do, so I do it;
it tells me how I am or it sometimes lies.
I hate it, I do it for pleasure, I'm not even part of it.

Though it's something like a frame, & I see through it.
I see you carrying on.
I see the part of your labor that must be your pleasure.[8]

I know few other poems about the writing process that are able to admit so many of its anxieties and contradictions while at the same time appearing to be so *unbothered* by them, and this seems to me the poem's small but resonant triumph. This is made possible in part because of the poem's syllogistic concision—it's a sonnet in all but name, leisurely moving toward its turn, teasing it out so that it comes to us in line ten. And of course there's Anderson's characteristic mash-up with tone—the regular-guy posture of the opening line gives way to the several lines of fluent pentameter that later occur. Notable too is the Heideggerrean trope of building that literally frames the poem, and allows Anderson to interrogate the motives for poetic construction in a way that is positively inquisitional, but presented with such nonplussed brio. The speaker sees his verse as a very poor cousin to labor, to friendship, to "perfectly talking" with his young son, to reading. Yet writing parallels these activities, ones which the poem sees as acts of intimacy and rapt attention. But the act of writing seems the very thing which also distances the speaker from these pursuits: "I don't start to talk or read the way I start to write." Yet as the argument of the poem unfolds, this breach is closed. Writing has permitted the poet to have the literal perspective to glimpse the friend's epiphanic "part of your labor that must be your pleasure." And the poet shares in this epiphany, an outcome that allows him to justify the act of poetic creation, to put up once again with the fickleness of the muse, and—most importantly—to not get all weepy about it: "it tells me how I am or it sometimes lies." Anderson's method may seem diffident, but by the end of the poem he has the audacity to rewrite St. Paul. Seeing through a glass darkly becomes seeing through a glass . . . quirkily. The radius of the poem expands to include all its disparate antinomies.

And I can't talk about this poem without seeing in my mind's eye the calm and always slightly bemused face of Jon Anderson as he sits at the end of a seminar table. It's thirty years ago. Around him are gathered David Rivard, Nancy Eimers, William Olsen, Tony Hoagland, and Michael Collier. He's uttering his Andersonisms: "Don't you understand that when you find your voice *you're stuck with it?*" (That one never made sense to me as a student—wasn't finding your voice something akin to being issued a union card? But now I understand his meaning all too well.) "That's a permission poem; it's about giving yourself permission to speak." (Also enigmatic, though I see today he was defining the function of the ars poetica, the very thing I'm trying to do here.) "The task of poetry is to say the hardest thing." (That one I understood even then, though I understand it better now.) They're wry and serviceable statements, the kind you carry with you and make part of your own teacherly toolkit. I probably trotted most of them out to my class of onanist Herbert haters, and I hope these plagiarisms did them some good.

And in memory I also travel to the Minneapolis apartment of James L. White, where he is reading to me his newest poem. It's 1975 or 1976. It's the poem that eventually will open his brilliant, heartbreaking collection *The Salt Ecstasies*, which will be issued after his death. He has no way of knowing this, but mortality, and poetry's cabalistic but essential capacity to help us reckon with our vanishing—that most ancient of themes—is what almost all of Jim's best poems are about:

An Ordinary Compose

I question what poetry will tremble the wall into hearing, or tilt the stone angel's slight wings at words of the past like a memory caught in elms. We see nothing ahead. My people and I lean against great medical buildings with news of our predicted death, and give up mostly between one and three in the morning, never finding space large enough for a true departure, so our eyes gaze earthward, wanting to say something simple as *the meal's too small: I want more.* Then we empty from a room on Intensive Care into the sea, releasing our being into the slap of waves.

Poems break down here at the thought of arms never coupling into full moons by holding those we love again, and so we resort to the romantic: a white horse, set quivering like a slab or marble into dancing flesh.

Why remember being around a picnic table over at Brookside Park? We played softball that afternoon. My mother wore her sweater even in the summer because of the diabetes. Night blackened the lake like a caught breath. We packed things up. I think I was going to school that fall or a job somewhere, Michael'd go to Korea. Before we left I hit the torn softball into the lake and Michael said, "You can't do that for shit James Lee."

Going back I realized the picnic was for us. It started raining in a totally different way, knowing we'd grow right on up into wars and trains and deaths and loving people and leaving them and being left and being alone.

That's the way of my life, the ordinary composure of loving, loneliness and death, and too these prayers at the waves, the white horse shimmering, bringing it toward us out of coldest marble.[9]

As with Anderson, White's stance toward poetic composition is ambivalent. Poetry can make no alchemical claims—it cannot "tremble the wall into hearing," and when "confronted by the news of our predicted death," poetry simply "breaks down." We may "resort to the romantic," but only as a kind of desperate act, in the manner of a deathbed conversion. White's marble horse is not Pegasus; it's more akin to the pale horse with pale rider which we know from the Book of Revelation. This is a heady symbolic flourish, surely, yet in some ways its most important function is to trigger the more prosaic but more affecting memory of the family picnic, which is rendered with a calm precision. And White wrote about the past with a special acuity; his masters were those great poets of memory, Cavafy and James Wright. I think he came to Cavafy because, as a gay man growing up in the pre-Stonewall era, the spare, unfussy out-ness of the Alexandrian poet was a stance he could aspire to, though not without great personal cost. And Wright's emotional honesty, coupled with his ability to wrest the rhapsodic from the most tawdry and ordinary Midwestern landscapes which the two poets emerged from, became a standard White applied to all of his mature poems. That honesty and directness becomes the saving grace of "An Ordinary Composure." It raises a "picnic over at Brookside Park," the mother's sweater, and a brother's gentle needling—"You can't do that for shit James Lee"—to the status of vision, a Wordsworthian "spot of time" that is aggrandized but not sentimentalized; the quotidian is sanctified in much the same way that it is for Herbert's partisans on the eve of their execution. "Going back I realized the picnic was for us." "We'd grow right on up into wars and trains and deaths and loving people and leaving them and being left and being alone." And it is from such realizations that our white horses are brought to life within their marble; poetry again offers its bittersweet redemptions. Jim was fond of quoting a remark attributed to Cavafy—"If poetry cannot absolve us, then let's not expect mercy from anywhere."

I am not sure I believe this statement, although I think Jim did. I also recall another visit to his apartment, several years later, after yet another of the many heart attacks that would bring him to intensive care. He was told on release that he had only a few months left. I am standing with the poet Tess Gallagher—who was a great champion of Jim's work—the three of us admiring the galley proofs of Jim's book which arrived a few minutes earlier by courier. Tonight Jim will die in his sleep, alone in that apartment, the proofs of his book on the bedside table. Like so many books of poetry, even ones of great value, the fate of *The Salt Ecstasies* will be uncertain, but the likelihood is that one day it will be buried as completely as those twenty thousand cuneiform tablets in Ashurbanipal's palace library—buried completely, but not irrevocably. And not yet. Yes, *The Salt Ecstasies* has been out print for some time, but next year a new edition of the collection will be issued in a series Mark Doty edits which reprints neglected books of American verse. Another bittersweet redemption; to the betrayed world, another garland, offered in dead earnest.

Postscript

In the months since I began these speculations, a hot and dry summer has begun. My students dutifully submitted their ars poeticae, and finished their semesters, most of them receiving Bs—Darth Howard would no doubt have been appalled at such generosity. Some of them will never write a poem again, though a few of them will, and will continue to do so, and their tutelage under yours truly will probably have done them no damage. Various panels have been appointed to investigate the tragedy at Virginia Tech, and Zbigniew Herbert, although he has been dead for almost a decade, still holds out his blossom to the world, a gesture that others still scorn, and the exquisite new translation of his *Collected Poems* sits now on my desk. (*I* think it's exquisite, at any rate; some snarky not-so-young poet who knows no Polish recently authored a review in *Poetry* that eviscerates the quality of the new translation.) My mid-South, mid-life crisis/malaise/ writer's block seems to have abated somewhat, and its treatment has not involved a higher dosage of my meds, the purchase of a parasail, or the desire to play drums in a garage band. The notebooks are starting to fill again, and, standing in a receiving line with a couple of other writers from my Commonwealth, I shook hands with Her Majesty, Queen Elizabeth II, who was on a state visit to commemorate the four hundredth anniversary of the founding of Jamestown. The president of the College of William and Mary introduced us to her, referring to us as "prize-winning Virginia poets," a designation that made us seem for all the world like big rutabagas pinned with ribbons at the state fair. "You are prizewinners for *what?*" asked the queen. "For poetry, Your Highness," replied one of our number. "Oh, poetry," said Her Majesty, and walked on to shake hands with the William and Mary glee club. Had this been Ashurbanipal, he'd probably have stopped awhile to talk shop with us, but a monarch's life is a busy one. Last but not least, I'm reading poems again, with renewed engagement and excitement—reading not only old favorites, but a number of new poets I've never encountered before. The other day I came across a lovely ars poetica by one of them. His name is Howard Nemerov:

The Blue Swallows

Across the millstream below the bridge
In shapes invisible and evanescent,
Kaleidoscopic beyond the mind's
Or memory's power to keep them there.

"History is where tensions were,"
"Form is the diagram of forces."
Thus, helplessly there on the bridge,
While gazing down upon those birds—
How strange, to be above the birds!—
Thus, helplessly the mind in its brain
Weaves up relation's spindrift web.
Seeing the swallows' tail as nibs
Dipped in invisible ink, writing . . .

Poor mind, what would you have them write?
Some cabalistic history
Whose authorship you might ascribe
To God? to Nature? Ah, poor ghost,
You've capitalized your Self enough.
The villainous William of Occam
Cut out the feet from under that dream
Some seven centuries ago.
It's taken that long for the mind
To waken, yawn and stretch, to see
With opened eyes emptied of speech
The real world where the spelling mind
Imposes with its grammar books
Unreal relations on the blue
Swallows. Perhaps when you will have

Fully awakened, I will show you
A new thing: even the water
Flowing away beneath those birds
Will fail to reflect their flying forms,
And the eyes that see become as stones
Which never tears shall fall gain.

O swallows, swallows, poems are not

The point. Finding again the world,
That is the point, where loveliness
Adorns intelligible things
Because the mind's eye lit the sun.[10]

2008

Notes

1. Howard Nemerov, "The Art of Literature: Poetry," in *The New Encyclopedia Britannica: Macropaedia,* 15th ed. (Chicago: Encyclopedia Britannica, Inc., 2007).

2. Wyatt Prunty, introduction to *The Selected Poems of Howard Nemerov,* ed. Daniel Anderson (Athens: Ohio University Press/Swallow Press, 2003), p. ix.

3. Quoted in Andrew Hogan, "Racing against Reality," *The New York Review of Books* 54, no. 11 (June 28, 2007): p. 42.

4. Zbigniew Herbert, *Selected Poems,* trans. Czeslaw Milosz and Peter Dale Scott (Harmondsworth: Penguin Books, 1968), p. 58.

5. David Damrosch, *The Buried Book: The Loss and Rediscovery of the Great Epic of Gilgamesh* (New York, Henry Holt, 2007), p. 185.

6. Damrosch, *Buried Book,* p. 186.

7. Bob Perelman, *The Marginalization of Poetry* (Princeton, NJ: Princeton University Press, 1996), p. 127.

8. Jon Anderson, *The Milky Way: Poems 1968–1982* (New York: Ecco Press, 1983), p. 39.

9. James L. White, *The Salt Ecstasies* (St. Paul, MN: Graywolf Press, 1982), p. 9.

10. *The Selected Poems of Howard Nemerov,* p. 82.

"And Not Releasing the Genie"

The Poetry of Stuff vs. the Poetry of Knowledge

Sexing chickens, which is apparently a finely honed skill. "Ice pick" lobotomies, as evidenced in no less than three efforts, one a rather lengthy sequence on the lamentable career of Walter Freeman, the psychiatrist who—on a annual summer joyride in his station wagon that took him to dozens of states and state hospitals—performed the procedure on upward of three thousand patients. Amy Winehouse, a triolet. A painting by Rousseau, a painting by Walton Ford, a painting by Poussain showing the flaying of Marsyas, five Cornell boxes, and one act of oral sex performed on Cornell late in life by one of his young admirers. A '67 VW bus, rusting in a field. The Neanderthal burials in Shinidar Cave—that the pollen on the necks and skulls is evidence of rodent activity, not the floral necklaces archaeologists had originally thought were adorning the burials. No Flower People, these Neanderthals. Amy Winehouse, a Miltonic sonnet. Murder Scene photo of Sam Cooke—he's slumped in a doorway, wearing only a raincoat, the linoleum ensanguined. Gregor Mendel, Moondog, Papa Neutrino, Evel Knievel. Facial tattoos among the Maori of New Zealand. The killing of a two-year-old boy by African wild dogs in the Pittsburgh Zoo—this from the point of view of one of the dogs. Jack White takes his solo—o boy, got a front row seat. Homeless lady, mistaking the speaker for Meg White. Io, Moon of Jupiter. Amy Winehouse, free verse version. Pac Man, evoked in a manner Wordsworthian. Super Mario Brothers, rendered in similarly Wordsworthian fashion. Titan, Moon of Jupiter. The headscarf of Tupac Shakur. A witchcraft museum in Cornwall. Tzcatilpoca, Aztec god. Ganymede, Moon of Jupiter. Ode to the speaker's parents' collection of British prog rock albums, an undertaking that seems to have been accompanied by the near-heroic act of listening to an Emerson, Lake and Palmer album in its entirety. How the preponderance of discarded tires in sub-Saharan Africa breeds mosquitoes that carry dengue fever, an illness whose symptoms are described in exquisitely gratuitous detail. Amy Winehouse, a double sestina.

The paragraph above, dear reader, is not free association. There is nothing at all arbitrary about this list. It is instead a catalogue of some of the subjects which graduate students of mine have recently chosen for their poems. I render this list in a spirit little short of awe. It is, by any stretch of the imagination, a wildly inventive set of topics and remarkable for its variety—pop culture, surely, but "high culture" as well, and history. The subjects are drawn from science, from mythology, and from both topics at once. And who would have thought that sexing chickens could be a topic of some interest? And I can tell you now with great conviction that dengue fever is something I wouldn't ever want to be stricken with. And it is good to be reminded that one of the occupational hazards of living fast and dying young is to then be the subject of an endless stream of elegies. Yes, the list makes me feel a little old and in the way, insofar as I can wax Wordsworthian about eight tracks, but not Pac Man or Tupac. And I have taught long enough to be witness to several historical phases of dead pop star poems. They're stratified, in layers like Troy. Amy Winehouse may characterize Level Seven, but dig down a bit and you find Kurt Cobain; dig further and the John Lennons appear; and way, way down, in the equivalent of Troy One and Troy Two, the paeans to Joplin, Hendrix, and even Jim Morrison come into view.

Yet this list tells us more than the fact that I am now quite a bit older than my students, or that they have grown quite inventive in their choice of subject matter. The list tells us something about how much the nature of contemporary poetry has changed in the past two or three generations. But it is also indicative about how much the very nature of reality has changed for us in recent decades. And poetry, although it's often called the most conservative of art forms—conservative in the best sense, one hopes, not in the Fox News and Paul Ryan sense—has changed in order to reflect these developments. The changes are both exhilarating and a bit scary. Where do the poems on the list I have offered come from? Obviously not from self-scrutiny and the sort of research that is a precursor of knowledge. They come from Google searches. Google "how to sex chickens," and you find 6,690,000 results.[1] And of course there are several dozen instructional YouTube videos, a couple of which have had over a hundred thousand views. Google "ice pick lobotomy," and you will be directed to a PBS documentary on the good Dr. Freeman.[2] It's posted on YouTube as well and has attracted 1,150,000 viewers. Interestingly enough, Dr. Freeman looks quite distinguished and avuncular, and always seems to be chomping down on a pipe—he's a dead ringer for Marcus Welby, M.D. (Although a reader not of a certain age will need to Google "Marcus Welby" to understand this allusion.) Google Emerson, Lake and Palmer, and you'll not only see how jaw-droppingly kitschy their album covers are, but you'll encounter a bit of synchronicity regarding the group and Dr. Freeman—one of their best-selling efforts, and arguably the one with the most garish album art, is entitled "Brain Salad Surgery."

What an astonishing array of *stuff* is just a keystroke or two away. A few weeks ago, after reading Tim Weiner's *Enemies*, a quite terrifying history of the FBI that included some very intriguing material on the agency's surveillance of political dissidents, I thought it would be interesting to find a way, perhaps via the Freedom of Information Act, to see what files Hoover's people had on three politically activist poets—George Oppen, Robert Lowell, and Muriel Rukeyser. It turns out that a copy of Oppen's file resides with the rest of his papers at the University of San Diego Library. Lowell's file seems to be unavailable. But if you Google "Muriel Rukeyser's FBI file," a 121-page document materializes, courtesy of the FBI's own web site.[3] It's badly scanned, and heavily redacted in places, but it shows the agency was following Rukeyser's activities from 1938 until 1973. The FBI records "vault" also exemplifies why Google searches can be so creepily addictive: a 1964 file that seeks to determine whether the lyrics to "Louie, Louie" are obscene is only two pages shorter than the one on Rukeyser.[4] And several agency typists were employed at various times to set down exactly the spurious "dirty" lyrics to the song. Interestingly enough, the Rukeyser file contains no examples of her poetry, though the FBI's exegesis of the Kingsmen's "Louie, Louie" is quite thoroughgoing. And the Kingsmen's gloriously indecipherable singing seems to have confounded the staff of the G-men's crime lab: "Because the lyrics of the song on the record . . . could not be definitely determined in the Laboratory examination, it could not be determined whether [it] is an obscene record."

Is it any wonder, then, that Google searches have produced Google poems, poems that derive from superficial knowledge about an endless number of things but deeper knowledge about very few. I'll call this sort of poem a "Stuff" poem rather than a Google poem, if only so that Google's lawyers, a very active bunch, don't go after me. And I fear the Stuff Poem is with us to stay. Its development derives from several factors. Some of them have to do with current aesthetic fashion. A few years back, in a sly essay entitled "Fear of Narrative and the Skittery Poem of Our Moment," Tony Hoagland described the current period style in this way: ours is a moment of

> great invention and playfulness. Simultaneously, it is also a moment of great self-consciousness and emotional removal. Systematic development is out: obliquity, fracture, and discontinuity are in. Especially among young poets, there is a widespread distrust of narrative forms, and, in fact, a pervasive sense of the inadequacy or exhaustion of all modes other than the associative. Under the label of "narrative," all kinds of poetry currently get lumped misleadingly together, not just story but discursion, argument, even descriptive lyrics. They might be called "The Poetries of Continuity."[5]

If you're a teacher of poetry writing, and have been doing it for as long as I have, the dominance of what Hoagland calls the "skittery" poem and the widespread suspicion of narrative (and largely unrelated stylistic approaches that somehow get lumped with narrative), is especially troubling on a pedagogical level. It's not altogether uncommon to see students feel a great deal of anxiety when they seek to break the conventions of skitteriness, or when they try to deliberately mask situations which call for clarity of dramatic situation and context in the trappings of irony and discontinuity. Every semester I encounter a couple

149

of instances in which a graduate student poem of great verbal energy but baffling obliquity gets defended and explained by the author saying that if she'd stated what the poem was "really" about it would be "too confessional"—or worse, "too sincere." And, sometimes, "too linear." I have started to label this condition "Contextophobia," after one of the Latin terms for continuity—*contextus.*

The problem here lies in some degree with the fickleness and limited shelf life of any period style. But it also has to do with the way we live now. The poetics of skitteriness in no small measure reflects the fact that we have become a culture of multi-taskers. My students treat their smart phones as something akin to a body part, and not an insignificant organ like the appendix. When they're at their laptops they're moving from the paper they're composing to their email; they take a breather from this and watch a YouTube video, then check their Facebook accounts, and they are fully capable of texting on their phones with one hand while still plying the computer keyboard with the other, a skill which requires rather astonishing dexterity. Media critic Jessica Helfand says this about the college students she works with: "You just have to wonder to what degree are they actually assimilating anything? . . . My big concern is how deep anybody can go if they're spread so thin, if they skim everything. . . . .This is the culture of narrative deprivation."[6]

A mind that is predisposed to skimming may well be a mind that is literally hardwired to resist an ability to read in a deep and discerning manner. In a brilliant and troubling "natural history" of the reading mind, entitled *Proust and the Squid,* cognitive neuroscientist Maryanne Wolf charts how the reading mind has evolved—and seems to have done so in a complex and quite radical fashion—since the time of the Sumerians. In trying to recapture the evolutionary development of how our species has learned to read, Wolf also hopes to cast light upon reading processing disorders such as dyslexia. One of the most important of Wolf's observations, at least for the purposes of my argument here, is that the developmental process of reading among children follows two essential stages. Wolf labels the first stage, which begins around the time of kindergarten and persists until about fifth grade, the time of "decoding reading."[7] The child reads with an understanding of words and sentence structure, but not in a manner that is nuanced or geared toward capturing the larger implications of the reading experience. The purpose of decoding reading is to garner facts and information. Any reading pleasure comes from the facts alone, an observation Wolfe makes while noting the immense popularity of the various iterations of *The Guinness Book of World Records* and those lavishly illustrated *DK Discovery* books among third- and fourth-grade readers, especially boys, who tend to eschew the demands of storytelling books in favor of compendiums of marvelous facts—Tom Sawyer and even *Diary of a Wimpy Kid* may make too many demands upon the decoding mind. But to know a man in India is able to lift an eighty-seven-pound anvil with his ear may not. In most cases decoding readers begin, around the age of ten or eleven, to become more discerning in their approach. They become what Wolf calls "fluent" or "comprehending" readers—able to see beyond the surface words and recognize, for example, the sly motives for Tom getting his pals to pay him to whitewash Aunt Polly's fence, or why Harry Potter's status as an orphan can make him so vulnerable as he confronts the evil Voldemort. The trouble, however, is this: isn't the Internet, in several essential ways, a vast and immensely labyrinthine version of *The Guinness Book?* Much of the time we use it in order to decode information rather than to analyze it. Worried about that mole on your thigh that's started to darken? Then check out the Mayo Clinic site. MapQuest the directions to a friend's house, and you'll know how to get there, but as you come down her street you'll be too busy reading the tiny print on the directions you've printed out to wonder if the neighborhood houses are haunted by white nightgowns or if somewhere down the block an old sailor is dreaming of tigers in red weather. And it will never occur to you to *remember* the directions to your friend's house. Next time you visit, you'll MapQuest the directions all over again, or decide to pop for a GPS. In a 2007 study of the British public, it was discovered that only one-third of the populace could recall the phone numbers of their own home landlines without pulling them up on their cells. And 30 percent of British adults couldn't recall the birthdays of more than three immediate family members.[8]

Does this matter? I think it does, for it signals that we exist in an era when we seem only able to negotiate the immense complexity on contemporary existence through superficial knowledge of many things, but deep knowledge of only a few. And it has been argued at least since the time of Classical Greece that superficial knowledge is not really knowledge at all. It's interesting that both Wolf and the eminent twentieth-century scholar Frances Yates—in her magisterial cultural history of mnemonics, *The Art of Memory*—quote from the same passage in Plato's *Phaedrus,* in which Socrates rails against what he sees as the corrosive effects of that problematic new invention, the written word:

> For this invention will produce forgetfulness in the minds of those who use it, because they will not practice their memory. Their trust in writing, produced by external characters which are not part of themselves will discourage the use of their own memory within them. You have invented an elixir not of memory, but of reminding and you offer your pupils the appearance of wisdom, not true wisdom, for they will read many things without instruction and will therefore seem to know many things, when they are for the most part ignorant and hard to get along with, since they are not wise, but only appear wise.[9]

Yes, Socrates was wrong, and yes, it is reductive to say these warnings apply in any more than a partial way to how knowledge has been debased in the digital age.

And yes, it surely can be argued that one of the functions of "the skittery poem of our moment" is to critique such debasement. Good poems, after all, are supposed to be on some level difficult and challenging, or we will have no inclination to re-read them. And many of the profundities of poems arise from their very skitteriness, as James Longenbach notes so eloquently near the beginning of his wonderful little study *The Resistance to Poetry:* "poems do not ask to be trusted. Their language revels in duplicity and disjunction, it is difficult for us to assume that any particular poetic gesture is inevitably responsible or irresponsible to the culture that gives the language meaning: a poem's obfuscation of the established terms of accountability might be the poem's most accountable act—or it might not. Distrust of poetry (its potential for inconsequence, its pretention to consequence) is the stuff of poetry."[10] But there is a difference between a distrust of poetry that is the stuff of poetry—such as the decidedly subversive guidance that informs Frost's "Directive," in which the narrator tells us he "only has at heart your getting lost"—and a *poetry of stuff,* in which disjunction is replaced by mere juxtaposition, often of an almost Pavlovian sort, by mere enumeration of special facts, allusions, tidbits, bric-a-brac, tonal and dictional shifts of no strategic value, and self-portraiture of the sort that's suggested by your iPod's playlist rather than from any important degree of self-reckoning. I speak of a poetry of superficial erudition whose readership is the superficially erudite reader whom so many of us have become today. And it is hard to resist the pull of such superficiality, for its pleasures are often immediate and in some cases enthralling. But these pleasures are very short-lived, the equivalents of sugar highs or—for the generations a few decades removed from mine—chugging a couple cans of Red Bull on top of a few shots of flavored vodka.

The newly anointed crown prince of stuff poetry seems to be Michael Robbins, whose *Alien vs. Predator* was issued earlier this year. Robbins has all the bona-fides that in the eyes of his advocates qualify him to be the Next Big Thing (or, if you're not an advocate, the next Flavor of the Month). Robbins is just short of forty, and *Alien vs. Predator* is his debut collection; it's published by Penguin, a not-too-shabby house, and he's placed his poems in both establishment journals like *Poetry* and the *New Yorker* and the trendier little magazines, places like *Fence* and *Court Green.* He has done a fair amount of reviewing as well, following the predictably Oedipal path of young-poet-on-the-make by, for example, hammering Robert Hass's *Selected Poems* in the pages of *Poetry* ("the dewy piety . . . makes it impossible to read many Hass poems with a straight face").[11] His jacket blurbs come from all the Right People, among them Sasha Frere-Jones, the poetasting pop music critic of the *New Yorker,* and fellow up-and-comer Ange Mlinko, who has this to say about the book: "Faster than you can rhyme stegosaur/megastore, Robbins code-switches between the English canon and Top Forty, Nirvana and Blake, The Clash and Yeats, creating a political and social commentary that will make the hair stand on your head."[12] (Over-the-top blurbs are a minor sin, and I have committed it myself, but someone might have pointed out to Mlinko that hair "stands" on the head of anyone who is not bald or shaved-headed.) The book jacket's self-description is similarly hyperbolic—"Equal parts hip-hop, John Berryman, and capitalism seeking death and not finding it, Michael Robbins' poems are strange, wild, and completely unlike anything else being written today. As allusive as *The Cantos*, as aggressive as a circular saw, this debut collection will offend none but the virtuous."[13] Given poetry's marginal status in the publishing world, it's common for the author of a poetry collection to compose his or her own jacket copy. If this *is* Robbins himself talking, he's not half-bad at self-characterization. And it shows us far we have come from Pound demanding that poetry be at least as well written as prose, or Charles Bernstein, in the 1990s, asserting that poetry needs to be at least as interesting as television. Robbins would likely claim that poetry has to be at least as interesting as your average Google search. Does his poetry meet this standard? On some occasions I suppose it does, but most of the time the writing can best be characterized as Name-Check Doggerel.

Here in its entirety is the title poem, which opens the collection:

Praise *this* world, Rilke says, the jerk.
We'd stay up all night. Every angel's
berserk. Hell, if you slit monkeys
for a living, you'd pray to me, too.
I'm not so forgiving. I'm rubber, you're glue.

That elk is such a dick. He's a space tree
a ski and a little foam chiropractor.
I set the controls, I pioneer
the seeding of the ionosphere.
I translate the Bible into velociraptor

In front of Best Buy, the Tibetans are released,
but where's the whale on stilts that we were promised?
I fight the comets, lick the moon,

pave its lonely streets.
The sandhill cranes make brains look easy.

I go by many names: Buju Banton,
Camel Light, the New York *Times*.
Point being, rickshaws in Scranton.
I have few legs. I sleep on meat.
I'd eat your bra—point being—in a heartbeat.[14]

What a Cuisinart of allusion this is—a title drawn from a drawn from a 2004 film, one that tries quite clumsily to reinvigorate two exhausted movie monster franchises; it's a kind of twenty-first-century *Abbott and Costello Meet Frankenstein.* But line one alludes to high culture—and not just to the *Duino Elegies,* but to John Berryman's snide assertion in "Dream Song #3" that Rilke was a "jerk" and perhaps to Alan Dugan's "Orpheus," which begins with the memorable lines "Singing, always singing, he was something / of a prig, like Rilke, and as dangerous / to women . . ."[15] As the poem progresses, the allusions roll along, Best Buy, Camel Lights, reggae singer Buju Banton, jargon phrases like "point being." Some of the lines seem pure surrealism ("The elk is such a dick. He's a space tree"); others seem cribbed from the Dean Young Songbook (although there's a pathos in Young's poetry that Robbins's studiously avoids). The rhymes are of course immensely clever—"chiropractor" and "velociraptor," "Buju Banton" and "rickshaws in Scranton," being the most appealing. And they're more than a bit reminiscent of the playfulness of Paul Muldoon, whom Robbins has spoken of admiringly—and who ran this poem in the *New Yorker.* But who is speaking in the poem, and what is at stake in all the wordplay and name-checking? When we arrive at the last two lines—"I have few legs. I sleep on meat. / I'll eat your bra—point being—in a heartbeat"—we can't help but be a little creeped out. We hear in the implicit misogyny the voice of Frederick Seidel, another poet Robbins has cited as an influence. Yes, the closing may bespeak mere horniness, but when we recall the title we can't help but wonder if we have just read a dramatic monologue, spoken by the Alien or the Predator as it zeroes in on its next meal. Here's a salutary poem that does not so much invite the reader in as characterize her as prey. I suppose this is meant to be a transgressive gesture, a warning that there will be no dewy pieties in the book which follows.

But as anyone who has tried to read the Marquis De Sade quickly learns, if you've seen one transgression of this sort you've seen them all. And what follows in *Alien vs. Predator* is more of the same wildly inventive wordplay that is at the same time stultifyingly tedious. And there's more, much more, allusion mongering—the book's second poem borrows from both Iggy Pop and Philip Larkin, and for titles alone Robbins purloins Guns 'n' Roses, Neil Young, Whitman, Ashbery, Spicer, Hass, Berryman, Madonna, the Talking Heads, the Rolling Stones, the Eagles, and the theme song from *Mash*. When he's not trying to eat the reader, Robbins seems to want her to undertake a kind of rhyming version of Trivial Pursuit. Advance two spaces if you remember that Prefab Sprout's best album was *Steve McQueen,* two more if you catch the line from James Wright in the stanza above that reference. Go back three spaces if you don't recognize both Sartre *and* Charlton Heston in the line "If hell, like soylent green, is people." If Robbins's point is that pop culture and high culture are equally important in our existence, he's telling us something that we've known at least since the Armory Show. If Robbins's intention is to show how much he loves all this stuff, he usually fails at his goal, perhaps because the allusions seem to be listed rather than set forth with any urgency. And Robbins's sophomoric penchant for the scatological doesn't help his case. Given a choice of having to read a poem about an ice pick lobotomy or a Robbins effort entitled "My New Asshole," I'd likely choose the former.

Mind you, it is sadly typical of poets of a certain age like myself to rail against what the hot younger poets are doing—it's a way to make you feel that you're not old and in the way. And it's clear that Robbins is not without talent—in fact he has talent to burn. And although his criticism of Hass is a cheap shot, some of Robbins's others reviews are first rate. He has written about Geoffrey Hill (a poet even more allusion-heavy than Robbins himself) with a sensitivity and discernment that I haven't seen in the writing of any other American reviewer.[16] And when

I discovered through an interview that Robbins had dedicated his collection to his *cat*, I wondered if there was an emotionally tender strand in his writing that I had missed.[17] And I am happy to say that in a further reading of *Alien vs. Predator* I found it, though it manifests itself only in a single poem. It's the one that references Prefab Sprout and James Wright, but the Rolling Stones and John Donne make appearances too. The poem even finds a way to steal a couple of lines from Bob Dylan's "Just Like Tom Thumb's Blues" *and* "All Along the Watchtower." None of this is atypical for Robbins, but the poem is framed in an actual *context*, and a venerable one at that. The Beloved has left the speaker. The poem is entitled "Sway," and it suggests what Wyatt's "They Flee from Me" would look like had he been given access to iTunes. Here are the final three stanzas:

> Mick Taylor's solos and Prefab Sprout
> taught me more than John Donne about
> how to do within and do without.
> And since the enamored fish will stay
> I count the hours since you slipped away.
>
> Words don't hold you. I'm thirty-five.
> I shine quietly to the riot moon.
> "That demon life has got me in its sway"?
> A bit rich for early afternoon.
>
> Still, there's one thing for sure: there must
> be some kind of way out of here, I trust.
> It rains in Juarez. It's Eastertime too.
> You're in my light. What is it then between
> our buttons? I reach for *Steve McQueen*.[18]

I think it is safe to say that the Poetry of Stuff has come to be a dominant mode in contemporary poetry, as evidenced not just in my students' work but in countless journals and scores and scores of first and second books. I don't feel the need to offer further examples of the mode, since Robbins's work is so representative of it. And, despite his various limitations, he's better than the average Stuffist, and could well be poised to grow out of the mode. But how do I define the other sort of poem that

I refer to in my title, a Poem of Knowledge? A poem that, to echo the concern of Socrates, does not simply *appear* wise, but aspires to something like genuine wisdom. Wise and not wise-ass. The Poem of Knowledge, like the Poem of Stuff, values the strange, the particular, the special fact, but not merely for the sake of novelty in the manner of circus side shows or the *Guinness Book*. The Poem of Knowledge picks such facts and particulars out not because of a desire to dupe and mystify the reader, but because some facts are better than others, and it is the task of poetry to draw meaningful combinations, not arbitrary ones. The poem of knowledge derives from a desire to synthesize—or alchemize—one's learning and command of craft into a new reality, a new reckoning. This is no easy task during a time when both literature and facts themselves are debased. Mitt Romney's presidential campaign was Stalinist for many reasons, but especially Stalinist in its blatant propagandistic indifference to factual truth. As Romney advisor Eric Fehrnstrom infamously put it, all the campaign needed to do was hit "the reset button," and the viciously reactionary Romney who bested the other candidates in the Republican primaries would morph into a moderate. "Everything changes," Fehrnstrom asserted to CNN. "It's almost like an Etch A Sketch. You can kind of shake it up and we start all over again."[19] Let's airbrush the Commissar from the Kremlin viewing stand; tomorrow we will tweak the Soviet Encyclopedia and drop all references to him in the next edition. In a time of such imaginative malevolence, literature may seem puny and beside the point. But this condition instructs us to value literature all the more highly. There's a time to be wise-ass in our poems, a time when we can revel in translating the Bible into velociraptor. But now is not the time. Prissy as it sounds, I happen to agree with something Gombrowicz says in his diaries: "literature is a lady of very strict habits, and one should not go around pinching her in the ass."[20] If we grant literature some essential dignity—a goal that is now very much out of fashion—perhaps then we can go about separating useless learning from authentic understanding. To distinguish this difference takes enormous discernment, but I would go as far to say that it is one of the primary tasks of poetry at this particular juncture in our literary history. In Geoffrey Hill's words, how do we, as poets, strike "the personal note amid the acoustical din that surrounds us all"?[21] And need it be added that this acoustical din is deafening and stupefying? It is made up of Fox News, Facebook, Limbaugh, Angry Birds, Michael Robbins, and Taylor Swift. I could go on with this list and never run out of trochees. But rather than doing so, let me offer a few examples of poetry that doesn't derive from Stuff, but from learning of a different sort, a learning that seeks to still, for a moment, the acoustical din.

Exhibit A is a poem from Linda Bierds's 1994 collection, *The Ghost Trio:*

The Whim Gin

Helmets, flint wheels,
our thick-toed boots, each
with its stubble of coal dust;
the flames of canaries, the lunch tins,
our pickaxes, water cans;
our voices, someone's whistle, inward,
so the lips retreated, everything
plied into whim baskets, raised,
lowered, the horses tight
on a circle above us
pushing the whim beams,
winding the rope that drew us
like beads from a sorcerer's mouth;
tight in a circle above us,
unwinding the rope that lowered us,
the whim gin creaking, slipping
a little, the sky a pale plate
of nothingness—nothingnerss—
then the cirrus cloud tails
rushing through.[22]

This is the sort of poem which Bierds has been writing, always with great accomplishment, for some three decades. As with Richard Howard and Norman Dubie, she has almost completely eschewed the autobiographical lyric in favor of monologues and character studies, most of them historical. And, like Howard, she has a special interest in Great Britain in the nineteenth century. Yet her poems are never effete, and have none of the versified *Masterpiece Theatre* qualities which sometimes trouble Howard's work. "The Whim Gin" is in fact a ferocious and decidedly political work—and one doesn't need to know what a whim gin is to recognize this. One of the eerily subversive pleasures of an initial reading of the poem is that the reader knows *exactly* the function of a whim gin—without Googling the term, without consulting the OED. Bierds conveys this knowledge for us not through explication of any sort, but through a relentlessly kinetic, indeed cinematic, enactment. The miners who narrate the poem speak chorally, and the fact that they all experience the same brutalizing ride down to the mine is the only element of the poem which affords them a sense of humanity. They have been reduced to boots, pickaxes, lunch tins, helmets. They are machinery, just as the canaries who will signal the presence of CO^2 have become and the horses whose endless circling allows the infernal device of the whim gin to operate with such cruel efficiency. We're of course reminded of a similar device from the era, one that also bespeaks the horrors of modernity and the Industrial Revolution, Bentham's panopticon. But the panopticon only watches and controls us. The whim gin sends us down to hell, and with such mechanistic precision the miners can only be resigned to their fates—they're too preoccupied, too beaten down, to ever bewail their condition; one of the primary effects of Bierds's decision to make the poem unfold as one long sentence fragment of twenty lines is to suggest that the speakers have almost been deprived of the power of speech. In its quietly controlled sense of inevitability the poem is a far more impressive linguistic tour de force than any of Robbins's glib rhyming. And Bierds makes her points not only through her pall-mall syntax, but also through her imagery. Most of her metaphors are grimly Dantescan—the "flames of canaries" and the "inward" whistling that causes the lips to retreat. But she also offers tropes that in any other context would seem too exquisitely chiseled, even precious. Yet here they arrive with the grimmest sort of irony—the miners are lowered down the shaft "like beads from a sorcerer's mouth," and the sky, as they glimpse it a final time before their descent is complete, is a "pale plate of nothingness." And in this most economical of poems, only the word "nothingness" is deemed worthy of repeating. Why Bierds did not include this remarkable effort in her recent *Selected Poems* is a mystery to me. One thing that is not a mystery for the reader, however, is that she will never forget the function of the whim gin, nor ever desire to take a ride in one. This may not be a complex or intricate lesson, but it is surely a resonant one.

This is one type of Poem of Knowledge; let's label it a poem about what that unintentionally brilliant wordsmith Donald Rumsfeld called, during the Bush administration's bumbling efforts of capture Bin Laden, "known unknowns." We may not have previously heard of whim gins, but now we have, thanks to Bierds, a new way to envision the brutalities of cutthroat capitalism—not just in Merrie Olde England but in modern culture in general. But you'll recall that Rumsfeld also told reporters that there was such a thing as an "unknown unknown."[23] (These comments of Rumsfeld's were so brilliantly surreal that they presented the extremely gifted young poet Nick Lantz with both a title and even a structural underpinning for his debut collection, *We Don't Know We Don't Know*.) Perhaps we can only truly respect knowledge when we admit that neither superficial learning nor deep learning can make us any more discerning as we peer out from the shadows of Plato's Cave. One crucial form of comprehension is the sort which physicists and theologians of a certain stripe confront unceasingly—the knowledge that our ignorance is dumbfoundingly vast. Here's a poem from Albert Goldbarth's most recent collection, *Everyday People*, and it speaks of this condition with great inventiveness and pathos:

The Lamps

What the TV says, and the Web Page says, and the fifteen-member Committee
on Reimagining the Product . . . But I'm thinking

of the story in which the Rabbi is done with the long day's draining
nineteenth century labor and drops insensible to his sleeping-straw

still wearing the dung-flecked clothes of the field, then suddenly looks down at himself from the air, the way the bright release

of oil-light must look down on the smudged and heavy glass
for a minute and then, the Rabbi ascends for the night

through the level of Cloud, and past the sword-bearing
    Guardians
with their riddles, and finally unto the gates of Eternity itself.

wherein he wanders until his earthly body reels him back
along a thread of *kasha*-steam, which we'd call being

downloaded into hard copy, for this is our language
here, the language of buying and selling the lamps,

and not of releasing the genie.[24]

Readers familiar with Goldbarth's vast oeuvre might be surprised that I have chosen one of his efforts, for there is no other American poet who crams so much factual detritus in his poems. His reference-laden concoctions, filled with all the sorts of high- and low-culture name-checking, and his tendency to swerve, often within a single poem, between a tone of glibness and deadly earnestness, suggests a superficial resemblance to writers such as Robbins. After all, Goldbarth proudly entitled his most recent selected volume *The Kitchen Sink*—and his tendency is not to throw in everything *but* that sink; it goes into the mix as well. Because the poems so lavishly display the author's seemingly encyclopedic knowledge and so vividly evidence the working of what must be an eidetic memory, sometimes we leave his poems mainly with a sense of their associative wildness and oddball learnedness but nothing more. (It's from Goldbarth, for example, that I've learned that paper money is typically only in circulation for about three months. But I could not for the life of me locate the poem from which I drew this info.) But Goldbarth's learnedness at its best is of a different order, deriving from true smarts rather than glib smarts: he understands the difference between Knowledge Poems and the verse of Stuff. Goldbarth has in more than one interview stressed that he does not even own a computer, let alone the tablets and smart phones that are now poised to be the laptop's replacements; writing a poem from the results of a Google search would be anathema to him.[25] The sensibility at work in Goldbarth's poetry has read deeply but eccentrically, and that eccentricity is one of the sources of his shape-shifting pyrotechnics. Furthermore, as a poem such as "The Lamps" tells us, his best work comes from a stance of moral seriousness and—in the case of this poem, an urgent critique of the limitations of our knowledge, our assumptions, and our belief that learning will ever offer us any sort of material success. Most of all, the poem questions whether knowledge is even *related* to facts, let alone derives from them. And, without explicitly stating it, the breezily rendered list that begins the poem suggests that the degradation of facts, their bowdlerization into ad copy or propaganda, now seems almost inevitable: "What the TV says, and the Web Page says, and the fifteen-member Committee / on Reimagining the Product . . ." The last of this triad seems, with its capitalization and high-handed jargon, less the language of Madison Avenue than the lingo of Orwell's Newspeak or the Great Leap Forward. This is *not* what knowledge looks like, though the forlorn and exhausted Rabbi who now appears, and "drops insensible to his sleeping-straw," seems not to know what knowledge looks like either. He is not a character who magisterially interprets the Talmud or espouses the impossibly intricate esoteric systems chronicled in Gershom Sholem's legendary *Major Trends in Jewish Mysticism*. No, this rabbi collapses into slumber, still wearing his horse-shit-spattered shoes. But suddenly he embarks upon a mystical hegira, rising into the various levels of the heavens, "through the level of Cloud, and past the word-bearing Guardians / with their Riddles." He ascends to the pinnacle of the world beyond, though not comprehendingly. He is still insensible; eternity is a place where he merely can "wander." And when his earthly body "reels" him back, the experience of his otherworldly visit offers him no insight, only a paltry, partial, and fraught account, which may be "downloaded into hard copy." But what is the use of that? We are not the hard gem-like flame, but the smudged glass which happens to contain it. We may know commerce, may know the "the language of buying and selling the lamps," but of the light itself we are wholly and woefully ignorant. The genie may exist within the lamp, but we

163

do not even know it can be released. This is truly a poem about unknown unknowns, and it insists upon one crucial thing—the nature of wisdom is often undistinguishable from sorrow. And could it be that sorrow persists longer than knowledge, longer than wisdom, and certainly longer than Stuff? Milosz, that wisest of poets, says as much in an ode to Heraclitus: ". . . he tortured himself, unable to forgive / that a moment of consciousness will never change us."[26]

In light of this I'd like to offer up one final poem for discussion, an effort from a highly accomplished first collection by Andrew Allport, entitled *The Body of Space in the Shape of the Human.* Like Goldbarth, Allport is a rangy poet, bound to no single style or approach; the book contains a series of moving and stately elegies for the poet's father, a translation from a section of *The Purgatorio,* a kind of cento cribbed from Augustine's *Confessions,* and a deeply endearing little lyric entitled "Keats, Listening to Van Morrison." But the poem I have in mind is more harrowing—and, perversely, although the good Dr. Walter Freeman is not its speaker, he surely seems to be a major player:

Poem Ending with an Ice Pick Lobotomy

Laid out in a white envelope.
I heard his bone hammer,

the tapered orbitoclast
a silver letter opener

sliding between gummed flaps,
a crack of daylight between hollow

and tissue, an entrance of instrument,
the bulbs smashed in their sockets.

Lions, water, the dark—
they said I was scared of everything

unreal. Even then, informally arranged
on the dining room table, I admit

to dreaming
when the dull pencil intruded.

Nights, I have been to the river,
I have seen the eyes of lions

bright with menace.
Then I lay on the bank

counting stars.
Then there were none.[27]

What makes this a Poem of Knowledge? Above all, the events it depicts are seen not as the product of gratuitous exoticism, but of tragedy. The descriptions are spare, and, given the context, one might even call them restrained—the surgical instrument is a "tapered orbitoclast / a silver letter opener // sliding between gummed flaps." The lobotomist performing the operation is not so much vilified as viewed as a distant and almost god-like presence; his hammer is not seen but heard, like the far-off rumble of thunder. The speaker of the poem offers only the most brusque sort of self-portraiture. We do not even know the speaker's gender, only that "they said I was scared of everything / unreal," and invariably the effect of the procedure is to offer not relief from the speaker's visions of "menace," but an oblivion that is indistinguishable from abjection. Although Allport's poem is considerably shorter than Randall Jarrell's dramatic monologues, its ending recalls one of his greatest such efforts, "Seel im Raum," whose speaker is also nominally "cured" of madness, and is left only with the aggrieved knowledge that "to be at all is to be wrong."[28]

In one of his final works, the posthumously published fragments entitled *On Certainty,* Ludwig Wittgenstein ultimately concludes that certainty and knowledge cannot be distinguished from mystery, bafflement, and confoundedness. "One is often bewitched by a word," he writes. "For example, by the word 'know.'"[29] The poems we return to, the poems which instruct us, the poems which I have so egregiously and inadequately termed the Poems of Knowledge, similarly bewitch us. And of course, bewitchment suggests discomfort. Stuff, on the other hand, is not even sufficiently substantial as to serve as spiritual or psychological comfort food. Whether it's someone boasting he will translate the Bible into velociraptor or the cheese-slathered curly fries you can Supersize at Arby's, it's all empty calories. About that, one *can* be certain.

2012

Notes

1." Sexing Baby Chicks," http://www.youtube.com/watch? v=ZGYP 3dUaVrQ. (Dec 12 2012).

2. "Lobotomy—PBS Documentary on Walter Freeman," You Tube. Web Jan. 27, 2008. (Dec. 12 2012). http://www.youtube.com/ watch?v=_0aNILW6ILk.

3. "Muriel Rukeyser," http://vault.fbi.gov/Muriel%20Rukeyser. (Dec. 12 2012).

4. "'Louie Louie' (The Song)," http://vault.fbi.gov/louie-louie-the-song/louie-louie-the-song/view. (Dec 12 2012).

5. Tony Hoagland, *Real Sofisttikashun: Essays on Poetry and Craft* (Minneapolis, MN: Graywolf Press, 2006), p. 174.

6. "The Future Of 'Short Attention Span Theater,'" Oct 26, 2012, http://m.npr.org/news/Technology/163649283?page=0.

7. Maryanne Wolf, *Proust and the Squid: The Story and Science of the Reading Brain* (New York: HarperCollins, 2007), p. 136.

8. Joshua Foer, *Moonwalking with Einstein: The Art and Science of Remembering Everything* (New York: Penguin, 2011), p. 138.

9. Francis A. Yates, *The Art of Memory* (Chicago: University of Chicago Press, 1966), p. 38.

10. James Longenbach, *The Resistance to Poetry* (Chicago: University of Chicago Press, 2004), pp. 1–2.

11. Michael Robbins, ""Are You Smeared with the Juice of Cherries?: Uneven Pleasures in the Work of Robert Hass," http://www.poetry-foundation.org/poetrymagazine/article/239972. (Dec. 12 2012).

12. Ange Mlinko, jacket copy for Michael Robbins, *Alien vs. Predator* (New York: Penguin, 2012).

13. Jacket copy for Robbins, *Alien vs. Predator.*

14. Robbins, *Alien vs. Predator,* p. 3.

15. John Berryman, *The Dream Songs* (New York: Farrar, Straus, and Giroux, 1969), p. 5; Alan Dugan, *Poems 7: New and Complete Poetry* (New York: Seven Stories Press, 2002), p. 44.

16. Michael Robbins, "Three Books," http://www.poetryfoundation. org/poetrymagazine/article/242900. (Dec. 12, 2012).

17. Michael Robbins, "Perdita: Why Cats Are Better Than People," http://www.poetryfoundation.org/poetrymagazine/article/244232. (Dec 12 2012).

18. Robbins, *Alien vs. Predator,* p. 66.

19. Michael Wolrich, "Why Etch A Sketch Gibe Will Be Hard for Romney to Shake," Mar. 23, 2012, http://www.cnn.com/2012/03/23/opinion/wolraich-etch-sketch/index.html.

20. Witold Gombrowicz, *Diary,* trans. Lillian Vallee (New Haven, CT: Yale University Press, 2012), p. 47. (Vallee has the author warn against pinching Lady Literature's "parts"—"ass" seems more tonally authentic to me.)

21. Geoffrey Hill, quoted in Dennis O'Driscoll, *Quote Poet Unquote: Contemporary Quotations on Poets and Poetry* (Port Townsend, WA: Copper Canyon Press, 2008), p. 85.

22. Linda Bierds, *The Ghost Trio* (New York: Henry Holt, 1994), p. 55.

23. "Donald Rumsfeld, Known Unknowns," Nov. 27, 2006, http://www.youtube.com/watch?v=_RpSv3HjpEw

24. Albert Goldbarth, *Everyday People* (Minneapolis, MN: Graywolf Press, 2012), p. 99.

25. "Backchat: Albert Goldbarth in Conversation," http://www.poets. org/viewmedia.php/prmMID/21390. (Dec 12 2012).

26. Czeslaw Milosz, *Selected Poems,* rev. ed. (New York: Ecco Press, 1973), p. 109.

27. Andrew Allport, *The Body of Shape in the Space of the Human* (Kalamazoo, MI: New Issues Press, 2012), p. 35.

28. Randall Jarrell, *The Complete Poems* (New York: Farrar, Straus, and Giroux, 1969), p. 39.

29. Ludwig Wittgenstein, *On Certainty,* trans. Dennis Paul and D. E. M. Abscome, http://web.archive.org/web/20051210213153/http://budni.by.ru/oncertainty.html. (Dec 12 2012).

The Coast Is Never Clear

On the Poetry of Happiness

Not long ago I had an interesting but also somewhat unsettling conversation with some other poets. I teach in a low-residency MFA program, which employs about a dozen of our kind, and one of the pleasures of teaching in such a place is that you have good company—my colleagues are not only writers I admire; many of them are also lifelong friends. True, the residencies can be taxing; after all, for two weeks you're far from home; you're working long hours, and living in a dormitory whose furnishings are Spartan at best. (I've heard that some lo-rez programs house their faculty in ritzy hotel suites, but our dorms resemble gas station restrooms with mattresses tossed into a corner.) Yet the conversations you have with colleagues in those dorm rooms, especially late at night when you've finished teaching, meeting with students, and attending the endless round of readings and lectures, are almost always a delight. I'd like to report that these conversations are primarily high-minded and intellectually stimulating, but that's not always the case. Sometimes you just bullshit and shoot the breeze. And so it happened that one night our chatter turned toward antidepressants, and quickly became one of those oddly partisan conversations of the sort you get when the Mac users take sides against the PC folks. The Cimbalta folks were needling the Paxil crew—"Paxil's so *twentieth century."* The Welbutrinites were giving it to the Citalapramers on the subject of "sexual side effects." And my own rhapsodizing about the virtues of Xanax was quickly shut down when it was pointed out that Xanax was a mere *tranquilizer,* not a "true" antidepressant. The conversation grew curiouser and curiouser, until someone commented upon the most obvious but also the most remarkable aspect of the discussion. Eight male poets and two male fiction writers were gathered in a room—and all of us were on some form of antidepressant. And although it was close to midnight, we decided it was time for an informal survey. Someone was dispatched to the floor where the women faculty were staying, and who were also apt to be kibitzing long into the night. The messenger returned with the news that all the women faculty he'd spoken to were on antidepressants as well. That night's survey of some twenty writers found that all but two of us had at one time or another gotten their serotonin levels tweaked. Only one among us—a fiction writer—had never been treated with an antidepressant. The other was someone taking St. Johns' wort, which didn't really count, or suggested a certain self-delusion, like Bill Clinton insisting that he smoked the weed but never inhaled.

No one reading this anecdote will find it surprising, As Lionel Trilling put it, the notion that creative people suffer from mental disorders is "indeed one of the characteristic notions of our culture."[1] There is also clinical evidence for this. A Dr. Nancy Anderson of the University of Iowa once conducted an intriguing survey of some students, faculty, and alumni of the Iowa Writers' Workshop, and reached the conclusion that 80 percent of her subjects met "formal diagnostic criteria for a major mood disorder." This figure strikingly contrasted with a control sample of academics and professional people who did not work in arts-related fields. Only 30 percent of them were afflicted with mood disorders.[2] One could make a case, I suppose, that this problem may have something to do with the Iowa Writers' Workshop and not brain chemistry, but other studies have yielded similar results. A Memphis State University survey of writers and artists concluded that 50 percent of its subjects had suffered at least one major depressive episode. Poets may draw comfort from the fact that another Tennessee study—of blues singers—came up with similar statistics. Upward of 50 percent of them are depressives, too: the prevalence of those bad poems we all wrote about Robert Johnson now makes a certain sense.[3] And if you want to know why so many of us pen brooding odes to the likes of Trakl and Celan, an oft-cited German study of 5,000 creative *volk* may help to explain: only 113 of those surveyed were labeled as "pyschosocially normal." And with typical Teutonic precision, the Germans tried to determine *which* artistic disciplines were most likely to invite "abnormality." Here's the breakdown: "The highest rates of psychiatric abnormality were found in the poets (50%) and musicians (38%); lower rates were found in painters (20%), sculptors (18%) and architects (17%)."[4] The above studies are only a handful of similar ones cited in Kay Redfield Jamison's *Touched with Fire,* an exhaustive survey of mental illness and the artistic temperament. Some of the figures she trots out get downright surreal: we find that debilitating mood swings are ten times more common among artists than among the general population; that the siblings, children, and grandchildren of depressed and bipolar artists are also likely to be depressed and bipolar, even if they themselves are not artists; that the suicide rate among artists is thirteen times that of the general population—that is, if you count single-vehicle car accidents as "suicide equivalents."

I read Jameson's book some years back, and I'd for the most part forgotten about it until a few weeks ago, when I wanted to consult it for the sake of a writers' conference panel I'd been asked to participate in—more on this momentarily. Jameson had obviously made an impression on me, since I'd filled the book with underlinings and margin notes, many of them simply expressions of incredulity or shock: lots of double exclamation points and comments such as "Yipes." The panel topic was a simple one: "Are Happy Poems Possible?" The panelists had been asked to respond to Philip Larkin's famous reply to an interviewer who asked the poet why his work was so melancholy: "Happiness writes white," he said, adding glumly that "deprivation is for me what daffodils were to Wordsworth."[5] We were also asked to bring to the panel an example or two of happy poetry. On the one hand, the panel subject was vastly more interesting than the usual fare at conferences, where you're apt to address issues involving po-biz rather than poetry itself, mostly benumbing variants on "How Do I Get Published?" Should I write "First North American Serial Rights" in the upper right corner of my submission? Is it okay to double submit? And so on. My friend the poet Ron Smith, who had come up with the panel topic and was moderating the event, clearly understood that this was a perversely challenging subject, and I came to it as a sort of wary agnostic about the question. Yes, I dug up a happy poem or two, but they were by no means easy to find. And in doing my research for the event I came to suspect that happy poems and happy people are not just rare but downright suspect in the eyes of most creative people. Or maybe most people in general: it's not for nothing that *Invasion of the Body Snatchers* has been remade four times. And not long ago, while I sat in the waiting room of my shrink's office—it's a big practice, so there are always a handful of people in the waiting room—the 1980s station the receptionist had on started to play REM's "Shiny Happy People." There was a couple across from me, a burly fellow with tattooed arms and his partner, a thin woman with long stringy hair who scarcely took her eyes from the floor. But she did perk up when the song started, turning to her tattooed hubby and saying, "Sure isn't our song, huh?" All of us in the room exchanged knowing smiles, though they could not be construed as "happy" ones. And who can forget those scathing words of Chekhov in his great story "Gooseberries":

> There ought to be behind the door of every happy, contented man, someone standing with a hammer, continually reminding him with a tap that there are unhappy people; that however happy he may be, life will show him her laws sooner or later, trouble will come to him—disease, poverty, losses, and no one will see or hear, just as now he neither sees nor hears others.[6]

Put this way, happiness becomes something not merely hard to achieve, but a condition almost sinful, something akin to lassitude, sloth, the selling of indulgences, or an excessive admiration for the poems of Charles Bukowski. Faced with this warning—beware the little man with the hammer!—I took my place on the panel. I began with the anecdote I started with here, rattled off some of the grim statistics I'd gotten from Jameson and others, and read my "happy" poem. Admittedly, its title doesn't exactly suggest it was written in a state of happiness:

My Funeral

Will my funeral start out from our courtyard?
How will you get me down from the third floor?
The coffin won't fit in the elevator
and the stairs are awfully narrow.

Maybe there'll be sun knee-deep in the yard, and pigeons,
Maybe snow filled with the cries of children,
maybe rain with its wet asphalt.
And the trash cans will stand in the courtyard as always.

If, as is the custom here, I'm put in the truck face open,
a pigeon might drop something on my forehead: it's good
    luck.
Band or no band, the children will come up to me—
they're curious about the dead.

Our kitchen window will watch me leave.
Our balcony will see me off with the wash on the line.
In this yard I was happier than you'll ever know.
Neighbors, I wish you all long lives.[7]

This is Turkey's Nazim Hikmet, who lived from 1902 to 1963,
and surely ranks among the greatest poets of the previous century. It is one of his last poems, written during a period of relative ease in his life. Dying in exile in Cold War Moscow—not
long after contemplating how your corpse will look with its face
bespattered in pigeon shit—will not seem to American readers a
particularly enviable fate. But for Hikmet, exile was far prefera-
ble to the Istanbul penitentiary where the leftist poet spent thirteen years as a political prisoner. There many things I love about
this poem, and they are all characteristic of Hikmet at his best,
whether he is writing from his prison cell or from his wanderings
in exile. The speaker's vision of his death is rendered with a kind
of wry objectivity. Good dialectical materialist that he is, Hikmet
has no interest in contemplating the afterlife; he instead focuses
on practicalities, small questions that in this context grow to be
grand ones—and simply to utter them requires courage: How
will they get my corpse to the courtyard? How will it look to the
curious children? In essence, Hikmet writes a poem in the man-

ner of "Ozymandias," yet he spares us Shelley's loftiness. *Look thee now upon my fate.* I'm no different from the trashcans in the courtyard, the rain on the pavement, and the wash that's hanging from the line. And they are more or less permanent features of the landscape—in contrast to the corpse of the poet, which will soon get jostled off into the streets of Moscow, and placed into what Ivor Gurney called that "six-foot length [we] must lie in, sodden with mud."[8] The sentiment of the poem's penultimate lines is uttered with the utmost conviction.

The audience, however, did not look as though they were buying it. And I suspect that some of them, perhaps rightly, thought of my choice as further evidence that most poets are indeed afflicted with "mood disorders": elderly Turkish poet, dying in exile, contemplating how his corpse will look and be treated. Yeah, that's joy for you. And my fellow panelists? Well, they must have seemed to suffer from mood disorders as well. Elizabeth Seydel Morgan read a sly and bittersweet poem by Wislawa Szymborska. And Claudia Emerson, unbeknownst to me, had also chosen a poem by Hikmet, this one dating from his years in prison. And Ron Smith, our moderator? He offered a poem by Larkin, of all people, one of the grim master's final poems, "The Explosion," which closes his last collection, *High Windows*. The title refers to a mine disaster, and though it is not one of Larkin's best-known efforts, I remember turning to it in the days after 9/11. "On the day of the explosion" the miners head for work as usual:

> Down the lane came men in pitboots
> Coughing oath-edged talk and pipe smoke,
> Shouldering off the freshened silence.
>
> One chased after rabbits; lost them;
> Came back with a nest of lark's eggs;
> Showed them; lodged them in the grasses.
>
> So they passed in beard and moleskins,
> Fathers, brothers, nicknames, laughter,
> Through the tall gates standing open.

But, precisely halfway through the poem, the event predicted in the title occurs:

At noon, there came a tremor, cows
Stopped chewing for a second; sun,
Scarfed as in a heat-daze, dimmed.

The dead they go before us, they
Are sitting in God's house in comfort,
We shall see them face to face—

Plain as lettering in the chapels
It was said, and for a second
Wives saw men of the explosion

Larger than in life they managed—
Gold as on a coin, or walking
Somehow from the sun towards them,

One showing the eggs unbroken.[9]

The audience, by this point rather puzzled by how in the world we previous panelists had come to think of our poems as "happy," was thoroughly dumbfounded by this one. First, the poem is authored by the very person who more or less claimed that happy poems are an impossibility, an oxymoron, a poem written by the Arch-Priest of Grim, the Leona Helmsley of twentieth-century verse. Second, it describes the violent, senseless, and utterly unpredicted deaths of a group of innocents. And it reminds us, contrary to what the authors of the *Left Behind* series would have you believe, that apocalypse is always personal, and always small. In this Larkin joins two of his predecessors who explored this theme: just as Auden in "Musée des Beaux Arts" insists that for the rest of the world the fall of Icarus was "not an important failure" and that violence is largely ignored—there's always "the torturer's horse," who "scratches its innocent behind on a tree"—so Larkin casts the mine explosion as a mere tremor; something that makes the cows stop chewing their cud, but only for an instant.[10] And although I doubt if Larkin knew the work of Milosz or would have cared for it much if he did, I hear echoes of the closing lines of Milosz's magisterial "Song on the End of the World," written during the Nazi occupation of Poland:

No one believes it is happening now.

Only a white-haired old man, who would be a prophet,
Yet is not a prophet, for he's much too busy,
Repeats while he binds his tomatoes:
There will be no other end of the world.
There will be no other end of the world.[11]

All well and good, but what does this dark but sublime sub-genre have to do with happiness? Ron offered an impassioned but somewhat tentative answer, quoting that famous dictum of Frost's "strongly spent is synonymous with kept." Frost's statements on poetry always tend to be impish, and this one certainly falls into that category: if we take "strongly spent" to at least in some degree refer to technique, to offering us delight through a skillful display of prosody, then "The Explosion" is nearly flawless. The descriptions are evocative but spare as the lingo of old telegraph missives from Western Union—or, for that matter, text messages on your cell. Larkin establishes a loose but fluent tetrameter in the poem's opening lines, but then immediately undercuts it with a mad rush of spondees and caesurae: "One chased after rabbits; lost them; / Came back with a nest of lark's eggs; / Showed them; lodged them in the grasses." The meter is troubled but never dissonant, a sonic foreshadowing of the explosion, which is evoked as movement rather than as sound—a "tremor." When the meter grows more regular in the poem's concluding stanzas, after the italicized passage which seems to be a pastiche of the Psalms, the turbulence is over; the sun doesn't just come out after the storm, but blazes with radiance. The dead are countenanced—they are kept and preserved in a transfiguring moment. The eggs are unbroken, and the poet furthermore signs off on the poem with a bit of punning self-portraiture: Larkin's lark's eggs. It's akin to Michelangelo putting his own face among the risen dead on the Sistine's *Last Judgment*. No doubt about it, here "strongly spent is synonymous with kept." But is strongly spent synonymous with joy? Ron seemed to think so—and how can you be a poet and not believe this? And, as the discussion continued, Claudia trotted out a similarly memorable quote, this from Djuna Barnes: "the unendurable is the beginning of the curve to joy." (And, bless her, quoted a verse from the immortal Townes Van Zandt's "To Live Is to Fly.") Earlier that week, a student of mine had in a very different context recited to me his favorite lines from Elizabeth Bishop. It's that well-known passage in "The Moose," where the bus passengers stop their nattering dialogue and descriptions of the moose, and the moose, in the fashion of Rilke's torso of Apollo, starts to *stare back* at them: "Taking her time / she looks the bus over, / grand, otherworldly." Note here that Bishop, that most precise of writers, allows into this passage what the prose style manuals call "a squinting modifier." Is it the moose who is grand and otherworldly to the bus passengers, or is it the bus that is grand and otherworldly to the moose? Good question. But the question which follows it is even better: "Why, why do we feel / (we all feel) this sweet / sensation of joy?"[12] As the panel began to field questions, this passage came back to me: it perfectly illustrates why happy poems are possible, why the individual and the collective can sometimes be indistinguishable, why the self and the world can—sometimes—be indistinguishable as well. Intimations of that sweet sensation of joy are indeed a part of my life: they happen when I'm spending time with my children or my wife; they happen—sometimes—when I write. But, dear reader, I thought of this and kept my mouth shut. If you're generous toward me, you can blame this lapse on my brain chemistry. If you're of a sterner disposition, you can call it an ethical lapse, or a failure of courage. The panel concluded; an audience member shook my hand and allowed that the discussion was "great fun." And I sheepishly walked away— "slunk" may be a better term. My fellow poets had all moved to the front of the bus; they had all stared at the moose while the moose stared back; they had all felt the sweet sensation of joy. But I stayed in the back, stewing and brooding, waiting for the Xanax to come on, and watching Elizabeth Bishop's grammar. I had learned that even Larkin had, in his way, come to believe that happy poems were possible. But I was at best an agnostic. I did not need Chekhov's little man with the hammer to remind me of my shortcomings. I could instead beat myself up, and do just fine.

Over the next few weeks, I frequently found myself pondering the poems the panelists had discussed, searching, I think, for patterns. What made this decidedly mixed bag of poems somehow share the "sweet sensation of joy"? A couple of provisional conclusions arrived. All of the poems shared a militant disdain for solipsism. This quality may not have allowed the poems to be happy—but it certainly distinguished them from most efforts in the period style; twenty-some years ago the late William Matthews rightly claimed that the template for the majority of contemporary poems is "I went out to the woods today and felt a little, you know, spiritual." This sort of Wordsworth Lite, this deification of the pathetic fallacy, may earn Mary Oliver a legion of readers, but Oliver is never really engaged in any sort of dialogue with her readership. She simply carries us along with her on her excursions into the scrub pine forests of the Cape—we're treated like the contents of her canteen, the granola bars in her backpack. Contrast this with Hikmet's farewell salute to his Moscow neighbors, or Larkin's miner showing off his lark's eggs to his comrades before they all pick up their lunchboxes and check the batteries on their helmet lights. Bishop wants to know why the moose elicits joy, but she emphatically asserts that this joy is collective, and underscores that assertion with one of her storied parentheticals: compare "(we all share)" with the legendary *"(Write it!)"* in the final line of "One Art." The poems recognize and rail against what Oppen called "the shipwreck of the singular." This much I could recognize fairly easily, but my other realization about the poems was more vexing—the sweet sensation of joy *never lasts.* Don't kid yourself—the eggs will break; Larkin by no means suggests that a couple of cute little baby larks will emerge from them. And the spell cast by the moose lasts only for a fleeting moment: the driver (literally) shifts gears, and the collective vision is (again, literally) left in the dust. Of course, the poems are intended to preserve those moments, in all of their bittersweet radiance. But the man with the hammer and my brain chemistry keep asking whether the poems achieve such radiant preservation of the joyful moment, or whether they simply mummify it. And the man with the hammer obviously is a critic rather than a poet. We live in a digital age, after all; everything can be preserved forever—so why are *these* moments so damn special? The little man with the hammer seems to have read Walter Benjamin; he stops hammering for a moment and chatters about "Art in the Age of Mechanical Reproduction." He tells me to forget about the notion that the poems might possess that "aura" which Benjamin thought the essential ingredient of a meaningful artwork, and which he predicted would be lost now that art—just like everything else—can be endlessly replicated. What's so jaw-dropping about a goddamn moose, anyway? And pigeon shit on the face of the dead Nazim Hikmet? Sure, we can download the image onto our hard drives, but so what? I'd gotten myself into quite a quandary. Here is a passage from the last paragraph of the last piece of writing Weldon Kees ever published, a review that came out in the *New Republic* in July of 1955, a few days before he took his leap from the Golden Gate Bridge. The title of the piece is "How to Be Happy: Installment # 1053." Kees performs one of his characteristically wicked eviscerations, this one of a pop psychology tome, *Love and Hate in Human Nature,* by a Dr. Arnold A. Hutschnecker, a name so deliciously pompous it could have been invented by Kees and placed in one of his bitterly resonant sonnets or villanelles: "The liberal assumption that self-knowledge will lead to 'adjustment' and 'happiness' is a curious one. "[13]

Self-knowledge, feeling "a little spiritual"—none of these conditions generally lead to happy poems, although they may lead to the consolation prize, in the form of a poem that laments the impossibility of happiness. Great poets along the lines of Tu Fu, Baudelaire, and Cavafy made their careers out of this sort of poem. We're painfully familiar with the condition which the kind of artwork I am referring to arises from; it derives from what the painter Donald Evans called "the *why* of art and the *I-give-up* of finding love or happiness."[14] It's a venerable sub-genre, to be sure, so much so that it's hard to take a new approach to it. This is why I find the following poem by the criminally underrecognized Ron Padgett to be such an acrid delight:

Standoff with Frosty

Every time I sit down to do some serious work
my stomach tells me it's time to go downstairs
and see what's in the fridge, but when
I reach in there an icy hand

grabs my wrist and thrusts me away
from the territory of the snowman.
Yes, Frosty himself.
He lives in there with a banjo and a carrot.
He plays the banjo and thinks about the carrot,
but it is a dull existence, and he is disgruntled.
How can I make him happy? There is no way
for he can neither hear nor understand my words.
I cannot reason with him, describe the arctic nights
which gave him "life," nor lure his melancholy world
away from him. He is stuck and so am I.[15]

I'm not going to insult this wacko ars poetica with a lengthy
exegesis, but once you read the poem it's hard to sit down to
your desk—hoping "to do some serious work" perhaps—and
not think of yourself as Frosty moping in his fridge, strumming
on the ol' banjo while coming up with end-rhymes for "carrot."
Never again can you call yourself "Keatsian." And yet, corny as
it sounds, Padgett wants to reach out to Frosty; he's concerned
about poor Frosty's happiness. The poem ends with a gesture
that's not that far removed from the end of the Hikmet's "My
Funeral." Frostys of the world, I wish you all long lives!

At some point in this process, again through a somewhat
desultory method of paging through books in my library that
might address these matters, I hit pay dirt, in the form of a very
judicious little selection of Freud's musings on aesthetics, called
Writings on Art and Literature. I came back to the book in part
because I suspected his well-known essay on the uncanny might
do something to address my problems. Unfortunately, that particular piece seemed windy and oblique, and other essays in the
collection—such as "The Moses of Michelangelo"—served only
to remind me how very eccentric the esteemed doctor's views on
artistic creation could often be. But then I came upon a humble
little piece—just four pages long—entitled "On Transience." In
form it's more a sermon than an essay, and a very wise one indeed.

And its opening is hilarious. Although the examples Freud
relates in his well-known essay on jokes seem either badly trans-
lated or a little lame, he had a finely honed sense of the comic,
and the essay starts with an anecdote that recalls a time-worn

genre of jokes—you know the sort: "A rabbi, a priest, and Mormon elder go into a bar . . . ." "A deconstructionist, a new historicist, and a feminist critic go into a bar . . ." "Hilary Clinton, Sarah Palin, and Michael Jackson go into a bar . . . ," etc. Here's the opening paragraph:

> Not long ago, I went on a summer walk through a smiling countryside in the company of a taciturn friend and a young but already famous poet. The poet admired the beauty around us but felt no joy in it. He was disturbed by the fact that all this beauty was fated to extinction, and that it would vanish when winter came, like all human beauty and all the beauty and splendor that men have created or may create. All that he otherwise would have loved and admired seemed to him to be shorn of its worth by the transience which was its doom.[16]

This scene is funny not merely because of the unintentional humor of calling a poet—and a young one at that—"famous." Picture Freud and his silent buddies ambling down a bucolic country path in what the essay's editors identify as the Dolomites. Freud's doubtless got a stogie lit up, and you can't help but wonder what the good doctor would have regarded as casual wear, what the *fin de siècle* version of Hawaiian shirt and Birkenstocks would have been for a well-heeled Viennese Jew. Jodhpurs? One of those Sherlock Holmes deerstalkers' caps? And you wonder who the oxymoronically famous poet was. The editors of *Writing on Art and Literature* say that the identities of Freud's companions "cannot be established." To give the joke's setup a little more texture, we want him to be Rilke, but we know from Rilke's letters than he was fascinated yet repelled by Freud. (As he wrote to his muse Lou-Andreas Salome, an ardent Freudian who kept bugging Rilke to go on the couch, "I could hardly expect anything good to come of it. Something perilously close to a disinfected soul is the result.")[17] But let's imagine the famous poet to look a bit *like* Rilke, something of a dandy, and with those big pouty Angelina Jolie lips that always made him look as though he'd been getting injections of collagen gel. In surveying the distant reaches of the landscape, he straps on his pince-nez for a better view; he's carrying a little volume of Hölderlin, and where-

180

as Freud and his buddy have gone the casual route, the poet's doubtless a bit overdressed. The doctor and his companion ooh and aah about the mountains and streams, while the poet lags a little behind, saying nothing until they return from their hike, at which point his hand-wringing pronouncement about beauty being "fated to extinction" must have tumbled exasperatingly out. I don't imagine Freud as having at that point argued with the poet. He instead wants to revel in the glorious landscape, wants to reach that tavern down the road for a stein of the local pilsner. But you can tell that this event impressed him deeply: partly out of sympathy for the poet's dilemma; partly because it pissed him off. For all his much-vaunted pessimism, Freud was a glass-half-full kind of guy, as the essay's second paragraph very eloquently attests:

> The proneness to decay of all that is beautiful and perfect can, as we know, give rise to two different impulses in the mind. The one leads to the aching despondency felt by the young poet, while the other leads to rebellion to the fact asserted. No! it is impossible that all the loveliness of Nature and Art, or the world of our sensations and of the world outside, will really fade away into nothing. It would be too senseless and presumptuous to believe it. Somehow or other this loveliness must be able to persist and to escape all the powers of destruction.

I love the emphatic "No!" here, and I love the slight tentativeness of his phrasing. He knows the poet has a point, but he is not going to compromise on this one. He continues:

> But this demand for immortality is a product of our wishes too unmistakable to lay claim to reality: what is painful may nonetheless be true. I could not see my way to dispute the transience of all things, nor could I insist upon an exception in favor of beautiful and perfect. But I did dispute the pessimistic poet's point of view that the transience of what is beautiful involves any loss of its worth.
>
> On the contrary, an increase! Transience value is scarcity value in time. Limitation in the possibility of enjoyment raises the value of the enjoyment. It was incomprehensible, I de-

clared, that the thought of the transience of beauty should interfere with our joy in it. As regards to the beauty of Nature, each time it is destroyed by winter, it comes again next year, so that in relation to the length of our lives it can in fact be regarded as eternal. The beauty of the human form and face vanish forever in the course of our own lives, but their evanescence only lends them a fresh charm.

Freud then makes a similarly spirited argument regarding creative endeavor. Our statues and paintings may "crumble to dust." But they should not lose their worth to us because of "temporal limitation." What seems to me most notable and moving about Freud's presentation of his views is their sheer passion. "On the contrary, an increase!"—the second exclamation point within a page, this from a writer not at all given to gush. And he hones his argument with epigrammatic precision: "Transience value is scarcity value in time." Freud knows, I think, that he's a bit out of his league, arguing aesthetics with a "famous" poet. Although *Writings on Art and Literature* testifies to the doctor's lifelong passion for literary criticism of a psychological sort, and although his judgments on art were sometimes quite acute—he found the writings of Breton and the surrealists to be odious, despite the groups' great admiration for his work—Freud knows this is not his area of expertise. Furthermore, the third member of the party seems to be going over to the poet's side. The doctor wraps up his argument, and, to his astonishment, it falls on deaf ears: "These considerations appeared to me incontestable; but I noticed that I had made no impression either upon the poet or upon my friend."

So the debate ends at best in a standoff. Doubtless the trio makes it to the beer garden they'd been heading for; more cigars are lit, the steins are drained. They all agree to change the subject—why spoil such a lovely hike in the mountains? Freud gets the last word, but only in retrospect:

My failure lead me to infer that some powerful emotional factor was at work which was disturbing their judgment, and I believed later that I had discovered what it was. What spoilt their enjoyment of beauty must have been a revolt in their minds against mourning. The idea that all this beauty was transient was giving these two sensitive minds a foretaste of mourning over its decease, and, since the mind instinctively recoils from what is painful, they felt their enjoyment of beauty interfered with by thoughts of its transience.

Freud then grows a little more Freudian, seeing this tendency toward preemptive mourning as a function of the libido, which is ego-directed in infancy and childhood, and later "diverted from the ego onto objects." Attaining emotional health—as we all were told in that chapter in our college intro to psych class texts about Freud—is a process of divesting ourselves of that fixation on objects. But it isn't that easy, as he now insists in one of the essay's most eloquent passages:

> But why is it that this detachment of libido from its objects should be such a painful process is a mystery to us and we have not hitherto been able to frame any hypothesis to account for it? We only see that libido clings to its objects and will not renounce those that are lost even when a substitute lies ready at hand. Such then is mourning.

These observations are given an even greater urgency in the essay's final two paragraphs. "My conversation with the poet," he tells us, "took place in the summer before the war. A year later war broke out and robbed the world of its beauties." Freud is writing in 1919, and the Great War's destructive consequences seem beyond belief: he begins to sound more like Jeremiah than the Father of Psychoanalysis: "It destroyed not only the beauty of the countrysides through which it passed, and the works of arts which it met in its path, but it also shattered our pride in the achievements of our civilization. . . . It tarnished the lofty impartiality of our science; it revealed our instincts in all their nakedness and let loose the evil spirits within us. . . . It robbed us of very much that we loved, and showed us how ephemeral were many things we had regarded as changeless." The poet's sense of preemptive mourning has been amplified a thousand-fold, replaced by a vast collective sense of loss; almost everything the culture held in its esteem is shown to be "so perishable and so unresistent." But Freud refuses to concede to this view: "I believe that those who think thus, and seem ready to make a permanent renunciation because what was precious has proved not to be lasting, are simply in a state of mourning for what is lost. Mourning, as we know, however painful it may be, comes to a spontaneous end." This too will pass; our libido will "replace the lost objects with fresh ones equally or still more precious." He concludes the essay with a passage of rhetorical zeal that wouldn't seem out of place in a presidential candidate's stump speech:

> When once the mourning is over, it will be found that our high opinion of the riches of civilization has lost nothing from our discovery of their fragility. We shall build up again all that war destroyed, and perhaps on firmer ground, and more lastingly than before.

That the good doctor can express such views despite his achingly keen understanding of the deep cultural pessimism that followed the war strikes me as near heroic. I can't help but wonder if Auden didn't have the above passage in mind in his wonderful elegy for Freud. Compare the essay's conclusion to these lines near the close of Auden's poem:

> . . . some hearth where freedom is excluded,
> a hive whose honey is fear and worry,
> feels calmer now and somehow assured of escape,
> while, as they lie in the grass of our neglect,
> so many long-forgotten objects
> revealed by his undiscouraged shining
> are returned to us and made precious again[18]

How does this "undiscouraged shining," an action that both illuminates and terrifies, compel us to continue, to shed our mourning clothes, and build our world again, "on firmer ground, more lastingly than before"? This is the question which the poems of Hikmet and Larkin seek to answer, the question which our panel sought to address, the question which is really posed when we ask if "happy poems are possible." Regarding the command of undiscouraged shining I am still far too ignorant, but as to the question of whether happy poems can exist, "On Transience" served to convince me that the answer is yes.

This leads me to three conclusions. And they are, in a certain sense, simple ones:

1. Happy poems are possible, desirable, necessary, and extremely hard to write. Hard to write because
2. You have to acknowledge the existence of the little man with the hammer, but write the poem anyway.
3. You have to decide that, as Freud insists, "the transience of what is beautiful" does not involve "any loss of its worth."

It's a tall order to try to fulfill all of these demands. My list of poems that do so now includes the Hikmet and the Larkin, but it sometimes feels as though the remainder of the list can be counted on your fingers. I will keep trying to find poems to add to the list, however, and from time to time author a list-worthy poem of my own.

In the meantime, just to show that I'm trying to fulfill this promise, I want to offer a third poem as a way of concluding this discussion, a poem notable because it so abundantly fulfills the three rules I've devised, and because it comes from a very unlikely source, a poet I always have difficulty with, Mark Strand. Furthermore, it's an uncollected poem, one Strand didn't see fit to place in any of his collections. I have difficulty with Strand's poetry because it often seems to me arch and under-achieving. Strand possesses astounding prosodic resources, but you always feel that he's reluctant or a bit too lazy to fully exercise them, and thus a poet who aligns himself with the great poets of philosophical query and depth—he's very much a successor to Wordsworth and Stevens—comes across as an extremely gifted student who does nothing over the course of the semester, finally studies a bit on the night before his final, and scrapes by with a B-, despite the immensity of his talents. "Feckless" is a word Strand often employs in his poetry, and that comes as no surprise. What does surprise me is that the poem I want to share with you lends the lie to all of my criticism of Strand. It's my favorite poem of his, and one of my favorite poems, period. It's called "Viewing the Coast," and it appeared over twenty years ago in an issue of the now-defunct *Grand Street*, then later in one of the Pushcart annuals. A while back, when I taught as a visitor at the University of Chicago, Strand was nominally my colleague, although I taught in the English Department, and Strand taught in an elite university-within-the-university called the Committee for Social Thought, with the likes of Saul Bellow and other big shots—they were the U of C's equivalent to Saddam's Republican Guard. Every now and again I'd pass Strand on campus, and whenever I'd meet him I'd accost him about "Viewing the Coast." He never put it in a book, he'd say, because it "didn't feel finished." Later, we'd pass on the sidewalk or encounter each other in a bookstore, and the first words to come out of his mouth were the likes of, "I'm working on the poem, honest." Eventually, he'd see me coming and turn in the other direction. This may be the first occasion in history in which someone felt that he was being stalked because of an unfinished poem.

But Strand was wrong about "Viewing the Coast." Here's the opening section:

> Sailing a ragged shoreline strewn with rocks
> And broken timber silvering in sunlight,
> And remembering, not clearly enough, a house
> Where roses on the walls have peeled by now,
> And ceiling leaks have spread their maps to let
> The sky inside, and a Chinese lantern that swung
> On the front porch is just a skeleton
> Of rusted wire, I wonder at the half-sleep
> Of a calling in which I spent so many days
> Offshore. The water's phrases break and bubble
> Into nothing, long undulating leaves
> Of kelp lean one way and in their shade
> Small silver herring glide. If I could see
> Beneath them to our least beginnings drifting
> In the tidal sway and see myself,
> What would I know? That what is most remote
> Is also best forgotten? This creaking boat
> Moves alongside islands that appear
> Then slip from sight. Wedge Island, like a shelf,
> Slides into view, and the top of Mosher Island.
> Then both are gone. The midday spreads a film

Of light over the whole watery scene,
It shines but seem less clear; while I,
Drawn from facts of the actual world into
A dream where there are no facts, only shapes
Resembling them, find that I desire less.
A deeper music darkens what I see,
And now at noon, parting from this shine,
These islands, I am sure that what was here,
The happiness I had, cannot return.
The land is gone. I have no past to speak of;
The history of this moment is this moment.[19]

This may nominally be the environs of Prince Edward Island, where Strand spent much of his childhood, but the setting quickly becomes allegorical—the landscape of memory, of pathetic fallacy, of the poet battling Freud's "revolt in [the] mind against mourning." And, although the passage is written in a slow and stately pentameter, the descriptions all suggest a hidden turbulence, a kind of kinesthetic undertow which always turns present into past, and prohibits any sort of objective view of the shoreline which the poets sails past. Everything is movement, paradox, uncertainty: the empty house is something out of Edwin Arlington Robinson's "House on the Hill" or Frost's "Directive"—impossible to imagine as anything but in its present state of ruin, much as the poet would like to invest it with nostalgia. But what is nostalgia, what is the past? Once the leaves of the kelp part and the school of herring glides by, the poet believes he might now "see himself"—but instead he is merely staring into the black depths of the sea. And when the poet turns his gaze upward, his perceptions are similarly confounded: "The midday spreads a film / Of light over the whole watery scene, / It shines but seem less clear. . . ." The ending of the section, refusing both the consolations of memory and any belief that the happiness of childhood could return in some transfigured form, is desolate and resigned: "The history of this moment is this moment." Freud would attest that the speaker's insights about the landscape are more realistic than those of the poet in "On Transience." But what consolation does his knowledge bring?

The poet's answer to this dilemma comes in part two of the poem. Its beginning will seem to those who share my reservations about Strand to almost be a primer on why he seems to waste his talents on cheap shots and easy ironies. But bear with me for a moment:

> Now when I said those things about having lost
> My happiness, I meant that I couldn't remember
> Clearly enough the happiness I had.
> I was so far away that nothing was clear,
> And I said a few high-sounding things without
> Intending to. The fact is that when one wants
> To go back, no matter where, the coast is never
> Clear. One is bound to see haze or ruins, and that,
> As I said, is a little sad. Take the house
> I mentioned. What good would it do to be living there now,
> Stuck on the shore, watching someone like me
> Sail by? And all that stuff about not seeing
> Down to our least beginnings, as if anyone could,
> And trying to reinforce and even deepen
> The longing I felt, was only me trying
> To impersonate what one might say in such
> A situation. . . .

The tone shifts radically: the solemnity of the opening section is replaced by something flip and wise-ass. Strand lampoons his earlier assertions: it "was only me trying / To impersonate what one might say in such /A situation. . . ."; "I said a few high-sounding things without /Intending to. . . ." And there's the egregious pun in "the coast is never /Clear." Strand's approach to the line changes, too: the pentameter has loosened to admit a great many triple feet and enjambments. The effect of all this is jarring, to say the least: Strand has cried wolf; he's indulged in the rhetorical contrivance of saying, "I'm lying. Do you believe me?" It's a masterful sleight-of-hand, but I for one am angered by it. Yet not so much as to be indifferent as to what happens next: smitten as we are by the gravity and Stevensian music of the poem's opening section, we can't quite believe that Strand is going to demolish his whole enterprise in this fashion. And he doesn't: here's the poem's conclusion:

> Sometimes when I write,
> Things get a little out of hand, which is
> What I meant when I said I was drawn

From facts into a dream resembling them.
You see, I am not unhappy, but unhappiness
Must have its say, and a poem is often
The appropriate means for this. Now as to
Desiring less and settling for the dark,
I always say that towards the end of poems
When, having committed myself to a line
Of argument, I see what is no longer
Possible, or rather what is no longer
Possible to speak of. But now that I
Have spoken, all that has changed; the history
Of that moment has lengthened to include this moment
And that makes me happy, as so much does.

What strikes me as remarkable about this passage is Strand's ability to very genuinely fuse the poem's two points of view. When he tells us that "unhappiness / Must have its say, and a poem is often / The appropriate means for doing this," I take him at his word. When he tells us that "settling for the dark" is a statement uttered because he committed himself "to a line / Of argument," Strand seems to have struck a credible balance between the two tonal extremes he earlier set forth in the poem. We believe both that "a deeper music darkens" what the poet sees, but also that when he writes, "Things get a little out of hand." By the end of the poem, we understand that these are not mutually exclusive stances, and that in fact their coexistence helps to assure us that the transience of what is beautiful does not involve any loss of its worth. And with this understanding we very willingly accept the sincerity of the poem's last sentence. And isn't the process of writing poetry *always* a means to make one moment "lengthen" to include another, and because of this despair may indeed turn to radiance, and the shipwreck of the singular may beach us on the shores of the collective, the communal? Unhappiness must have its say—and once it does, a myriad of other states may follow it, happiness being one of them, a happiness that cannot linger but can endure—and that absolutely does not write white.

—For Ron Smith

2009

Notes

1. Kay Redfield Jamison, *Touched with Fire: Manic Depressive Illness and the Artistic Temperament* (New York: Free Press, 1993), p. 55.

2. Jamison, *Touched with Fire,* p. 73.

3. Jamison, *Touched with Fire,* p. 75.

4. Jamison, *Touched with Fire,* p. 60.

5. Philip Larkin, *Required Writing* (New York: Farrar, Straus & Giroux, 1984), p. 47.

6. Anton Chekhov, *Anton Chekhov's Short Stories,* ed. Ralph E. Matlaw (New York: W. W. Norton, 1979), p. 192.

7. Nazim Hikmet, *Poems of Nazim Hikmet,* rev. ed., trans. Randy Blasing and Mutlu Konuk (New York: Persea Books, 2002), p. 269.

8. Ivor Guerney, *Selected Poems* (New York: Oxford University Press, 1990), p. 82.

9. Philip Larkin, *Collected Poems,* ed. Anthony Thwaite (New York: Farrar, Straus & Giroux, 2003), p. 154.

10. W. H. Auden, *Collected Poems,* ed. Edward Mendelson (New York: Vintage, 1991), p. 179.

11. Czeslaw Milosz, *Collected Poems 1931–2001* (New York: Ecco, 2001), p. 56.

12. Elizabeth Bishop, *The Complete Poems 1927–1979* (New York: Farrar, Straus & Giroux, 1983), p. 173.

13. Weldon Kees, *Reviews and Essays, 1936–55,* ed. James Reidel (Ann Arbor: University of Michigan Press, 1988), p. 201.

14. Willy Eisenhart, introduction to *The World of Donald Evans* (New York: Dial Books, 1980), p. 15.

15. Ron Padgett, *How to Be Perfect* (Minneapolis: Coffee House Press, 2007), p. 64.

16. Sigmund Freud, *Writings on Art and Literature,* ed. Werner Hamacher and David E. Wellbery (Stanford, CA: Stanford University Press, 1997), p. 176.

17. Rainer Maria Rilke, *Selected Letters, 1902–1926* (London: Quartet Books, 1988), p. 198.

18. Auden, *Collected Poems,* p. 273.

19. *Pushcart Prize XII: Best of the Small Presses,* ed. Bill Henderson (Wainscott, NY: Pushcart Press, 1988), p. 502.

"If You Have to Be Sure Don't Write"
Poetry and Self-Doubt

Tattoos begin to lose their luster in middle age. After a couple of decades of wear and tear, even permanent ink begins to fade, and middle-aged flesh, more prone to flab and loss of muscle tone than the taut skin of youth, is apt to become a poor display case for your body art. The roses and the bluebirds and the prancing tigers sag, and soon you're wearing one of Dali's melted watches—now the incised skin shouts *tempus fugit.* A friend of mine, who has just passed the other side of fifty, has given up her habit of receiving an annual tattoo, opting for a yearly branding instead. Scarification tightens the skin, and therefore your brand will never sag. She tells me there's a wide array of designs available, should I ever want to try the procedure myself. But I'm not much interested in body art, neither tattoos nor brands, not even decals or henna. Yet I am very interested in a tattoo which my student J. recently affixed to his left arm. He's a do-it-yourselfer, and I hadn't realized this particular pastime had many adherents outside the slammer. You could hardly liken J.'s latest creation to your average prison tattoo, however. Over the summer, for god knows how many hours, J. labored to ink into his inner arm the following passage from Paul Celan:

A word—you know
a corpse

The presentation of this is more elegant than you might think. The letters are fairly large, fourteen-point or thereabouts, with the *A* slightly larger. As tattoos go, it's not really garish. But it's also unsettling. In some ways it makes sense for a tyro writer to

191

adorn himself with verses, but J. chose a stanza from one of the most hermetic of poets, a passage that, like so much of Celan, laments the inadequacies of language. As my theorist colleagues would say, in their exasperating jargon, this "problematizes" J.'s gesture. And the more you think of it, the more curious it gets. The inner arm, you'll remember, was the place where concentration camp inmates had their numbers tattooed, the place where a sequence of digits was doubtless inked into the flesh of Celan's mother, Fritzi Antschel, and into that of his father, Leo Antschel. Did J. know about this grim ritual of the Nazis? He isn't Jewish. But how could J. *not* know, for he chose to mark himself with a passage by the most famous poet to have survived the Holocaust? I should have thought to ask about this, but seeing Celan reduced to body decoration left me too stunned. Instead, pedant that I am, I asked J. what translation of Celan he used. Michael Hamburger? John Felstiner? Heather McHugh? And what does it mean to tattoo yourself with translation rather than something in its original tongue? If, as Frost famously said, poetry is what gets lost in translation, is poetry then doubly lost if it is replicated in a foreign tongue, and then painstakingly etched into skin, maybe during nights of TV watching, the way other people knit? Or is something of poetry's essence even more insistently preserved in this bizarre transport? It could be argued that J. has rewritten Celan, offering up another form of translation; in a very literal sense he's made the poet's lines his own. And his version is a definitive one, a final draft; nothing short of laser surgery can remove the tattoo. J.'s text cannot be revised, only erased.

But does J. possess a text or something more akin to a trophy? "Body artists" often talk of their tattoos as souvenirs of the time and place of their execution, pointing to them in much the same way that hunters speak of the eight-point bucks they've mounted above their mantels. To think of the Celan tattoo in this manner makes J.'s decoration quite distressing. For the Nazis had their trophies too, some of them lampshades made from human skin. (And it's known that the Nazis especially valued tattooed skin; a "hide" with a tattoo embossed upon it made for a uniquely pleasing lampshade. Eichmann reportedly instructed his Auschwitz *kapos* to be on the lookout for inmates with interesting tattoos;

they were then separated from the gas chamber–bound prisoners and executed by gunshot—Zyklon-b tended to discolor the skin and make it unsuitable for tanning.)

Of course J. will have a lot of time to consider the myriad ramifications of his Celan handiwork. And it makes me glad that I never went in for tattoos myself. But how brazen is the confidence that allowed J. his Celan. The doubts and regrets will come later: that's the way it is with youth, and the way it also is with tyro poets. But I am a middle-aged member of the middle class, and a poet in mid-career, and I must admit that something in me envies J.'s cavalier disregard for the long-term consequences of his body decoration. Yet I'm glad I'm not in my twenties anymore, glad as a writer that I'm no longer a candidate for those endlessly replicating anthologies of young, younger, or "new" poets, those monotonous gatherings of versifying by "the next generation," many of whom are rarely heard of again. I can no longer decorate my body; I instead have to maintain it, following an intricate regimen of Lipitor and Welbutrin, visits to the gym and to the shrink, annual readjustments of my bifocals, and encounters with M.D.s—or sometimes machines—skilled in the art of unpleasant probings of the lower tract. And everything is about consequences—Have I made the right choices in my CREF account? How will my wife and children fare if I die in an accident? Can I really afford this Victorian white elephant of a house? As I write this I am staring at a bucket placed beneath the leak in my study ceiling. It's raining outside, and the water beats down a different sort of tattoo. Consequences, doubts: of these I now am made. Of course, if you're a middle-aged member of the middle class who is also a poet, such doubts are not supposed to affect your writing life. The conventional wisdom has it that literary expertise improves with age and practice. You step onto a marvelous Hegelian escalator—if you keep writing, you're supposed to get better all the time. Doubt shouldn't trouble you. I want to debunk that notion. More important, I want to give doubt its due, to see it not as a nagging (or relentless) occupational hazard of the writing life, but as a necessary, if unwelcome, writerly tool. And not a glamorous tool, not some garish and decorative thing engineered along the lines of Keats's negative capability, but something humbler—something versatile, functional. A doubt you must live with, put up with, and in the end learn to wield with a certain facility.

Naturally, there are various kinds of writerly doubts, some more profound than others, and ones that a writer who writes long enough will eventually learn to overcome. Call them the expected doubts, the ones to which you affix a small *d*. There's the doubt that assails you as you try to hammer out a first draft of a poem: as Anne Lamont bluntly asserts, you must understand that "all first drafts are shitty first drafts." It takes time to learn this lesson, but the fear that what you write is shitty attends you every time you sit down to write a poem, and it only goes away—in provisional fashion—as the drafts pile up and the poem resembles something like poetry. But over the years you learn to live with this sad fact.

There's the related but more terrifying condition of writer's block: William Stafford's cure for this was to counsel you to "lower your standards." I've always thought of Stafford as an avuncular windbag, Polonius in a cardigan sweater, but here his advice is sound, especially because Stafford insists that you cure writer's block not simply by "lightening up" and doing free writing and improvisations, etc., but instead that you be wary of competing against "your last good poem." There is furthermore the doubt that comes from rejections—also a tough one. If you write long enough and invest the requisite emotional energy and time into the activity, you are apt to get better. You are apt to find your voice (whether that is a blessing or a curse is another question entirely). You've worked hard: Yet why are the editors and judges of the poetry book contests not recognizing your hard work? Why do the grants and book contacts and teaching jobs go to the less worthy? Perhaps it means you're not really that good after all. Your exasperation turns to envy, your envy to self-doubt and finally to self-laceration. Yesterday you felt okay about your career—the call from the Nobel committee may not have been coming on that particular morning, but at least you had a body of work you could take pride in. But today you're a deluded fool. You're not successful because you're not any good, and so on. It takes effort to remember that your contemporaries are all for the most part mediocre, no better and no worse than you are, that editors and grants-giving committees are schooled at best in preserving and replicating the blandest pieties of the period style, that your writing life is about your writing and not your career, that the cover of *APR* is not an indication of your arrival upon Parnassus. These are the daily doubts, the ongoing doubts, but ultimately they are trivial. You learn to write better by rewriting. You conquer writer's block by writing. You overcome careerism by attending to writing and not to career.

But you will write and write, and still it won't be good enough. You will write for years and for decades, and it still won't be adequate. You fail from lack of character, you fail because the language itself may not be able to say what you want it to say, you fail from lack of talent—although lack of talent is the least likely thing to hobble a dedicated poet. For whatever the reasons, you feel that what you want to say can't be said, and what you've already said was never good enough. This condition is a crisis more profound and more terrible than writer's block or lack of recognition, and it afflicts both the most lowly and the most esteemed writers. This is the sort of doubt I want to speak of here, and try to demystify. This is not an easy task, as you will see.

I want to begin with Ivor Gurney, a figure almost wholly unread in America, but well regarded in his native Britain. As with Wilfred Owen, Siegfred Sassoon, Robert Graves, and Edmund Blunden, Gurney served in the trenches, and saw more than his share of horror. He was wounded in action, gassed at Passchendaele, and finally discharged after a mental breakdown—or "deferred shell-shock," as it was called in those days. Like his fellow war poets, his aesthetic affinities are with the Georgians rather than the Modernists, and even within his most horrific descriptions of battlefield carnage he presents some oddly bucolic interludes. The spirit of merrie olde England always prevails. In "First Time In," a group of fresh recruits are met in the trenches by a welcoming committee of crooning Welshmen:

> and there the boys gave us kind welcome,
> So that we looked out as from the edge of home.
> Sang us Welsh things, and changed all former notions
> To human hopeful things. And the next day's guns,
> Nor any line-pangs ever quite could blot out
> That strangely beautiful entry to war's rout;

Candles they gave us, precious and shared-over rations—
Ulysses found little more in his wanderings without doubt.
"David of the White Rock" and the "Slumber Song" so soft,
    and that
Beautiful tune to which roguish words by Welsh pit boys
Are sung—but never the more beautiful than there under
    the guns' noise.[1]

We can't help but wonder what those "roguish" lyrics might have
been, but they seem roughly equivalent to the "dirty" version of
"Louie Louie." Of course, "roguish" words can only be alluded
to rather than quoted in a poem such as this. The tone is tender and consoling, but to contemporary readers it seems a bit
schmaltzy. Not schmaltzy at all, however, are many of the poems
from the later years of Gurney's career. Gurney's poetry and music compositions brought him a brief period of success in the
early 1920s, but his mental illness worsened. From 1922 until
his death in 1937 Gurney was an inmate at the City of London
Mental Hospital, and, following in the tradition of British poets
such as Christopher Smart and John Clare, the asylum became
a kind of writer's retreat for him. He wrote steadily, both music
and poems, and penned unsuccessful "appeals" for his release.
Certain of these poems have a truncated majesty reminiscent
of Dickinson. They share, too, Dickinson's penchant for tonal
reversals. The eight-line "Between the Boughs" begins with a
bittersweet stanza which evokes all the watered-down romanticism which makes the writings of the Georgians so dated. The
speaker recalls two lovers staring at a night sky of "numberless
stars" glimpsed among leaves "wonderful in blackness." We expect the rest of the poem to continue along these lines; soon the
author will grow wistful and nostalgic, and doubtless will pine
for his lost love. What, he asks, could possibly diminish the lovers' reveries? By line seven we have our answer, a telegraphic
vision of dread: "The aloofness, the dread of starry majesties /
The night-stilled trees."[2] How puny these lovers seem beneath
the vast impersonality of the stars. Why say anything more?
    Gurney's later poems do not so much subvert our expecta-
tions as they deride them through their brusqueness. Familiar
lyric premises are set forth, but the poet refuses to develop

them. The initial couplet of "April Gale" seems to promise some predictable conceit, but the poem barely gets going before Gurney says to hell with it. We find the speaker and Rover on an amble through a spring field. The wind frightens poor Rover, but the speaker delights in the gale—that is, until the poem's fourth and final line. Suddenly Gurney confesses that "My coat's a demon, torturing like life."[3] The awkwardness of this closing does not allow us to see it as a sudden insight: a haiku this is not. The end of the poem does not make what Robert Bly used to call an associative "leap"; instead it seems to bypass—out of impatience and exasperation—the methodologies of traditional conceit. It's as if Gurney began to write a sonnet but by line four lost faith in his project. The fourth line, clumsy as it may be, has a certain abject bravery. "Why not dispel the lies of mere neat poetry?" it seems to say. Why take fourteen lines to tell you my life feels like torture? Read in this way, many of Gurney's poems look less like botched efforts at lyrics in the manner of Graves or Edward Thomas and more like harbingers of post-modernism. Fractured, often seeming to stutter, thanks to their syntactical inversions and belabored rhymes, and time and again lamenting the insufficiency of the lyric impulse and of language itself, certain of Gurney's later poems very much resemble those of Paul Celan—although I doubt if "April Gale" will ever be etched into somebody's arm. Poems are repeatedly seen as "embers of a dream," "scrawls on a vain page," and "the sentimental fib of light and day." Lest my analogy seem farfetched, let me turn my attention to "Moments," another eight-line poem, and one which has haunted me for years. Here the "loathed minutes" of daily life serve only to remind the speaker of his existential despair and mortality. They can do nothing but point to "that six-foot length I must lie in." Only death will bring him a kind of solace; only then will he not "grieve again / Because high autumn goes beyond my pen / And snow lies inexprest in the deep lane."[4]

Unlike "April Gale," which ends before the writer can tell us the source of his suffering, Gurney here makes a very specific claim—*writing* is the cause of his problems. Upon first encountering "Moments," a reader is likely to misread its conclusion: setting down the poem just now, I keyed in "unexpressed" for

Gurney's oddly anachronistic "inexprest." But the difference between the two words is significant. "Unexpressed" can mean "unattempted," as in "I never tried to tell you what the snow looked like." "Inexprest" suggests inadequacy: "I tried many times, but I never got my descriptions to sound right," completing the trope that begins in the previous line. Failure is the issue here, not mere writer's block.

Like Hölderlin in his later poetry—work which also emerges from years of acute mental anguish—in the final phase of his career Gurney replaces lyric polish with writing that is fragmentary, piecemeal, stunted. Yet, as in the case of Holderlin, these final unfinished efforts remain their writers' most interesting and resonant work. Is it their madness which speaks to us in their late poems, a force which prevents the authors from writing in the manner that they once did? Perhaps in some degree it is. But along with their madness Gurney and Hölderlin were bestowed with the dubious gift of an acuity that sometimes comes with bereavement and self-doubt.

But what happens when a writer encounters that same bereavement and doubt and can manage to wrest from it something larger, and even transformative? Gurney, like many writers of the past century, arrived at an aesthetic based upon permanent crisis. Confusion and uncertainty were never resolved over the course of his career; instead, the confusion and uncertainty intensified. But there are other writers who are able to face such traumas and who learn to partially overcome them. Their doubts do not stunt their writing; in fact, their writing may be deepened by their doubts.

Often this deepening is the result of a poetic mid-life crisis. In mid-career, "in the middle of life's journey," the author renounces his or her early work, and seeks to write from a totally new perspective. Dante famously ends *La Vita Nuova* with the statement that his praise of Beatrice has been inadequate, and that he cannot write of her again until he has relearned the craft of poetry. This knowledge, Dante tells us, comes literally in the form of a vision, one which arrives after he has written the highly self-questioning sonnet which appears in the penultimate section of the book. "A strange new understanding that sad Love / imparts" has occurred for Dante, but he "cannot understand the subtle words / it speaks."[5] The final section gives us a Dante who is chastened and humbled, who tells us that Beatrice is the great subject of his writing, but that he is not yet capable of writing of her in the way that he must: "After this sonnet there appeared to me a vision in which I saw things that made me resolve to say no more about this blessed one until I would be capable of writing about her in a more worthy fashion. And to achieve this I am striving as hard as I can." But a few lines later the tone shifts, suggesting ambition and even arrogance: "I hope to write of her that which has never been written of any woman."[6] Beatrice may indeed be "inexprest" here, but the book ends with what Dante biographer R. W. B. Lewis calls "the foreshadowing of some enormous poetic endeavor."[7] Yet Dante suggests that this new project can only be achieved through a total renunciation of his earlier poetic self. As if to make this point absolutely clear, early manuscripts of *La Vita Nuova* conclude with the medieval equivalent of a film's closing credits:

HERE ENDS
THE
NEW LIFE
OF
DANTE ALIGHIERI[8]

The new life is in reality the old life, and it is over. Dante completed this book around 1295; the first cantos of the *Comedia* date from around 1309. Obviously the project of learning to write about Beatrice as no woman has ever been written of before took Dante a good bit of time. When Dante first encounters Beatrice in Canto XXX of *The Purgatorio,* she berates him about his failings of character, while at the same time slyly alluding to the inadequacies of *La Vita Nuova:*

. . . such, potentially, was this man

in his new life, that every right disposition
would have come to marvelous proof in him,
    but the more vigor there is in the ground

> the more rank and tangled grows the land
> if the seed is bad and tilling left undone.[9]

Even on the threshold of paradise, Dante is reminded that he cannot leave his old selves and his old writings completely behind. Even in his renunciation of them, he understands that they must be grafted to his new self and new poetic project, grafted not in a fashion which bespeaks triumph, but instead with a sense of ongoing crisis and uncertainty. The transformation can never be complete.

American culture is of course reluctant to admit to the sorts of unease which the example of Dante suggests are inherent to writerly self-transformation. One of America's enduring myths is that you can truly make yourself over, that Gatsby will never be James Gatz again, nor John Wayne be Marion Morrison. This myth has become such a received truth that we even apply it to poets' careers, most egregiously to many of the poets who matured in the late 1950s and early 1960s: Lowell, Merwin, Rich, Wright, and Carruth, to name the more obvious examples. Schooled in the impersonal academic formalism of the New Critics, these writers offered debut collections buffed to a glossy High Modernist sheen, whether it is, in the case of Wright and Rich, a Modernism deriving from Frost and Robinson or, in the case of Lowell, a more cantankerous Modernism following in the lines of Eliot and Hopkins. The conventional wisdom attests that this group soon left the frigidity of High Modernism completely behind; Merwin and Wright made themselves over as Deep Image writers, Lowell and Rich as writers of a confessional mode, and so on. In reality, these changes were never the radical departures which critics saw them to be at the time, neither thematically nor formally. For example, Lowell in *Life Studies* and Rich in volumes from the 1960s like *Snapshots of a Daughter in Law* practice a kind of autobiographical poetry which had been already been published in the 1950s by writers as different from one another as Allen Ginsberg, W. D. Snodgrass, and Robert Penn Warren. Furthermore Lowell, Wright, and Carruth never entirely abandoned rhyme and meter for free verse. There are a fair number of poems in traditional form in every one of James Wright's books, and Lowell's 1967 volume, *Near the Ocean*, is written largely in tetrameter couplets modeled on Marvell. In an interview published shortly after the publication of *Life Studies,* Lowell allowed that his new work did not represent a conversion to open forms: "I seesaw between something highly metrical and something free."[10] More important, though, these writers changed their methods slowly, unmethodically, and often at significant personal cost. At certain points in the 1960s Wright and Carruth were unable to write at all. "My writing was at a dead end," says Carruth, "themes scrambled and uncertain, sense of a creative locus hopelessly lost."[11] And Wright's now-legendary break with tradition between his second volume, *St. Judas* (1959), and the Deep Image free verse of *The Branch Will Not Break* (1963) has been shown by the poet-critic Kevin Stein to be an exhausting process. Midway during the four years which passed between the publication of these two books, Wright submitted to his publisher a volume with a singularly unpromising title, *The Amenities of Stone* (he had earlier given the book an even more unfortunate title, *Now I Have Awakened*), containing a mixture of poems in his early formalist manner and efforts in his later Deep Image mode. But after the book was accepted Wright got cold feet, and withdrew the manuscript. In examining Wright's papers, Stein gives us a portrait of a writer afflicted with grave uncertainties about his writing:

> Doubting a poem's worth was not uncommon for Wright. He was not easily satisfied with what he produced, be it a single poem or a collection of verse. Between 1959 and 1963 Wright did not work on *Amenities* alone; in fact, he tinkered with no less than six separate manuscripts in that period, placing side by side and in myriad combinations some 113 different poems in that four-year span. Various tables of contents reveal that twenty-eight of the forty-five poems in *Branch* originate as early as the previously mentioned 1960 manuscript *Now I Have Awakened,* and in the March 1961 draft of *Amenities.* Thus, it would seem that Wright's struggle was equally a matter of learning to write some new style, and a slow process of eliminating from his manuscript those poems that did not stylistically cohere with the deep image poems which later formed the crux of *Branch.*[12]

Wright never fully abandoned his early style, and he continued to engage in an aesthetic and stylistic argument with his early manner throughout his career. "St. Judas," the heretical retelling of the biblical story which is the title poem of Wright's second collection, is later alluded to and critiqued in Wright's 1972 volume, *Two Citizens.* Yet "Son of Judas" compares poorly with its predecessor. The earlier poem makes Judas a tragic figure, an existential hero in the manner of the outcasts and loners who populate Wright's other poems of the 1950s; it is also an impeccably written hybrid sonnet. "Son of Judas," by contrast, seems to grope for both a form and a clear sense of purpose. Wright specifically alludes to several of his earlier poems—in addition to "St. Judas," he references "A Blessing" and "To the Muse"— but the poem neither stands on its own nor enlarges our understanding of these earlier Wright efforts. But, as in the case of Dante's reappraisals of *La Vita Nuova,* we sense that Wright's project in the poem is an ambivalent one—he must deny the significance of his earlier writing while at the same time asserting that it predicts the directions his new work will take. Such a process does not always make for successful poetry, but it can frequently invest a new sort of urgency and a more rigorous self-appraisal in the career of a "writer of a certain age."

In the pages that follow, I want to examine some individual poems by three writers who in mid- or late career address their self-doubt in a fashion similar to Wright's, but who do so in poems which are of greater interest than "Son of Judas." The three poems, by Robert Lowell, Larry Levis, and W. S. Merwin, have much in common. Each is a kind of ars poetica, explicitly or implicitly alluding to its writer's earlier poetry and aesthetic presuppositions—and often doing so in a decidedly harsh fashion. The poems do not seek to deny their writers' earlier productions as much as they hope to reconfigure the early work in the context of a new and considerably altered aesthetic. They are, like all ars poeticae, aesthetic credos, but in this case they are written not to articulate their authors' belief in poetry, but to *re-assert* it. They are poems in the manner of Dante's "strange new understanding."

"I am tired. Everyone's tired of my turmoil." So ends "Eye and Tooth," a stark lyric from Robert Lowell's 1964 volume, *For the*

Union Dead. Unlike the often lapidary poems of childhood and family history which are to be found in Lowell's earlier and most famous collection, *Life Studies,* the poems of *For the Union Dead* are jagged and relentless—the lines are short, and the writing lurches from baroquely intricate metaphors to bald statements such as the one above. But of course the turmoil in his life and writing continued onward through the various editions of his *Notebook* sonnets and into the frequently awkward efforts of Lowell's final volume, 1977's *Day by Day.* This collection, however, contains one of Lowell's most compelling individual lyrics, its final poem, "Epilogue."

The voice of the poem is plaintive. Lowell begins by asking why the "blessed structures" of "plot and rhyme" can no longer serve him as he attempts to create "something imagined, not recalled." He seems to lament his entire oeuvre, bemoaning that it seems merely snapshot-like, "heightened from life / yet paralyzed by fact." He immediately retracts this statement, however. "Why not say what happened?" he asks. But factual truth is seen by the end of the poem as something far different from the often self-lacerating autobiographical writing which we associate with Lowell:

> Pray for the grace of accuracy
> Vermeer gave to the sun's illumination
> stealing like the tide across a map
> to his girl solid with yearning.
> We are poor passing facts,
> warned by that to give
> each figure in the photograph
> his living name.[13]

Day by Day is a valedictory collection, steeped in elegiac feeling; one senses that Lowell suspected that this book would be his last. Lowell pays homage to friends and fellow writers, living and dead, among them John Berryman, Peter Taylor, and Robert Penn Warren, and mourns the collapse of his second marriage, to novelist Elizabeth Hardwick. He also paints a quietly turbulent picture of his marriage to Lady Caroline Blackwood, for whom he had left Hardwick. Lowell's previous two collections,

The Dolphin and *For Lizzie and Harriet*, tell the tale of this triangle, but they are agonized and unseemly books; their tone is one of manic relentlessness. A more subdued ambivalence prevails in *Day by Day*. In writing of the collection, Richard Tillinghast astutely observes that "in poem after poem, [Lowell] says goodbye not only to friends but to old ideas—the ruling ideas of his time. He continues to feel ambivalent about the third of his troubled marriages. Ambivalence was Lowell's characteristic stance—a stance that positioned him to embody many of the conflicts of his period."[14] This remark helps us to understand the curious unease with which most readers will likely approach "Epilogue." Lowell was a supreme rhetorician; a casual tonal authority prevails in the lines, as it does in so many of Lowell's other poems. But here the meditation bristles with anxiousness; contradictions abound. No sooner does the writer make a statement than he begins to nullify it. Like Yeats, whose mixture of rhetorical swagger and acutely self-conscious ambivalence colors so many of his lines, Lowell has an uncanny capacity to wrest memorable statement from conflictedness. As Tillinghast notes, "the sense of 'Epilogue' becomes problematic almost immediately." Within the space of scarcely a dozen lines the author announces his allegiance not to memory but to the imagination, ascribes a quotation to himself to illustrate what he means (*"the painter's eye is not a lens, / it trembles to caress the light"*), criticizes the Polaroid-like tendency of his previous work, but then reverses himself: "All's misalliance," the quasi-Shakespearean interjection which occurs in the middle of the poem, seems especially fitting commentary on Lowell's jittery shuffling between dichotomies. The poem also manages to allude to the various earlier poetic incarnations of Robert Lowell—the formalism of the early poems, the severely "plotted" monologues of *The Mills of the Kavanaghs,* the recollective verse of *Life Studies,* and the reportorially immediate *Notebook* sonnets—all with a rueful tenderness. He is weary of these earlier selves, but is not seeking to completely disown them now that he is, as he puts it in "Thanks-Offering for Recovery" (the poem which appears immediately before "Epilogue"), "free of the unshakeable terror that made me write. . . ." Yet how does Lowell resolve his divided feelings toward his work, and the similar conflicts which now so trouble him? Like Proust, another writer preoccupied with the seemingly insoluble division between recollection and imagination, Lowell turns to the painter Vermeer. The canvas to which Lowell alludes is one of the painter's most haunting and enigmatic ones, *Woman in Blue Reading a Letter,* where the light indeed appears to be "stealing like a tide across a map" behind its subject. *Plot* is "of no help" as we attempt to narrativize the painting—the girl, in profile and likely pregnant, holds a letter in her hand; on a table, atop the letter's envelope, glows a string of pearls. Richly implicit, the scene is, in the words of critic Edward Snow, "one of unresolved yet almost viscerally enforced contradictions."[15] This rendering of delicate stasis may be the "grace of accuracy" which Lowell seeks in line seventeen of the poem, for the poet appears to regard the painting as a "snapshot" which avoids the pitfall of being "heightened from life but paralyzed by fact." (It is worth remembering that Vermeer likely painted with the aid of a *camera oscura*—the paintings were in this respect a kind of ur-Polaroid.) With this invocation of Vermeer, Lowell suggests that he now must renew his artistry not by continuing the relentlessly personal writing for which he had become so justly famous, but by seeking a more intricate form of autobiography, one self-transcending but not self-negating. Despite the typically Lowellian agonies which prompt the poem, it ends on a note of quiet jubilation, a quality which Alan Williamson finds in many of the poems of *Day by Day*: "A curious, joyful feeling of being— not in the ordinary sense—beside himself, beside his own life."[16] One wonders if Lowell, who knew his century's literature better than almost anyone, had in mind as he reached the closing of his poem the famous reverie about Vermeer which Proust offers near the end of his novel:

> Thanks to art, instead of seeing one world only, our own, we see the world multiply itself and we have at our disposal as many worlds as there are original artists, worlds more different from the other than those which revolve in infinite space, worlds which, centuries after the extinction of the fire from which their light first emanated, whether it is called Rembrandt or Vermeer, send us still each one its special radiance.[17]

The Lowell of "Epilogue," the writer who seeks to send us not his history but his "special radiance," is a Lowell we have not seen before, a Lowell who, as he puts it in "Thanks-Offering for Recovery," "was created to be given away." How regrettable it is that he was not permitted to live long enough to exercise this new understanding.

Larry Levis did not live long enough, either, and with his death in 1996 at the age of forty-nine, American poetry lost a writer who might well have grown to be a figure of Lowell's stature. Although Levis's aesthetic allegiances were to writers other than Lowell, most notably the European and Latin American poets of the surrealist tradition, to whom he pays homage in several of his poems, he shared with Lowell a capacity for unsparing self-examination, and the autobiography which emerges in his poems also seems to share something of the older poet's "turmoil." Like Lowell, Levis often writes in response to domestic trauma—divorce, the deaths of parents and loved ones. He shares Lowell's outrage at social injustice as well, and as a writer keenly aware of his rural working-class roots, he is blessedly free of Lowell's elitism. But the trait Levis most acutely shares with Lowell is a searing ability to convey the experience of personal apocalypse—of the tumult which characterizes Lowell's "Eye and Tooth" and "Skunk Hour." In "The Two Trees," the poem which opens Levis's posthumously published *Elegy*, Levis describes a mid-life crisis, a *noche oscura*, replete with rueful allusions to the opening of *The Inferno:*

> Friends, in the middle of this life, I was embraced
> By failure. It clung to me & did not let me go.
> When I ran, brother limitation raced
>
> Beside me like a shadow. . . .[18]

The poet's "only acquaintances" are a pair of trees, which come to seem emblematic of the breech which exists between the speaker and the world: they perform much the same function as the skunk and her young do in the conclusion of Lowell's poem. Here are the concluding lines:

One, that seemed frail, but was really

Oblivious to everything. Simply oblivious to it,
With the pale leaves climbing one side of it,
An obscure sheen in them,

And the other side, for some reason, black, bare,
The same, almost irresistible, carved indifference

In the shape of its limbs

As if someone's cries for help
Had been muffled by them once, concealed there,

Her white flesh just underneath the slowly peeling bark

—while the joggers swerved around me & I stared—

Still tempting me to step in, find her,

And possess her completely.

This is a devastating poem, but I am more interested in another effort from *Elegy*, a poem which more obliquely addresses the doubt which informs "The Two Trees" and so many of the rest of the collection's efforts. "The Poem Returning as an Invisible Wren to the World" is a strangely majestic meditation on poetry's power to transform consciousness and solace human tragedy. It makes these claims while at the same time acknowledging poetry's insignificance within history and its inability to cure injustice. Almost as significantly, it achieves all this by rewriting one of Levis's earliest published efforts, "The Poem You Asked For."

Let me begin with the latter poem, first published in 1972 and typical of the neo-surrealist mode so fashionable in the 1970s. "The poem you asked for" is personified, alternately as a kind of fickle muse, a precious stone, a bird, or an animal: "My poem would eat nothing. / I tried giving it water. / but it said no. . . . I held it to the light / turning it over / but it only pressed its lips / more tightly together. . . . I cupped it in / my hands, and carried it gently / out into the soft air, into the / evening traffic, wonder-

ing how / to end things between us. . . ."[19] By the end of the piece
the "poem" has grown more decisive and strong, but abandons
the speaker, instead "going / over to your place." It's the sort of
effort you can read in any number of Charles Simic or Gregory
Orr poems of the period. The short lines are neatly parsed and
only rarely enjambed, but the clarity of presentation is meant to
counterpoint the poem's essential mysteriousness. Levis is careful
to make the conceit spacious, never letting his personified poem
remain in any one of its incarnations for long. By the final lines,
we well understand that Levis's personified poem is a metaphor
for something, perhaps the essential ineffability of poetic creation; the poem is finally about the poet's surrender to meaning's
changeability and precariousness. Yet ultimately the poem is arch
and formulaic. Of course, we might expect to encounter such
problems in the work of a poet barely out of his teens. Twenty or
more years later, Levis employs nearly identical conceits and rhetorical strategies for "The Poem Returning as an Invisible Wren to
the World." Again, poetry is personified as a mutable and shape-
shifting force. Here are the opening stanzas:

> Once, there was a poem. No one read it & the poem
> Grew wise. It grew wise & then it grew thin,
> No one could see it perched on the woman's
> Small shoulders as she went on working beside
>
> The gray conveyer belt with the others.
> No one saw the poem take the shape of a wren,
> A wren you could look through like a window,
> And see all the bitterness in the world
>
> In the long line of shoulders & faces bending
> Over the gleaming, machine parts that passed
> Before them, the faces transformed by the grace
> And ferocity of a wren, a wren you could look
>
> Through, like a lens, to see them working there. . . .[20]

Levis replaces the surrealism of his earlier poem with a different
approach to fantasy, with a fabular narration akin to magical realism. In contrast to the vapory imagistic transformations that "po-

etry" undergoes in "The Poem You Asked For," here it is seen as a force informed by paradox rather than by mystery. As it grows more insubstantial, it also grows wise, becoming the lens through which we may distinguish not only the woman factory worker and her partners on the assembly line, but "all the bitterness in the world." The force of poetry is thus sacrificial, destroying itself in the process of presenting the clarity it seeks to reveal. And this is not a clarity that aims to console us through a palliative romanticism. The final stanzas of the poem are insistent upon this point:

> This is not about how she threw herself into the river,
> For she didn't, nor is it about the way her breasts
> Looked in the moonlight, nor about moonlight at all.
> This is about the surviving curve of the bridge
> Where she listened to the river whispering to her,
> When the wren flew off & left her there.
> With the knowledge of it singing in her blood.
>
> By which the wind avenges. By which the rain avenges.
> By which even the limb of a dead tree leaning
> Above the white, swirling mouth of an eddy
> In the river that once ran beside the factory window
>
> Where she once worked, shall be remembered
> When the dead come back, & take their places
> Beside her on the line, & the gray conveyer belt
> Starts up with its raspy hum again. Like a heaven's.

The metaphorical transformations that the poem makes are complicated, partly because, like Lowell in "Epilogue," Levis seeks to divest himself and his readers of all of the conventionally romantic preconceptions of poetry's mission. The factory worker does not throw herself into the river, and Levis refuses to traffic in the imagery of cliched surrealist decoration—the poem is not "about moonlight at all." When the "invisible wren" of poetry departs from the poem, we are left with a scene of abjection. Moonlight does not survive, but the "curve of the bridge" and the "limb of a dead tree" do. The poem's final images describe a strangely desolate resurrection, a scene made visionary by the sheer intensity of its pitilessness. Yet it is this very quality which gives the poem its urgency, suggesting a perspective beyond uncertainty, of a curious imaginative triumph in its glimpse of *thanatos*. It's the stance we encounter in late poems of Stevens such as "The Plain Sense of Things," where the abandoned mansion, "the great pond and its waste of lilies . . . / Had to be imagined as an inevitable knowledge, / Required, as a necessity requires."[21] Levis refuses to charm us, refuses to offer the tidy blandishments we might have expected from his earlier self.

But this is not to imply that the cure for our doubts is merely to reconcile ourselves with mortality. Perhaps doubt is also mitigated by a reconciliation with our past selves, and "The Poem Returning as an Invisible Wren to the World" implies this as well: it is not a recapitulation of one of Levis's early poems as much as a reconstitution, and therefore an act of acceptance—the prodigal poem returning, forgiven and renewed. In "mid-career" and beyond, such perspectives are now possible for a poet, and a new kind of self-integration may arise in one's writing as a result. While attempts to correct or improve one's earlier selves are likely to fail—think of the aged Wordsworth's disastrous attempts to rewrite the poems of his youth—perhaps it is possible to glimpse as never before the multiplicity of selves which make up a writing career: and possible to write for all of those selves, past and present both. This seems to be the task which W. S. Merwin sets for himself in his astonishing "Berryman," a poem that manages to be a kind of Horatian ars poetica, a memoir of Berryman as teacher and mentor, and a retrospective self-portrait. And as for doubt, Merwin speaks of it straightforwardly and eloquently.

Merwin invokes Berryman "in the days before the beard / and the drink," when he was Merwin's teacher at Princeton. The portrait is a mixture of affection and awe. The advice Berryman offers the youthful Merwin about his poetic aspirations is sometimes grandiose, sometime merely eccentric. He counsels Merwin to "never lose [his] arrogance," and to "paper his wall" with rejection slips. He suggests that Merwin pray to the muse for guidance, "and he / said he meant it literally." But the closing of the poem offers some chilling advice:

I had hardly begun to read
I asked him how can you ever be sure

that what you write is really
any good at all and he said you can't

you can't you never can be sure
you die without knowing
whether anything you wrote was any good
if you have to be sure don't write[22]

All morning the page was blank. Yesterday, too, the notebook leaves were empty, and the day before that as well. But as morning turned to afternoon, I was able to put down onto the page a few lines that seemed to me interesting enough to return to later. Now it is later, and I've spent the afternoon telling graduate students why their poems worked or didn't work. Outside the streetlights have come on, and the snow predicted all week is finally upon us. The grimly intractable pewter of the sky is now going dark. I open the notebook to this morning's lines—or are they this *week's* lines? or the lines which the years and decades have always been leading me toward?—and they seem to me dull, static, derivative. Tomorrow I will have to start again. And it occurs to me that for weeks I have written about doubt while avoiding any discussion of my own doubts. How could I show you these mornings of silence, culminating in these paltry few lines, and the panic or fear or self-loathing which is this moment? And what point would there be in sharing this with you? Neither the lines nor the sharing are poetry, although perhaps at some point the mornings and the silences and gracelessly stuttering lines will coalesce into something which might become poetry, and be worthy enough to present to you. But how do I know they will coalesce? Perhaps I have no new poems to write, and can present to you only shards and fragments, glinting pieces of the vessels which once were my poetry, but which neither you nor I can hope to reconstruct. For one thing I do know about verse is that it is perishable, friable, and sometimes made precious because of this, whether it is written on paper, or with pixels on glowing screens, or inked into human skin. That it can be written at all is astonishing, and that it can survive its writing is astonishing as well.

2002

Notes

1. Ivor Gurney, *Selected Poems*, ed. P.J. Kavanagh (Oxford: Oxford University Press, 1990), p. 19.

2. Gurney, *Selected Poems*, p. 52.

3. Gurney, *Selected Poems*, p. 38.

4. Gurney, *Selected Poems*, p. 84.

5. Dante Alighieri, *Vita Nuova*, trans. Mark Musa (Oxford: Oxford University Press, 1992), p. 82.

6. Alighieri, *Vita Nuova*, pp: 83–84.

7. R. W. B. Lewis, *Dante* (New York: Penguin, 2001), p. 61.

8. Lewis, *Dante*, p. 61.

9. Dante Alighieri, *Purgatorio*, trans. W. S. Merwin (New York: Knopf, 2000), p. 299.

10. Robert Lowell, *Collected Prose*, ed. Robert Giroux (New York: Farrar, Straus and Giroux, 1987), p. 244.

11. Hayden Carruth, *Selected Essays and Reviews* (Port Townsend, WA: Copper Canyon Press, 1986), p. 106.

12. Kevin Stein, *James Wright: The Poetry of a Grown Man* (Athens: Ohio University Press, 1989), pp. 44–45.

13. Robert Lowell, *Day by Day* (New York: Farrar, Straus and Giroux, 1977) p. 108.

14. Richard Tillinghast, *Robert Lowell's Life and Work: Damaged Grandeur* (Ann Arbor: University of Michigan Press, 1995), p. 112.

15. Edward Snow, *A Study of Vermeer*, rev. ed. (Berkeley: University of California Press, 1994) p. 3.

16. Alan Williamson, *Eloquence and Mere Life: Essays on the Art of Poetry* (Ann Arbor: University of Michigan Press, 1994), p. 9.

17. Marcel Proust, *A Remembrance of Things Past*, vol. 3, trans. C. K. Scott Moncrieff and Terence Kilmartin (New York: Vintage Books, 1982), p. 932.

18. Larry Levis, *Elegy*, ed. Philip Levine (Pittsburgh: University of Pittsburgh Press, 1997), p. 3.

19. Larry Levis, *The Selected Levis*, ed. David St. John (Pittsburgh: University of Pittsburgh Press, 2000), p. 3.

20. Levis, *Elegy*, p. 14.

21. Wallace Stevens, *Collected Poems* (New York: Knopf, 1954), p. 503.

22. W. S. Merwin, *Selected Poems* (New York: Atheneum, 1988), p. 270.

Printed and bound by CPI Group (UK) Ltd, Croydon, CR0 4YY

09/06/2025

14685639-0001